Midwives of the Future

Midwives of the Future

American Sisters Tell
Their Story

Edited by
Ann Patrick Ware

Leaven Press
Kansas City, MO

Library of Congress Catalog Card Number: 84-82554

ISBN: 0-934134-11-1

Published by: Leaven Press
P.O. Box 40292
Kansas City, MO 64141

Printed and bound in the United States of America

IV

CONTENTS

This book is dedicated to the memory of the late

Sister Annette Walters, CSJ/SFCC (1910-1978)

Annette was one of the early leaders of the Sister Formation Movement which, long before Vatican II, began those changes which led to the entry of sisters into the mainstream of American society.

Sister Annette Walters is a breathing presence among us for she was

— unclouded in her towering vision

— creative in touching the core of our common concerns

— consumed by her thirst for equality and justice

—dynamic in her all-embracing love.

Preface

The idea for this book came in the midst of a discussion by sisters about the Vatican-initiated investigation of "religious life" in the United States. Sisters rightly felt that their mode of life was likely to be scrutinized more closely than that of religious congregations of brothers or of priests. How, someone wondered, are we to let the investigating commission know what renewal of religious life in the post-Vatican II church has meant to us? Even more pointedly, did we ourselves know what renewal had meant in our lives? How many of us had ever looked deeply and critically at the past 20 years and assessed the changes those years had brought?

At once a small group of us issued invitations to some 30 sisters, hoping to find a few who would undertake such a task and do it within a few weeks. The plan was then to issue a second and third round of invitations, forming a broad spectrum of sisters in varied ministries, of ethnically diverse backgrounds, and of different congregational experiences. Unexpectedly 19 of the original 30 at once agreed to write the story of how the renewal had personally affected them. Our book was now not only launched but of a size to brook no additions. Here, then, are the stories which answer the question that no one has ever asked American sisters: What have the vast changes during the years of experimentation in the post-Vatican II church meant in your life?

Many thanks are due to many people, but I want especially to mention two religious communities — the Sisters of Loretto and the Sisters of Mercy of the Union — who gave us small grants to help us launch this project, and one donor who gave generously from her pocket. A small committee helped with the final planning: Jane Boyer, Ritamary Bradley, Anne Mary Dooley, Anne Mayer, Terry McGreevy and Margaret Ellen Traxler. Cecily Jones is responsible for the interview with Mary Luke Tobin. All the authors have been faithful to their promise and unbelievably prompt. Our publisher, convinced of the importance of what we had to say, has rushed to make this book available.

The work of thoughtful and prayerful reflection has been its own reward. If it succeeds in making those who read it understand more clearly what American sisters are about, so much the better.

Introduction

Ann Patrick Ware

Ann Patrick Ware has been a Sister of Loretto for 43 years. Formerly associate director of the Commission on Faith and Order of the National Council of Churches of Christ, she now works part time for Church Women United and spends two days a week with women in jail or in court.

Of all the changes in the Roman Catholic Church in the past 20 years, no segment of it has undergone upheaval and transformation as much as those women known to all as "the sisters." Their life, characterized by the wearing of a medieval costume, by silence, by regulations about the smallest details of life, was largely incomprehensible even to close family members. Outsiders knew that, in most instances, sisters could not eat in their presence, that certain sections of convents were off limits to them, and that a thousand other differences set them apart. An esoteric monastic language shrouded conventual life in mystery: "cloister," "refectory," "cell," "habit," "chapter," "office," "the discipline."

Despite the fact that generations of American children passed under their tutelage daily, American sisters — what they thought and how they really lived — remained a great unknown. Occasionally films like *Come to the Stable* attempted to break through the secrecy. In the 1950s *The Nun's Story*, a book (and later a film) made a great impact by revealing all from the viewpoint of one who finally found the life intolerable and left it. In novels and movies sisters generally appeared as gentle, naive, well-meaning but somewhat dim-witted folk who were forever making preposterous demands, often of thugs or steely business tycoons, demands which somehow tugged at a forgotten heartstring and enabled the grace of God to move a stony heart. Not a bad image, all in all, but not the story as we would tell it.

Even when striking changes began to take place and sisters donned street clothes, took jobs on public university campuses, managed housing developments, stood on picket lines or ran for public office, it was not uncommon to have a TV or newspaper interviewer focus attention on a sister's makeup or choice of clothes and ask about the reaction of the Catholic public to this new image rather than get to the heart of changes and the reasons which prompted them. There were tired jokes about the new nuns who had "kicked the habit."

This book contains the story of those changes as related by 19 women who moved from the "before" to the "after" of renewal and who tell of the costs and rewards, the joy and the pain along the way. Sisters, brought

up in awe of authority and with a dedication to obedience, studied avidly
the documents of Vatican II as if they had been written expressly for
them. They, perhaps more than anyone else in the church, bent their
total attention to what it would mean to open the doors and let fresh
breezes blow. The council documents on the liturgy, on sacred scripture,
on religious life, ecumenism, and the church in the modern world affected
them profoundly. And when in 1966 Pope Paul VI issued a letter *Ecclesiae
Sanctae* mandating special assemblies for all religious within three years,
congregations of sisters fell to work with a vengeance to carry out the
task: All constitutions, books of customs and regulations were to be restudied under a quadruple lens — the life of Christ as presented in the
gospels; the spirit of the founder; the life of the church; and human
conditions in the modern world. This is the story of what that restudying
of religious life resulted in and how it has affected the lives of specific
individuals.

A certain sameness in the narratives points out how strictly governed
our lives were in the 1950s and early 1960s, not because religious communities of women had got together and decided to do things in a certain
way. No, the regulations came from the outside — from the male,
ecclesiastical outside — even though women freely embraced them. Intercongregational meetings were at that time almost unheard of. In fact, it
was commonplace even for branches of the same family of religious, those
who claimed the same founder and followed the same rule, not to have
much concourse between them or even to exist in competition with one
another. Old hostilities which had caused official ruptures sometimes
still festered.

Between other communities there occasionally existed ill will because
of the competitiveness of their enterprises — mainly schools and hospitals
— or because one community, refusing to bend to the will of an unreason-
able and crotchety pastor, could be readily replaced by another. I remember hearing tales, as a young sister, of the schools we "used to have,"
now staffed by other communities. Oftentimes this shift came about because of our Loretto policy not to take on sacristy work simply because
we staffed the parish school. I always felt that other communities, who
readily accepted additional burdens that we thought the parish should
be paying others to do, were akin to "strike breakers," though, of course,
we never got together to talk things over.

Some of the writers of these chapters declare themselves feminists and
are careful not to use solely male language for God. Others do not seem
to have any problem with masculine pronouns for God or with feminine
images and pronouns for church. Some have been grievously wounded
by the hierarchical, institutional church; others work happily within its
structures. Some of the writers have left their original communities and
joined others. One sister writes about her struggle to deal with truly
human love within the boundaries of a twisted understanding of the love
of God and of celibacy. In fact, she demonstrates on behalf of us all what
pain and distortion have been produced by silence on the subject of sexuality, especially for those who choose to live a celibate life. In short, not
everyone is in the same place. But that is the charm of storytelling.

One of the reasons for publishing this book at this time is that ominous signs are in the air. In 1983, the Congregation of Religious and Secular Institutes (SCRIS) issued a document, *Essential Elements of Religious Life*, which in effect would undo the work of renewal that religious communities of women have carried out. The present pope, John Paul II, has written a letter to preface the document in which he claims that superiors have asked for help in determining these essentials. The Holy See has appointed a commission of bishops to investigate religious communities in the United States to see why so few new members are entering. And in an unprecedented and frightening action, an auxiliary bishop of Brooklyn personally carried from the pope to a sister in Detroit an ultimatum demanding either that she give up the work which her community had authorized her to do or that she renounce her vows. Since then other sisters have been subjected to similar treatment.

A question for many religious women can now be put this way: Have we in all good faith and obedience taken to heart the words of one pope, Paul VI — to renew our lives in the light of the gospel, the charism of our founders, and the signs of the times, and this at great cost — only now to have our work, our best insights, our personal growth and the autonomy of our congregations destroyed at the word of another pope? And, if this is the case, what is to be the place of religious communities of women within the Roman Catholic Church in the future?

The reader will find numerous references to the Quinn Commission (the investigating bishops named above); to Sister Agnes Mary Mansour (the sister summarily presented with the dilemma of quitting her community-authorized job or having her vows nullified — and this with no possibility of dialogue); to the SCRIS document (a short way of referring to *Essential Elements of Religious Life* — also mentioned above). Each of these instances is described in greater detail in chapters where authors choose to deal with one or the other of them as paradigmatic of future relations with Rome. We have decided, despite the repetition, to let them stand, just as we have let stand the repeated expressions of joy and delight at what the Spirit has wrought in our lives. After all, one should be able to tell one's story in one's own way!

No Time for Tying Cats

Joan D. Chittister

*Joan Chittister is the prioress of the Benedictine Sisters of Erie, Pa.
She is president of the Conference of American Benedictine Prioresses, a
U.S. councilor-delegate to the International Union of Superiors General
and a past president of the Leadership Conference of Women Religious.
She holds a Ph.D. in communication theory from Penn State University.
Her most recent publication is* Women, Ministry and the Church *(Paulist
Press, 1983).*

It was a difficult and poignant conversation. The young nun announced
at the family dinner table that she would be leaving the convent the
following June when the teaching year was over and her obligations to
the school in which she taught had ended.

The father was Protestant. He had resisted her entering the convent
in the first place.

The mother was Catholic but committed to independence. She wouldn't
be crushed if there were no nun in the family.

The Sister was an only child. Most of the family thought she should
never have entered in the first place.

"I still love religious life," she said. "But I'm not leaving religious life.
It's leaving me. Everything is falling apart. Nothing is the same anymore.
There's no reason to stay. People don't want to teach; they don't want to
wear the habit; they don't want to live together. I have to leave while
I'm still young enough to be able to make a living."

Everything about their response was exactly what she expected: If she
was unhappy, of course she should come home. If this was what she
wanted to do, then indeed she should do it. If religious life wasn't good
anymore, then certainly she should leave. But they did suggest that she
not make a final decision until she thought through two additional questions: "Who would take care of the old Sisters if all the young ones left?"
the father said, and, "Did she really believe she could do anything of
substance without its changing in the course of the commitment? "You
don't think," her mother said, "that our relationship today is the same
as it was when your father and I were first married, do you? It isn't the
things you do that count; it's what you are. Don't think about what nuns
do; think about what nuns are before you make your final decision. Just
be sure you're not leaving for the wrong reasons."

I've been thinking about all of that ever since.

It was 1968, I think. The community had been in turmoil for years. Religious had begun leaving in droves — not after Vatican II was over as people so often now glibly assume — but long before it ended, not only in my own community but all over the country. The women who stayed were plunged into both uncertainty and excitement. The council was calling for the renewal of the church, and religious life had been singled out for analysis. In a group that hadn't changed much for centuries, anything had suddenly become possible. And that was exactly the problem. For many, the changes were already too late and they had left. For many, change was a welcome possibility and they would cooperate happily in its development. For many, change was the height of infidelity and they intended to resist with all their hearts. By 1970, uniform dress had been discarded and even the veil was optional. Sisters in "teaching orders" had begun to want to do other things. Community life was being interrupted by relationships outside the group — family, colleagues, even friends. A life that had been sunk in certainty was now awash with uncertainties. All the old absolutes had blurred.

Except perhaps the ones my mother and father had identified: community and commitment. Through these two filters I began to make a distinction between what was custom and what was charism. More than 15 years have passed since the conversation and every day I become more grateful for it. Without it I might have lost one of the happiest, most fulfilling, most demanding, most challenging, most spiritual and most genuinely Christian life-styles of the present time.

How renewal happened is a matter of record. In most communities, in-depth study by various commissions led to recommendations for change to the community chapter or superior. No area escaped experimentation and review: governance, community life, prayer, apostolic works, formation, vows. We asked ourselves, too, if that theology and those practices were the best we could do in our time as the Vatican document said "in the light of the gospel, the spirit of the founder, the needs of the members and the signs of the times." It sounds so neat and simple now; so ordered, so rational, so clear. That's why "how" is not the right question; only "what" and "why" get beyond not only renewal but the present resistance to returning to the past as well.

Let me try to describe it from my own experience, not as an isolated example of personal history but as a distillation of a general environment recounted though actual circumstances.

Governance

In 1964, obedience — strict obedience, military obedience, parental obedience — was the standard for the vow. Every Saturday I went to the superior's bedroom, knelt down in front of her and asked, "For the love of Jesus, sister, may I go over to school to work in my classroom on bulletin boards (or class projects or records or cleaning)?" Once every month — once every week for the five years before final profession — I "spoke fault." Last week the old list of permissions and faults fell out of a small notebook that has long been tucked away among old pictures and poetry and spiritual reading books. It went like this:

"Mother, for the love of Jesus may I have permission to:
wash my clothes,
air and press my clothes when necessary
give and receive small things,
lend and borrow small things,
read the newspaper,
use school and cleaning supplies,
take a bath,
trim my hair,
polish my shoes,
write letters and send feastday greetings,
go to my room and school when necessary,
use the telephone when necessary,
have toothpaste and soap,
get my shoes stretched this week.

And then, after unusual permissions were discussed, "Mother, *mea culpa* for:
making mistakes in the divine office, community prayers and
spiritual reading,
hurrying in the halls and on the stairs,
walking heavily,
failing to keep my hands under my scapular,
spilling food and water,
wasting paper and electricity,
talking loudly,
breaking silence,
making mistakes in my works of obedience,
using slang and nicknames,
crossing my feet,
spotting my clothing,
failing to mortify my eyes,
being late for prayer on Tuesday morning,
talking to seculars on the street,
sleeping in this morning.
For the love of Jesus, Mother, may I have a penance?"

I did that for 20 years. In 1952, at the age of 16, it made no sense to me. In 1972, it made even less. Were those really the great issues of the spiritual life that I had come to grapple with and grow through and grasp? And if virtue was supposed to be the by-product, who said that humiliation was a good substitute for humility or oppressiveness for obedience? It was a far cry from a home where I had been raised to be a part of all family decisions, to take accountability for them, and to be responsible for my own activities.

Every small detail of life was regulated, not in the name of community order which surely they served, but in the name of the vow of obedience. A sister with whom I lived was in charge of the forensic program and asked regularly and wearily for the permission to take the youngsters to diocesan speech tournaments which she was assigned to conduct. One night the superior came back with, "And what will you do if I say no?" And the sister answered simply: "Oh, would you please?"

Week after week we asked permission to do what we could not possibly *not* do. Formalism and legalism had completely replaced either spiritual direction or blessing. Every day life got smaller. Religious life had become the celebration of the trivial. While McCarthyism raged, I was told to guard myself from spiritual distraction by not listening to the news. While Martin Luther King began black sit-ins of white lunch counters in a country that routinely lynched blacks, I believed it when they said that had nothing to do with religious life and concentrated on darning my socks, a real sign of poverty, I was told. While troops were sent to Indochina and the United States invaded Cuba, I aimed at self-perfection and worried that making a phone call without permission might be a violation of my vows. A young woman who entered the community at the same time I did preferred to catch a red hot iron in mid-air rather than have to "speak fault" for dropping it.

When, abruptly, personal responsibility became the basis for obedience, religious communities found themselves with a whole population of the most educated women in the country who found decision-making a burdensome task. What doctor shall I go to; how shall I get into town; what cupboard should I use, all became major concerns for some. For a while everything went tilt. Some struggled with anxiety; others, it seemed, ran through life as if it were a candy shop, trying everything in sight and leaving the papers strewn behind them. Many found themselves torn between license and reaction. Most, finally, came to the realization that the proper content of obedience was the discernment of individual gifts in the context of the community charism and social concern. Now, though the concept of obedience has never been questioned in the community, it is hard to imagine that the purpose of a superior is to scold a woman like a child for dropping an iron.

Now I and all the other sisters in my community participate in the decisions that affect our own lives and bring to the decisions that affect others the standards of the gospel, not the requirements of a custom book long out of date that busied itself with directions about not sitting on beds or talking on the streets or swinging your arms or making solemn bows where simple bows should be. Now obedience has been elevated beyond the level of the parental to the level of the adult and has become a listening to the discerned will of God on both sides. Before renewal, obedience had become tightly regulated but trivialized; now obedience has become difficult but worth the effort.

Community Life

My first mission was in a rural area about 90 miles from the priory. At 19, I was the only non-professed sister in the house of eight. Conversation between scholastics and the perpetually professed members of the community was strictly forbidden. So were visits to any other mission unless you were professed and then only four times a year. I made up a 30-day novena to St. Thomas the Doubter asking for a miracle to get me to the priory for Christmas where there would be a full liturgy and many of my peers. On December 21, the feast of St. Thomas, word came from the motherhouse that all non-professed were to be sent home to the priory for special meetings during the holidays.

There were many things about community life that did not make for community and "the common life" was no guarantee of them. Recreation was anything but. We sat around a table together in order of rank for 45 minutes a day and talked about vacuous subjects while we corrected papers. I was told to keep an account once of the amount of time I was spending with one specific sister — too much, the superior judged, for someone to be a good community member. The most time was 63 minutes in one week, all stolen from something else for the sake of business. I felt guilty for days and frightened that I'd be forbidden even that since I had to admit that I had spoken to her every day.

It's hard to talk the "common life" to those who lived it like this and get good, positive vibrations. Then, friendship was the enemy of community; today friendship is the basis of community. Time and space are not. Then we lived together day in and day out but learned little about one another and shared little about ourselves in the name of community. "The sisters should not speak of their families," the directives said. "The sisters should not talk about the things they did or learned when they were outside of the community" for fear these things would lead to distraction or temptation or arrogance or all three. We lived with people we never spoke to and wanted to talk to people who were missioned elsewhere and told to stay there for the year. We all lived alone together.

Now we live in self-selected groups where interests and schedules and needs match and we come together as a large group at the priory time and again throughout the year for liturgy, for community projects, for celebration, for discussion, for education, for retreat, for chapter concerns, for parties. We're getting to know one another in different, deeper ways. But in the process we've found out that there's a real distinction to be made between "the common life" and "community life." We're monastic and the two often intersect, but not always. The assumption that the two are the same can make a mockery out of religious life.

Ministry

The concept of interchangeable parts revolutionized industry. Products could be made faster and distributed more broadly. Multiple copies of specific parts were warehoused and retrieved for use as the original systems wore down or needed to be expanded. The idea was a great one and the American economy thrived under it. Unfortunately, it was often applied in the social system as well and the results were not the same.

I was studying for a degree in English literature and sent to teach double grades, fifth and sixth, for four years. A chemistry teacher in the community was taken out of her high school laboratory in December and transferred to a fourth grade in a completely different city in January. A concert pianist was sent to teach beginning piano students in a farm parish out of the city. A typing teacher was made a high school principal overnight. Sisters who wanted to nurse were told that they knew when they entered that we were a "teaching order" and prepared for classroom work whether they were capable or happy or not.

The important thing to remember is that the examples aren't bizarre. They were the norm. In a society where everyone dressed the same, looked the same, lived the same, functioned the same and believed the same, there was no reason to imagine that individual gifts and needs lurked anywhere beneath the surface or should, at least, be given any attention. Work undertaken in the "spirit of obedience" would be blessed and that was enough.

Though I'm sure it was blessed, I'm a great deal less sure that it succeeded as well as the nostalgia buffs like to recount. The Catholic school system grew and flourished, true, but someone has to wonder out loud what was under the multiple stories of its nun-teachers who hit children, or never smiled, or refused to talk, or wielded authority like a scourge. What was going on in those women who were moved willy-nilly from one parish and one professional area to another? Frustration? Unhappiness? Underdevelopment? Fear that came with constant lack of preparation? What did robotizing do to the human spirit and, even when you're taught to "offer it up" and submit to the "will of God," what effect did that have on the growth of the spiritual life? The Catholic community was as full of ridicule and scorn for the way religious lived and taught as they were respect. But when sisters began to leave the schools for new or different works in the 1960s, people constantly worried only about what would happen to the Catholic school system in the United States. Few people worried about what would happen to the new poor — the blacks, the Hispanics, the Third World, the planet — or the sisters themselves if they didn't. It's hard to believe that much of a sense of either public concern or personal charism was left alive in the church.

Some of our sisters joined demonstrations during the Vietnam war and then opened a soup kitchen, a hospitality house for homeless women and a peace and justice center to resist the nuclear buildup on a fragile planet. People, pillars-of-the-parish types, asked to be taken off the community mailing list or withdrew their children from our academy. They wanted nothing to do with a community that bred communists and radicals in its midst. Long forgotten was the fact that our community came to the United States to work with outcast German Catholic immigrants to whom the society of that day was also closed. They forgot as well that on the backs of those early nuns their own poorer ancestors had learned to read English, to vote, to work, and to succeed in this Anglo-Saxon Protestant culture. It made some of us wonder two things: what we had been teaching in the Catholic schools all those years that people were so ill-prepared for this kind of Christianity and, then, why was it — if the schools were so valued and valuable — that the people who had been trained in them for 150 years would not undertake their administration and their support themselves so that the sisters could attend to the newly deprived of this day. Was it we ourselves who had reduced the gospel mandate to the level of cheap labor for the sake of the established subculture?

The questions were hard and harsh and unrelenting. But we went on asking. After all, it was no less an authority than a Vatican Council that had instructed us to measure everything, *everything*, against the "standards of the Gospel, the charism of the founder, the needs of the members and the signs of the times." That couldn't be anything but right, could it?

Formation

It didn't take five minutes to get the picture. Before taking us into the community dining room for the first time, they had us put on the black shoes and cotton hose, the mid-calf dresses and shoulder capes, and the filmy mesh veils that had long been the uniform of candidates to the religious life. Then, in a less-used front parlor where we couldn't be seen, they lined us up according to birth dates and entrance applications from the oldest to the youngest. We learned how to cross our arms under our capes — the only accepted way to walk — and began the exciting move down the long, long halls in single file procession to our first community meal. Away from the parents we'd left at the convent door, away from the friends we'd grown up with, away from the activities and concerns and realities of the cities we'd lived in all our lives. I can still see the shadows of the girls in front of me bobbing up and down along the high walls of the sunlit hall. I was the youngest in this new group and so in the community. "I'm going to be following this crowd around at the end of this line for the rest of my life," I remember thinking. It wasn't a joy and it wasn't a sadness. It was simply an intuition that took years for its implications to emerge.

After that, routine, discipline and denial became the foundations of religious commitment. Sanctity, I learned quickly, lay in regularity of schedule, submission to the will of another in the minutest elements of the day, and constant suppression of any personal instinct even in the commonplaces of life. Sanctity was not riding in the front seat of the car with your father, not eating an orange between meals, not talking on the city streets, not being up after 9:30 at night, not being out after twilight, not missing prayer or meals, not breaking silence, not doing anything without permission. It was easy to tell what holiness wasn't; it was harder to tell exactly what it was. Formation was the standardization of behaviors rather than the internalization of values.

At the Chapter of Faults in the refectory on Friday nights we knelt in the middle of the community and confessed such things. The superior gave us a penance. I used to sit at the table and read a book, trying hard not to let myself hear the recitations. They embarrassed me, I think. They also raised a lot of guilt. I knew I would simply never be perfect. What was worse, I didn't even want to be if it meant mustering repentance for swinging my arms or laughing out loud or talking to people. Frankly, I was the joker in the crowd and those things were my stock in trade. Besides, I failed to be convinced of their moral value and I had a lot of reason to think that not too many other people did either.

Prayer

If one of the functions of good liturgy is to reflect life, then ours worked. Like us, it was half medieval monastic and half standard American. Out of a 17-hour day that began at 5:00 a.m. and went to 10:00 p.m., we were in chapel for prayer, meditation, or spiritual reading a total of four and a half hours daily. All official prayers were chanted in Latin. As time went by we prayed out of books that carried the Latin on one side of the page and its English translation on the other but there was little enlightenment that came from reciting in one language and trying desperately to see what you had just said in another. Over the years, the psalms became familiar; the long patristic readings at matins never did.

We were trained to bow at certain angles at certain phrases, to "kiss the pew" — tap the bench in front of us with our fingertips — when we made a mistake, to drop the proper thirds and fifths as we sang the lives of the saints in psalm tones, to read the Latin *Ordo* or official daily prayer schedule and mark our breviaries accordingly. Sort of. The definition of a novice became "someone who intones the wrong antiphon at the top of her voice."

Then after all that was done, we said a series of litanies and prayers and novenas in English, obviously to have some kind of community prayer that was clear and meaningful to us as a group. "Evening prayer" followed compline, the official evening prayer of the church and a little gem of faith and petition in psalmody but foreign to us. Instead every night one of us said aloud for the community a personal "ferverino" to Jesus that assured God, "I now retire to rest in order to please thee" (or as someone once announced with Freudian honesty, "I now retire to rest in order to please me").

Even at prayer, in other words, we were in another kind of world: formal, ritualized, and foreign. Even here where you would expect religious to be most involved we stood with one leg in one culture, one leg in another.

Nevertheless, I would probably never have survived if it hadn't been for prayer and reading. I never did completely understand all of the Latin prayers and passages but the rhythms of the choral psalmody were nevertheless quieting and the long spaces for prayer in a day full of physical labor and nervous strain were a godsend. So the fact of the matter is that it was actually the reading that counted most, I think. At least in my case. Only in the late 1950s did they begin to teach the younger members of the community theology. Theology was no subject for a woman, after all. Priests took care of that. We studied *Baltimore Catechism II* for novitiate religion and the *Catechism of the Vows* — the staples of religious formation for the women of the church until the Sister Formation Movement in 1956. But we read a lot. In the daily periods of meditation and spiritual reading, like water dropping on a rock, we learned the history of spirituality and the person of Christ in the gospels. In retrospect, I've often secretly thought that it may have been precisely our immersion in the "secular" subjects and in spiritual reading that eventually undermined the whole system. Thinking is always dangerous, especially in a society that doesn't foster it.

The thought began to form that religious life had to be about more than prayer formulas and schools and good order in the group. But what?

Vows

Before Vatican II vocations were either "higher" or "lower," not simply different from one another. And dualism was alive and well. There were the things of the world or the things of God; the things of the flesh or the things of the spirit; the sacred or the secular. One was in tension with the other. One worked to our good and one to our woe.

Life was divided into two mutually exclusive categories, spiritual or worldly, and there was little gray space between the two. To be a religious was to reduce the margin for error even more than most. Perfection, in fact, demanded that we "give up the world," even its more benign aspects: hamburgers at MacDonald's, swimming in a public pool, wearing second-hand cardigans. Religious were "signs" of consecration, of separation from the world, of everybody else's weakness. And women religious most of all who were never to go out without a companion, or into public gatherings, or to perform public functions. It protected their vocation; it developed their humility; it increased their respect, we were told.

I remember the downcast eyes of the 17-year-old boy who would not look at me to answer a question the day we first appeared in school after replacing our medieval headdress with a simpler pinned-back veil. When he left the office I said to the sister with me, "All we've managed to do in 1500 years is to make hairlines obscene." I had to begin to ask myself what we had really taught about the evangelical counsels of poverty, chastity and obedience. The world was starving; I was well-fed. I had never said a word about the injustice of it all, but I could point with pride to the fact, not that I spent a life of sharing and trying to assure that others would have enough, but that I never had a dime in my pocket. I kept myself away from people to preserve my chastity when a loving presence whose concern was celibate and unpossessing was the sign of Christ that was really needed. I did what I was told instead of doing what I should and called it obedience. Separation from the world, not insertion into its pain, was the theological vision of the time.

I remember the novice in our group who hid behind the stove in the kitchen in order to avoid breaking the rule by talking to her mother who was delivering a package at the back door of the convent. I remember watching the men of the parish take the television they had loaned us out of the community room when we couldn't get permission from the prioress to watch the coronation of Queen Elizabeth. I remember being told when we would all begin to wear our winter shawls, whether you were cold or not. I remember going only between the convent and the school, the school and the convent, every day of my life, with some opportunities to go to the priory or our other missions but never, never into the homes of seculars — even my family — and never to public places like restaurants, or movie theaters, or even meetings. I remember it all with pain and embarrassment.

And I remember the years of renewal, too. There was pain then as well.

Expectation was high during the council; surely some of these things would be changed. We would be allowed to pray in English, perhaps. We might at least be asked what works we would like to do. Maybe we would even be permitted to go to our homes to visit our parents. Some of them were elderly now and it was getting more and more difficult for them to always come to see us. We waited for a list of directives that never came. This time it was not going to be so easy. This time we were going to have to work it all out ourselves. And the order was from Rome.

Every area of community life was opened for experimentation by a general chapter made up of prioresses and community officials, the very people who, in authoritarian terms, had the most to lose. People began to dream new dreams out loud: If we wanted to know what poverty was about, why couldn't we have an allowance to buy our own toothpaste and powder and soap and get to know what kinds of choices people without money had to make? Why couldn't we apply for our own apostolic works and bear the responsibility for our own mistakes and make our own commitments as well instead of being sent like wooden puppets on a steel string? Why couldn't we live with the sisters we wanted to? Why couldn't we stay in regular houses, like the people we served and in the neighborhoods they did rather than in large, cold institutions far removed from the city? Why couldn't we take people in to live and pray with us, the poor, the tired, the frazzled, the wounded? Why was teaching the only thing we did when there were so many other gifts, so many other needs? If we wanted to identify with the people, why couldn't we wear ordinary clothes? Why did we have to keep reminding them that we were different, better, more chosen than they? Pandora's box was open at last.

Fear and frustration walked hand in hand. Blue blouses became a sign of scandal. New ministries were a type of treason. After all, these sisters were destroying the schools and with them, of course, the ministries of the rest of us. Money in the pocket was an overwhelming temptation to sin. At best, it would simply be frittered away. Why didn't people who wanted things like that just leave?

Young sisters cried in rage after every meeting. Older ones sank deeper and deeper into depression. The middle-aged agonized over the future.

At every community discussion, the blue blouses sat on one side of the assembly room and the veils sat together on the other. Like Esau and Jacob, two nations struggled to live while every day more and more peole left. My favorite line got to be, "I don't say good night around here anymore; I say goodbye. You never know if you're ever going to see anyone again." But the humor was quick to wear thin and I began to consider the possibility of leaving myself. It seemed that the tension would never end. But one day, for me, it did.

Governance

Discernment replaced maternalism. A good many sins had been committed in the name of "mother said . . . " over the years. To wheedle or weary something out of a superior was often the game of obedience. Since she was the community conscience no one else really had to have one. If she said it was all right, it was all right and if anyone questioned they questioned the wisdom of the superior, not the righteousness of the sister. Now, all the permissions in the world will not save me from a conscience formed in the context of community and the vows. I remember asking for new serge habits and three-foot square linen headdresses with aplomb. Four years later I could not allow myself to buy a leather coat on sale for less than the cloth ones because of what I thought that would say to people with no vow of poverty but no money either.

No, there are no public penances now; no routine permission system for pins and paper; no daily assignment sheets; no effort to create a series of false asceticisms (the Benedictine Rule has always maintained that there is more than enough of the real stuff to go around); no sense of military measures of the gospel life. I don't sit in the office and assign companions to sisters with doctor's appointments or listen to the recitation of formulas or content myself with checking the bedrooms or censoring personal mail before it's sent as prioresses had to do in the past.

But I do have long, deep discussions with people about their life direction and its relationship to the gospel, the rule and the vows. I do work hard at both listening and responding and searching together for the will of God for this community and for each of its members. I find real obedience much harder than lists and customs books. And on the days when nothing seems right, I get a new understanding and empathy for the Israelites in the desert and yearn for the lists and the customs books. Now lockstep is gone. In its place is the constant call of the prioress and community to strain toward the highest standards of the Christ and the stark, hard awareness of my own distance from that truth. The call now is to authenticity, not to conformity. It occurred to me years ago that every day of their married lives my father left home for work and my mother went about the business of running the house. They were neither policed nor directed by any outside force how to do that but the expectations were clear: Each night when they came together again they were to have been faithful to one another and to their marriage vows though they had not had the privilege of being protected from breaking them. Why should religious be expected to do less? Free love freely given is surely the only real standard of adult commitment.

In the first place, I went home to announce to my parents that I was leaving. In the second place, someone in the community began to circulate a petition requesting a split in the community. With those two incidents I got an insight into religious life that I had never been conscious of before: it wasn't *part* of the community, not even the part that agreed with me, that I had entered and loved and respected and drew strength and joy and inspiration from; it was the *whole* community that I wanted and either half alone was seriously deficient. It wasn't what they did or how they dressed or where they lived that counted. It was what they were. As my parents had said, it was community and commitment that it was all about. That's why the others hadn't left; that's why I wouldn't either. A basic love for the community itself was bringing us all back together. The sign of the first Christian community had been a simple one: See how they love one another. Funny how we'd missed that all this time.

After that everything became clearer. Anything that didn't meet those criteria wasn't religious life. Anything that did, was.

It wasn't that the past had all been bad. In fact, great women had emerged from it, all of them in some grand way exceptions to its rigidity and infantilism. It was simply that the past was past. Education, culture, theology — all conspired against the maintenance of a system that made children out of highly competent women. The young, of course, were the first to realize how completely out of sync with their expectations and hopes this life-style was: once they saw it up close, the novitiates and scholasticates of the country began to empty out. The middle-aged were professionally prepared enough to deal with the facts if they were psychologically prepared to cope with change. The elderly had themselves lived through less rigid times long ago and through other social upheavals of no small magnitude. From many of them came both faith and encouragement. Most superiors, who saw best the human underside of a life-style that cramped large-souled people, facilitated rather than obstructed renewal. And as the years went by, it became apparent that out of chaos had come a new kind of order, less confining than the past but in many ways more accountable and in all ways more mature.

Community Life

The common life still exists. Our pattern is to live and pray together in a spirit of monastic recollection; to operate only out of a common fund; to share responsibility for the community; to participate in its development and to function according to the policies that emerge in it. But the common life is not enough; community has come to enhance it.

In 1965, the schedule was always more important than the conversation. I lived with a superior who routinely turned the TV detective story, "Perry Mason," off at 8:15 rather than extend the recreation period 15 minutes so we could find out who did the who-done-it. After all, recreation was a time period, not an experience.

We were allowed to go to our own homes when people were dying, but not when they were alive. We could visit funeral parlors but not wedding receptions. (They were threats to our vocation; death apparently was not.) We could correct one another but we could not have personal friends. Anger was an acceptable emotion; love was not. We could keep the world out to keep it from breaking us down; we could not take it in to lift it up.

Well, that's all gone, too. Because of the support of their communities, people can live alone in the ghettos and back waters of the continent to make community for those who have none. We've changed community schedules so that those sisters who work late into the night in counseling, nursing work, care for the aged, administration, or education can come home themselves for prayer and presence and find them when they need and can profit from them most. We take vacation and development days together every year. Instead of living in subsets built only around a given work, we party and pray and process life together as a total group — not all the time but at significant times and regularly and often. We've moved out of convents into homes like those of the people we serve, taken them in with us and tried to be neighbor and sister as well as social worker and church functionary.

I remember when people were not permitted into our chapel to pray or into our dining room to eat because withdrawal from the world was something we practiced very selectively. Now we've come to understand the wedding feast at Cana as well as the 40 days in the desert, the days with Martha and Mary as well as the time at Nazareth. And the Christian community is fuller for it all. A 75-year-old sister says with firm assurance, "I'm just glad I lived to see this day."

Ministry

The myth is that sisters abandoned and destroyed the Catholic school system. The fact may well be just the opposite. Several years ago I discovered that though it was true that only half of the active members in my own community were still teaching in the parochial system, it was also true that if the other half had remained there our small community of 140 sisters would be an additional $100,000 in debt. The point is that for any sisters to be able to stay in the schools, some of us had to leave. In an earlier period, the community could live on the housing that was provided and the gifts of farm products or services or discounts that complemented the small school stipends. In 1966, the average sister's stipend in the parochial school system was $100 per month without benefit of health insurance or retirement monies. Nevertheless, women religious were responsible for providing their own food, shelter, health care and education. But within the past 20 years, religious communities, like the people around them, have been faced with compulsory automobile insurance, compulsory medical insurance, rising educational costs even at Catholic colleges, taxation, and increasing expenses for food and utilities. Everything had changed, in fact, except the community's economic base. More than that, the face of ministry changed as well.

For all practical purposes, the task that most communities came to this country to do had — with the accession of John F. Kennedy to the presidency of the United States — been completed. Through the school system, the faith had been preserved in a strange land; Catholics had been inserted into a Protestant culture; the church had a tightly organized catechetical base and major institutional system. But whole new pockets of poor and oppressed people have arisen in this society and women religious are attempting to start all over again with the same bias toward the poor of this generation as we brought to the poor of the last, this time with a commitment to systemic justice as well as to personal charity. We are beginning to see more and more religious working for full salaries to support their communities so that more and more religious can work again for people who can pay nothing. But to do that we have to put a lot of things down: so-called religious garb, institutionalism, withdrawal, a common apostolate in favor of corporate commitments to the global issues of peace, poverty, hunger, minority concerns, human rights and the equality of women.

Yesterday, as I wrote this, a 72-year-old sister stopped to tell me, "I clothed the naked today. Instead of going to the prison as we usually do on Wednesdays, we went to the prisoners' homes. No one thinks of how hard it is for their families and children so I take orders for clothing and toys and get the sisters to help me collect them." She's been doing that work for 14 years, long before it was "religious" to go into people's homes, long before it was religious to be something other than a teacher or a nurse, long before it was religious for a sister to work outside of the Catholic institutional system, long before it was religious not to wear a habit or a veil. I don't question her sanctity or her commitment to religious life and this community; it's her ecclesial legitimacy I'm worried about.

Formation

When I entered the community I was 16, full of good will, some intelligence, a great deal of spunk and an over-endowment of Irish wit. And that was all. I had no money, only half a high school education, little or no experience, and only the haziest notion of what I would like to do in life as well as be. Not that anyone cared.

My formation consisted mainly in waiting for me to grow up and in teaching me to behave as I did. That was what I needed and that was all there was. Ideas had already been shaped and closed long before my appearance on the scene. The structures were tried and true. No one, absolutely no one, needed my opinions on the great matters of life. They had all been solved a long time past without my help.

Oh, have times changed. In the first place, most women are entering between the ages of 25 and 35, much later than before. In the second, formation is no longer seen as a project to be completed by the time of perpetual profession but an activity to be engaged in throughout their entire community lives. In both cases, consequently, the emphasis is on values, not behaviors, and reasons, not directions. I spent an hour explaining patiently to a novice why, in a monastic community, novices did not go home for an overnight visit on Christmas Eve. She asked me how much formation I thought took place in bed. My answer was that it was not the activity that was in question but the need to begin early in community life to identify with and take responsibility for the community Christmas. Consequently, she could choose either time: all night and be home for prayer in the morning or all day and be home for the community party that night, but not both. She understood instantly and the novitiate and the vocation and I all survived. But she had to have the answer. My novice mistress would have sent me home for daring to raise the question. I prefer now. What we can't explain shouldn't be masquerading as religious life. So dealt Jesus with Thomas, with Mary Magdalene and with the disciples on the way to Emmaus. When the teaching persuades, force and fear are unnecessary.

That doesn't mean that policies don't exist, that accountability isn't an expectation, that the center of the life isn't still Jesus and not self. It means that being scolded for getting in after sundown, as I was 15 years ago at the age of 32, is not what religious life is about. It's about the gospel. It's a life-style for adults of the highest caliber.

Prayer

I remember the first time a beautiful, lithe sister of mine danced the alleluia banner down the middle aisle of the chapel at the gospel of the mass with her long-lined gown swirling, her head back and her hands up. I remember the feeling of prayer as she enabled us verse after verse to raise our hands in alleluia, too. I remember the first time a sister of mine gave the reflection on the gospel at a Sunday night vigil, dredged out of years of experience and quiet reflection. I had been taught both implicitly and explicitly that only priests, men, could expound the faith or know what the scriptures meant. I remember the first time a young woman in my office said she preferred to make commitment to religious life at prayer "where we'd be able to do it ourselves" instead of mass "with a strange man" in charge. I remember in all those instances learning something different about monastic community and how for women it had only been partially possible all these years.

So remote had prayer become for us, so formal and so unrelated to our lives, so acutely aware did younger women become of the gulf between them and God in chapel that it seemed for a while that community prayer and celebration of the eucharist were in danger of being lost. But whatever the tensions of style or theology, the liturgy of the hours and the eucharist remain the centerpiece of our daily lives together because now it's our prayer and our reflections that shape them. It makes me remember the great abbesses of the past and their administration and instruction of the dual monasteries of both men and women. That's the least we owe to the young women of our time who are looking for God in their own lives.

The Vows

In 1957, I took final vows. In 1979 I renewed them at my silver jubilee. The second time meant a great deal more than the first. Not only did I realize better then what I had done with my life but I also realized that I was re-committing myself to do the same thing differently.

I had lived in my lifetime two separate visions of the vowed life. The old vision said that it was a function of religious life to be a state of perfection. Nothing less than high level standard was allowed. We were to be perfectly silent, perfectly orderly, perfectly docile, perfectly capable in everything we were told to do. The new vision said that religious life is, like any Christian vocation, a state of search: open, listening, changing, growing, not a checklist of ministries, schedules and spiritual devotions. "Cookie-cutter" spirituality is gone. Sameness is no longer a synonym for sanctity. But growth is. And growth is what we foster. Growth in personality; growth in giftedness; growth in human community; growth in ministry; growth in God. A sister said, "It's not neat around here anymore but it's exciting."

I can't honestly say what I'll be doing 10 years from now or how I'll be doing it, as it seemed I could say in 1957, but there is one thing of which I can be sure: it will have something to do with spiritual development, community, peace and justice, the upbuilding of the kingdom, and the development of the gifts God has given to me to spend in this context. Those things will be the touchstones of the choices and that is enough to know right now. In that lies the Benedictine vows of stability and *metanoia*.

The old vision of religious life said that religious took vows to keep the law; the new vision says that religious take vows to gain life and give life. There can't be any more hiding behind stoves to avoid people. We have to take the life we get from the gospels, from the community, from the continual mantra of the common prayer and work to change the life of others for the better. That's a listening obedience.

The old vision said the function of religious life was to be a labor force, to do institutional work. But the new vision says that religious are not called to be a labor force but a leaven: a caring, calling presence that moves quickly into new needs. That's celibate love unbound.

The old vision of religious life said it was a function of religious life to take a stand against the things of the world. The new vision says that religious must stand for the good things of this world — not *against* property, flesh, and will but *for* the poor, for justice, for love, for accountability, for a positive, not a negative, spirituality. Like the Christ of Emmaus rather than the Christ of Transfiguration, many sisters go among the people of the area dressed from a rack of used clothes in the basement that are given to us regularly by the women of the city as they clean out the wardrobes or closets of their homes. Sisters carry money now — $55 a month — out of which they're expected to pay for all their toilet articles, books, clothes, recreational activities, private transportation, vacation expenses, gifts and private almsgiving. They know what it is not to have what other people have, not to be able to give what other people give, not to be able to have what you'd like. Poverty has become a closer thing. It means laying down your life without the return it deserves. That's poverty lived for others; not poverty lived for piety's sake.

The old vision of religious life said that the function of the religious is to transcend the world, to withdraw from it; the new vision of religious life says its function is to transform the world, to be in but not of it, as Jesus was. Every year our sisters, from our oldest to our youngest, present their covenant statements at the blessing of ministries ceremony. They record how they'll give themselves to both their personal ministry and the achievement of our corporate commitment to nuclear disarmament and the relationship between militarism and sexism ("by writing to congress to protest further proliferation of nuclear arms and being community health insurance coordinator"; "by studying the peace pastoral with others and by being parish music minister"; "by supporting demonstrations and vigils and being executive secretary"; "by making financial contributions and teaching the issues to third graders"). As I see our sisters making this commitment, I know that the kind of transformation religious life has always been about is still very alive, very well. As I pack my bag for speech after speech and meeting after meeting from this continent to the next, as I watch my sisters leave prayer every day for the soup kitchen, the food pantry, the grade schools, colleges and inner-city academy, the homes for the aged, the hospitals, the peace work, the retreats, the parishes, the prisons, the print shop, the fine arts studios, the energy conservation projects, the food bank, the minority day care centers, the local, state and national commissions, I know there's no going back. That the past was all prelude. That this is what incarnation and the God of history are all about. That this is what the vows are all about: the use of people, possessions and power in our own time. That, as my mother and father said, this is what monasticism is all about: community and commitment.

How can I be so sure in the face of so much uncertainty, so much criticism, so much past? There's a Sufi tale that impels me. It reads:

> When the guru sat down to worship each
> evening, the ashram cat would get in
> the way and distract the worshippers.
> So he ordered that the cat be tied
> during evening worship.
>
> Long after the guru died, the cat

continued to be tied during evening
worship. And when the cat eventually
died, another cat was brought to the
ashram so that it could be duly tied
during evening worship.

Centuries later, learned treaties were
written by the guru's disciples on the
essential role of a cat in all properly
conducted worship.

Having once discovered the real purpose of things, this generation is
not going to spend any more time tying cats.

My Pact with Camillus

Camille D'Arienzo

*Camille D'Arienzo has been a Sister of Mercy since 1951. Her profes-
sional experiences include teaching in Catholic elementary schools, producing instructional television programs, training lectors and providing
workshops for organizations wishing to improve their communication
skills. She is a frequent lecturer on a variety of topics, including women
and the life of the church, and has contributed articles on that topic to*
America *and* Commonweal. *Occasionally a visiting professor at the University of Michigan, she is a tenured associate professor in the television-
radio department of Brooklyn College (CUNY), an associate editor of* The
Tablet, *and Catholic commentator for WINS radio.*

Act One: Days of Decision

Scene One. Carrying my suitcase, I moved with the rush of weekend
commuters from the train platform, down the steps, toward the row of
doors leading to and from the waiting room of the Long Island Railroad
Station at Jamaica, New York. It was May of 1950, a month before my
high school graduation from Our Lady of Mercy Academy, a boarding
school at Syosset on Long Island, in which I had been enrolled six years
earlier, three years after my mother's death and two after my father's
difficult second marriage. I was 17.

As I approached the doors to the waiting room, the familiar words
above them assumed ominous implications:

"Enter."

"Do not enter."

This was the weekend I had determined to tell my father, the person
I loved most on earth, that I was going to join the Sisters of Mercy, a
semi-cloistered congregation. That decision would remove me from the
family circle and position me on the periphery of his life, in a condition
beyond the pale of his expectation or comprehension. Could I do it? Should
I do it?

Scene Two. Late Sunday afternoon that weekend I sat in my father's
car outside the same railroad station, talking with him as the time drew
near for my return trip to Syosset. He was, as ever, smartly dressed with
the dignity and assurance of the self-made man. He was an energetic 65
and the father of three daughters (the youngest of whom was seven),

with no thought of retirement. I was his firstborn and his concern in that quiet conversation carried on — miraculously, it seemed — above the pounding of my heart. He was inquiring about my plans for the future. Had I chosen a certain college? Was I interested in a graduation gift of a trip to Europe? A car, perhaps, as soon as I turned 18 in October?

I don't remember the words I used, but I did tell him that before my birthday, on September 8th to be exact, I wanted to enter the novitiate of the Brooklyn Sisters of Mercy. It would mean returning to Syosset for a few more years, this time for mutual trial, but I expected to last and to become a nun.

The pounding intensified as I waited. What would he do? Argue? Shout? Throw me out of the car?

The silence was terrible.

When he did speak, the words were astonishing. Never a churchgoer or a religious man, he was for me the best of fathers — responsible, caring, affectionate — across a thousand communication barriers between an American teenager and her old world father.

"This is not at all what I had planned for you. I want you to meet a good man who will love you and take care of you — someone who's a good provider. I want you to give me grandchildren. I want . . . I don't understand this . . . but if this is your devotion, I won't stand in your way."

That was it. That's all — except for tears and hugs and amazement on my part.

It wasn't until many years later that I learned how he cried before my aunt and uncle and how deep was his anguish.

For me, the road was clear. It was only after I made my application on the feast of Pentecost that I told my stepmother, actually my mother's younger sister. The scene was terrible. Because she continued to disapprove of my choice, I never dared bring my regulation trunk with its various required items of clothing into my home. All was stored at a friend's house.

None of that mattered. I was on the way now, as was my best friend and classmate, Pat. My favorite cousin, Stella, was on the same day to enter the Sisters of St. Joseph. We, who had grown up together, were planning similar life choices. It all seemed quite normal, quite predictable.

Scene Three. Stella and I had spent the hot July afternoon shopping for black oxfords at the store recommended by our congregations. As ugly as the shoes were, we had enjoyed the experience, marking as it did, a forward movement toward our entrance date. Soon after we arrived at her home, a hysterical phone call ordered me back to mine. My father had suffered a stroke and was in a coma. The date was July 22.

With my father's illness, everything changed. The paralysis affected his left side and, initially, his speech was impaired. His bright and resilient personality suffered permanent alteration. In the 11 years of his existence as an invalid, he experienced occasional hallucinations and regular indignities from without and within.

Scene Four. A year later I was in a parlor of St. Teresa of Avila, my home parish in Queens, N.Y., pouring out my heart to the popular young priest who had served as my spiritual director. I had not entered the community the previous September, but had stayed at home trying to cope with the loss of my father as I had known him and with the complexities of a very difficult home life. I didn't go out to work, but tried to make myself generally useful as driver, companion and home helper. At the same time I became deeply involved in the parish youth program. I taught a young adults CCD class, wrote and produced a parish play and made some very good friends, most of whom were somewhat older than myself. I had also fallen in love.

While my high school social life was good and included the regular complement of proms and dances, this was different. There was now someone who cared enough to ask me to marry him.

As I wrestled with that decision, I received a letter from the sister who had been my good friend and who was to sponsor my entrance into the community. Another September 8 was drawing near and I owed reverend mother the courtesy of a decision as to my association with the Sisters of Mercy.

The letter was short, but it hit me like an earthquake. I loved Tom but wasn't sure I wanted to marry him. I had begun to believe that my desire to become a nun was the pipedream of a romantic teenager. Still, I had been faithful to daily mass and felt a continued uneasiness in completely closing the door to religious life.

"Tell me what to do," I pleaded through my tears.

"No, that wouldn't be right," answered a very young and very pastoral Father James J. Tuohy. "That's got to be your decision. Suppose we spend the next three days praying about this and then have another talk."

When the time was up, I reported my decision.

"I've decided to enter the convent."

"That's wise," he said. "The truth is I don't think you'll last six weeks. But if you don't give it a try, you'll spend the rest of your life wondering if you should have."

Act Two: Learning the Role

Scene One. On September 8, 1952, friends and relatives, including Father Tuohy and Tom, accompanied me to Syosset. I was dressed in the postulant's dress, the black oxfords and, upon arrival, was given a cap with a short veil attached. En route, we stopped in Brentwood so I could say goodbye to my cousin, Stella, who was now a novice. Given the regulations of that period, we knew it would be years before we would see each other again. In fact, it would be about 15 years before we re-established the kind of loving, familial relationship that had characterized our life before entrance. The separation lasted longer than was required because of my attempt to remain "detached." That value was among many unnecessary and unnatural ideals that I had accepted in my effort to pursue the kind of perfection promoted as requisite for personal salvation and for the souls of others. Reclaiming relatives — including my sisters and their children — was a post-Vatican II necessity.

I was one of 15 postulants who entered a novitiate that would expand to embrace five sets of women entering over a two-and-a-half year period. At our peak, we would number more than 80 and be crammed into common rooms built to accommodate half our number. While we were novices an additional floor would be added and the construction of our spiritual development would be paralleled by the bricks and mortar climbing around us.

We lived a strict, conventual life. The horarium was practically inflexible, the physical labor much harder than was necessary, with hours spent washing the already clean and polishing the already polished. Minor infractions were perceived as indicative of monumental flaws. Psychic energy was expended on trivia, and endless hours were wasted in conversations and projects far removed from the reality of our friends and relatives in the real world. Contacts with family and friends were curtailed, and the most innocent of correspondence was deemed inappropriate.

The spiritual reading imposed upon us was reflective of the theology of the early 1950s with its mixture of strengths and weaknesses. Regular periods of prayer and classes designed to prepare us for the classroom were uneven in their opportunities for personal development.

Of the original band of 15, six remained. As sister after sister left during the novitiate, I would comment to my friend Kathleen, "All the beauty, brains and personality seems to be going home."

People look back on their formative years in community with a variety of reactions. Unlike some of my contemporaries, I harbor no bitterness for what I now perceive as waste of time and poor theology. What we received was what was available then. Those who formed us did the best they knew how within the range of their own limitations.

The long-term benefits for me, included an understanding of and dedication to the spirit of our Irish foundress, Catherine McAuley. Her gift was to respond to the needs of her time, sometimes while questioning authority. My devotion to the caring, truth-proclaiming Jesus of the New Testament intensified, and when, at the time of perpetual vows, we were permitted to have a quotation from scriptures inscribed on our wedding band, I chose a phrase from the Acts of the Apostles: "He went about doing good." As a motto, it was something I could treasure, a challenge I could live with.

A third spiritual benefit came with the choice of my religious name, Camille, after St. Camillus de Lellis. He was a soldier whose wounded leg motivated him to care for battlefield casualties, and his concern for the ailing caused him to set up an early version of a hospital. An anthology I read listed him as patron of the sick. I asked for "Camille" as part of a pact. I would pray to my patron each day in my father's behalf. In return I asked that he be granted the grace of a happy death.

Ten years later, in 1961, my father lay dying in a big hospital. He had suffered a broken hip and, in bed, had contracted pneumonia. The fireman father of one of my students drove me to the hospital for a very short visit and, in that moment of great anxiety, I asked my father if he would agree to see a priest. To my astonishment, he consented.

With panic over my dad's condition mingled with the short amount of time I had to search out a priest, I hurried out of his ward and literally walked into the hospital chaplain.

By the end of the week my father was dead. After the burial I ascertained the chaplain's name and learned, among other things, that he had a marvelous reputation for compassionate treatment of the dying. I sent him a thank you letter and a mass offering. In return I received a note that included the assurance, "You can be sure that your good prayers won for your father the grace of a happy death."

A few years later when updated, post-Vatican II theology encouraged sisters to return to their baptismal names, I refused. Community members who by then regarded me as one of the more liberal sisters, were astounded at my retention of my religious name. Indeed, Joan would have been easy enough to resume; however, I had a pact with Camillus and I continue to go by and think of myself as Camille.

Scene Two. The year was 1954. The neighborhood was Bedford Stuyvesant — all black. I was on yard duty during lunch hour, which is to say it's my turn to supervise the closed street where the children play.

A child's mother had come to bring her daughter's lunch. After giving her a thank you kiss, the little girl said to her mother, pointing at me, "Look, Mommy, that's my nun." A wave of surprise and pleasure swept over me. How did it ever happen that I could be somebody's nun?

Scene Three. Thanksgiving day three years later, one of the few times we were allowed to go for a walk. Our destination was a card store. An extraordinarily thoughtful superior had given us each a dollar bill with no strings attached. Several of us were heading to trade our money for birthday cards to send to friends and relatives. With cards still available at five to fifteen cents, we were in for some additional shopping.

Suddenly I caught sight of myself reflected in a store window. There were no mirrors in our convent and seeing myself in full, austere religious habit startled me. Almost at the same instant one of my students in this, my second mission, St. Agatha school, a blond-haired, blue-eyed fourth grader, tugged at her mother's sleeve and said of me, "Look, Mommy. That's my nun." The wonder returned.

Scene Four. Twenty years later, I was looking at the bulletin board outside the main office of the television department at Brooklyn College, on whose faculty I hold tenure. Debbie Greenberg, in graduation cap and gown, introduced me to her parents and said, "I want you to take a picture of me with my nun."

We posed and chatted for a while and, in the aftermath, I pondered how many people's "nun" I'd been. I felt a sense of awe that the years have held such unanticipated richness of ministry and friendship. I felt humbled and exhilarated all at the same time.

Act Three: The Play is Over

There's a kind of poetic justice in the fact that I am spending St. Patrick's Day, 1984, in writing this reflection on my life as a Sister of Mercy. In my local community of eight, I am the only one without Irish ancestry. Yet I baked the Irish soda bread for this St. Patrick's Day and for most of the 10 years we've lived together in this convent in East Flatbush. The Brooklyn Sisters of Mercy, probably more than or at least as much as any other branch of the Catherine McAuley's followers, reflect the national membership of the original band.

There was a time when this congregation refused admission to women of Italian descent. I was, in fact, only the fourth such person to be welcomed into the congregation. All that has changed, of course, as have many things in my life as a Sister of Mercy.

Until 1963, I had every reason to assume that I would spend the rest of my life as a teacher in the conventional classroom situation. I loved teaching and because I was good at it, my major superiors, responding to a request from the diocesan schools office to volunteer an exceptional teacher to audition for work in the newly developed educational television project, volunteered me. I wasn't dead set against the idea. I have always liked a challenge. But I was heartbroken at the thought of leaving my seventh graders in Queen of the Angels School, Long Island City, my creative writing club, and the school paper. I went to a workshop and a year-long, one-afternoon-a-week training program. In the end I was one of seven religious chosen from the original 60 recruits sent from the 30 or so congregations teaching in the Brooklyn diocese.

The period from 1964-69 was one of the most demanding and rewarding of my life. Under the leadership of Father Michael Dempsey, with technical assistance from laymen and support from religious who worked part-time with the television project, we broadcast quality programs of instruction and enrichment to meet the needs of and to compensate for the deficiencies in the 240 schools of the diocese.

There were many rewards from that career. I would cite three above all: We had a working model of the benefits that could result from cooperation among religious communities and with lay people, Catholic and non-Catholic alike. It broke down the provincialism naturally nourished by our local congregations and taught us a profound appreciation of people different from ourselves. In many instances that entailed interacting with institutions and individuals not associated with education, but responsive to its needs. It necessitated some degree of travel and attendance at conventions at which those of us who wore habits stuck out like sore thumbs.

The second major benefit was the cementing of enduring friendships. At the top of my list is my fruitful and continuously nourishing relationship with Barbara Valuckas, a School Sister of Notre Dame. She, more than anyone I knew, was receptive to questions and unintimidated by their answers. Without realizing it, she helped me break the shackles of blind obedience and mute acquiescence to the suffering-is-God's-will theology. I can recall the moment I took the quantum leap into a theology in which I would find myself at home.

My best friend in the community had died of a heart attack on March 31, 1968. Almost everyone in the congregation was attending an all-day education program that I had originated and was moderating. My friend, Sister Mary Benedicta, wasn't among the 500 or so who had come. I looked for her. Everyone from her convent expressed surpise that she wasn't in attendance; however all concurred she'd probably had some reason to visit her elderly mother instead. It was a Saturday and participation wasn't mandatory.

When the sisters returned home that night, they discovered that she had died early in the morning. For me the news was shattering. I reproached myself, "If only I hadn't pressed for this day, someone would have looked in on her . . .   she wouldn't have been alone."

A week after the funeral, Barbara and I were driving to a project-related destination and I was detailing some of my uneasiness. I had special praise for Sister Mary Benedicta's mother, Susan McMahon, at whose side I had been throughout the wake.

"Her faith is so strong," I observed. "She can live with the sudden death of her only daughter as part of God's will. I wish I could feel some of that."

"Now, Camille," Barbara chided, "do you really want the faith of an old Irish woman?"

In that instant, I was free — not only from the guilt, but from almost 20 years of trying to conform to a predominantly Irish spirituality.

The third benefit from my years in the Brooklyn Diocesan Television Center, primarily as a producer of programs in which Barbara was the on-camera talent, was this: "Celebrate your failures. The successes will bring their own reward."

As inexperienced pioneers in an educational venture which claimed every ounce of our energy and resourcefulness, our most dedicated efforts sometimes failed because of a malfunctioning camera, a missing prop, or an improperly cued segment of film. With editing kept to a minimum, it sometimes meant hours of overtime. Or cancellation. Rather than let such unavoidable occurrences dishearten us unduly, we would escape for a walk along the ocean or an ice cream cone or some other small pleasure. It helped.

My work in the TV center led my superiors in the congregation to send me on for a master's degree in the area I thought would be of greatest benefit to my apostolic commitment. After research and consultation, I chose the University of Michigan in Ann Arbor. I knew no one at the university and, indeed, no one who had even passed through the city that encompasses the university. I had learned that the television facilities were excellent and that the professional staff was experienced, dedicated, top notch. Most had worked in the industry and written the textbooks. So, in the summer of 1966 I left, wearing the full religious habit, for a world that was to become wonderful to me and a second home.

At 34 I was an older graduate student, mingling with ambitious younger people from all backgrounds and places. There were a number of religious visible on campus, but none in my immediate discipline.

From the outset, I loved every aspect of the experience. I found myself excited and challenged by the demands of radio and television, enriched and befriended by the faculty, and openly and warmly received by the other students.

It took me three years to complete my master's degree. During that period, I also worked part-time as department secretary, attended daily mass at the Newman center, participated in intercommunity activities with other religious students and moved out of my educational cocoon and instructed converts in Catholicism.

What my professors didn't understand was that from the time I entered religious life in 1951 until I started studies in Ann Arbor in 1966, I, as a member of my particular semi-cloistered community, had been extremely restricted in my interaction with world events. TV, newspapers, magazines, novels, or outside entertainment had been proscribed. Politics, cultural events, social interactions — all of these registered in my experience as a psychic zero. In the university setting, I had to keep running backwards to come near to catching up.

As the summer of 1968 drew to a close and my master's degree was at hand, Dr. Edgar Willis, who was one of my teachers, lectured me sternly about the absolute need for me to continue my studies and to get a doctorate. I resisted. There was no need for such a degree in my community. We had no college for me to teach in. He was adamant. He was sure I would receive a scholarship. In the end, he wrote to my superior general and convinced her to release me for two years of full time study. I thank him for two magnificent years during which I enjoyed a scholarship and a teaching fellowship. The friendships I made exceeded any expectations I might have had. And the joy of that studying was incomparable. For the first time I had no other obligations, other than my personal prayer life. I soared.

I've been back a number of times as visiting professor at that university and I continue relationships with students, sisters, brothers and priests as well as with the faculty. One particular joy I recently experienced was the invitation to speak at Edgar Willis' retirement banquet. He had requested me as his favorite student over a long teaching career. It was a singular honor for me.

For a number of good reasons, I never returned to the TV center in Brooklyn. Instead, I accepted an invitation to work as a part-time reporter for the *Tablet*, the weekly diocesan newspaper. My involvement with the *Tablet*, similarly, has been mind expanding and filled with opportunities to concern myself with social justice issues. The people who work there are dedicated and interesting. I have loved everyone. In terms of personal friendship and the evocation of new depths of commitment, I would have to credit the editor, Don Zirkel, for being a source of strength and inspiration.

With the *Tablet* as one of my touchstones, I have been able to be more closely attuned to the cry of the poor and to proclaim the reality of the evils of sexism and racism. I have reported on heroes and heroines like Daniel Berrigan and Dorothy Day. I have followed and joined the peace movement and have been kept alerted to changes in church and society. I have helped expose the plight of the homeless and aliens, the deceptions in high school ROTC recruitment and immoral practices of funeral directors who bilk the poor. I have been a mouthpiece for the good news and watchdog of the bad — and I have loved every opportunity that has come my way.

I have at this writing been associated with the *Tablet* for 17 years — always in a limited capacity.

My full time position for the past 11 years has been with Brooklyn College. After receiving my doctorate, I realized I wanted to return to teaching. Overqualified for elementary school, I applied to every local Catholic college. When all turned me down, I applied to the secular universities. Brooklyn College hired me on the first interview.

My major academic contribution is the teaching of courses in broadcast speech and writing. The textbook we use is one I wrote as secondary author to Dr. Willis, my former professor and colleague. In addition, I teach classes in mass media and television criticism. These and others offer me an opportunity to challenge young men and women to determine the extent of their interaction with the media that so affect them. We don't ordinarily address religious issues; however, we frequently explore human values and the meaning of life and death.

The extensions of my campus involvements have led to some places where, as the disciple writes, I would not choose to go.

I am remembering a gray December day a few years back. They were erecting the artificial Christmas tree in the lobby of Queens Crematorium. After a terrible day-and-a-half with one of the professors whose best friend and roommate had committed suicide, I was asked, as their one religious link, to conduct a service before the incineration.

The pain-filled faces of the victim's parents, relatives and small knot of friends will never leave me. They drew from my faith to mitigate their despair. I have rarely felt more humbled or more grateful. An exception was when I prevented a suicide. The young man who called me then was like a son to me. He came into my life when he was 16. At 30, he declared his homosexuality. Coping almost cost him his life.

Soon after I began teaching at Brooklyn College, a priest I know encouraged me to apply for the position of Catholic religion commentator at WINS, an all-news radio station serving the tri-state metropolitan area. The priest who had recently held that post had moved and there was an opening. The opportunity to offer a timely observation from a perspective of faith appealed to me. I astounded the news director by my request for an interview and an audition. ("Why yes, sister, we do have an opening but to tell you the truth, sister, we never considered a woman for that post."

I was invited for the interview September 24th, the day we celebrate the feast of Our Lady of Mercy, and began broadcasting two months later. I have never missed a Sunday and have enjoyed the weekly challenge to present some relevant reflections about the issues and events that affect people's lives.

I have no question that my life as a religious has been personally satisfying — not perfect, but satisfying. I have been the fortunate recipient of responsible leadership, have personally felt freed and enabled to follow what has for many years been the sound of a different drummer. I have felt trusted and respected.

In all the stages of the religious life I've lived with women who have given me good examples and opportunities to develop generosity. My local community of seven is particularly dear to me. I came upon it through the oblique direction of a woman not of my community, but a Dominican from Columbus, Ohio, Marjorie Tuite. I say "oblique" not because it in any way characterizes this most direct of women, but because I happened to be attending her workshop as a reporter, and the challenge she hurled at the group angled into my troubled conscience. "You've got to know who your people are," she said. "You've got to know what they believe in and if they'll stand behind you in the crunch."

At the time I was living in a community of 10 or so, good people, but many without any opportunities for awareness, or challenges for growth. We had "permission" from our leadership to invite lay relatives and friends to be our guests in community for prayer or meals. When such guests came to our convent they were often greeted with something less than cordiality. It bothered me.

Our congregational chapter had encouraged us to become aware of and responsible to social justice concerns. The sisters' senate was supporting a lettuce boycott as an aid to migrant workers. The sister who was food buyer for our house ignored the boycott because she didn't know what to believe and besides the sisters wanted lettuce. There were numerous similar circumstances.

I had tried to inform and persuade but had lost round after round. I was bringing fewer guests home and was back to keeping silence over the lettuce. Moreover, I wasn't satisfied with the quality of prayer or presence to one another. TV got first billing. Meals were seldom shared.

As I drove home from Marjorie Tuite's workshop, I told my two companions that I was going to move out of the convent and look for a place more in line with my views on religious life. The others listened and, eventually, we three and two others who shared our views came together to establish a new foundation in an old convent. Ten years later five of us remain. Three others have joined us. One of the three just left to join the Sisters of Mercy in Chile.

Our professions include teaching at the high school and university level, social work and nursing. Our life together rests on a firm foundation of prayer, presence to one another and hospitality. There have been frequent tests to these goals over the years, but we hold them as strong values and continue to work at them. We share life with one another — good and bad — and are glad to do so.

A high point each week is the night we set apart to celebrate the eucharist in our living room. This is the time we most frequently invite guests to share our prayer and the best dinner of the week. We are fortunate in knowing a number of priests with feminist leanings who are good friends to us and upon whom we can call with confidence.

This, of course, is not enough. For deeper, longer draughts of spirituality, we spend days in retreat. One place to which we have gone as a group and to which I have often returned alone and with friends is Mount Saviour, a Benedictine monastery in Elmira, New York.

It is for me a favorite place in which to sort out my stresses and values and to enjoy the spiritual nourishment that abounds. There are few such places that impress me.

One of my most nourishing visits to the monastery was during June of 1981. I had accepted an invitation from Bishop P. Francis Murphy of Baltimore to address the Bishops' Commission on Women in Church and Society on the matter of preaching. I wanted to present a strong case to open the ministry of preaching to qualified lay men and women.

Upon my arrival, Fr. Martin, the abbot, had in readiness for me commentaries on canon law, related reading material, a list of several people in the Rochester area who were women preachers and male liturgists with special insights into the possibilities. All had agreed to speak with me, and did so. The time spent at Mount Saviour and the prayerful support I experienced there, made my preparation pleasant.

My cousin Stella accompanied me to Chicago for that long anticipated meeting with the bishops. I expected to meet six bishops of the committee and several women who served in an advisory capacity. Only three bishops were present to hear me. None of those who ignored the trip I made at great personal expense (though aided by signed testimonies and small donations from a hundred supporters) apologized.

Bishop Murphy was encouraging throughout. The others, however, considered my presence and presentation out of line. I was disappointed, but not discouraged. I continue to publish and speak about the sufferings imposed by the church's sexism upon its members. I have often supported the ordination of women — both in personal presentations and on numerous radio and television programs.

Having easy access to media carries its liabilities as well as its assets. Some years ago a reporter I know called me for some comments about a popular woman religious. Dick Ryan, then religion editor for the *New York Daily News,* began his line of questioning with:

"Sister, what do you think about Mother Teresa?"

Before I opened my mouth I knew I was about to get myself in trouble.

I had no idea how much.

Carefully, I began:

"I think Mother Teresa is a holy and compassionate woman. There is no minimizing the good that she does for Calcutta's abandoned poor and dying. But I think she does many sisters a disservice by allowing the media and ecclesiastical authorities to promote her as the role model for all religious throughout the world, especially in the United States."

"What do you mean?" he pressed.

"We confront different needs, a variety of injustices," I explained. "Brooklyn, unlike Calcutta, isn't overwhelmed by the lepers and aged dying in the gutters. Sisters here — as in other places — must discover corporately and by themselves what needs exist and how to address them. And even in Calcutta, I added, someone ought to be figuring out who or what it is that causes so many people to perish in the streets. There have got to be direct ministers in the streets, but there must also be people who invade high places to learn why people die in the streets. There must also be sisters who find ways to change the killing systems wherever they are. There have got to be yet others who expose the evil."

That story made the wire services and the *Washington Post* and NC News. RNS and AP called me for more information. Articles abounded. News stories first, then editorials — 95 percent condemning me for stoning a saint and being jealous of Mother Teresa's popularity. Letters to the editor asked for my excommunication. Personal letters assured me I was going to hell and ought to get out of the church before I destroyed it from within. Several NBC television appearances fanned the flames. There were, of course, supportive words and letters, but rarely in the Catholic press. It proved an interesting summer. I stand by the statements I ventured then.

The interesting thing about my own life as I try to wind down these reflections is that with each year it seems to become fuller, more challenging. My God is a God of surprises.

The Mother Teresa episode not only motivated me to examine my concepts about religious life, it marked the beginning of a friendship between myself and a priest-correspondent. Puzzled by the public furor in which I was embroiled, he invited me to dinner, then to the rectory to discuss the issue with the priests who lived there. That initial effort to understand paved the way to an association that has been helpful to us both.

And it proved helpful to the family of another Theresa.

Almost a year after the Mother Teresa controversy, I attended a seventy-fifth anniversary Mass in St. Agatha's parish, where I had, more than quarter century earlier, spent a half dozen years teaching fourth grade.

After the liturgy, I found a couple waiting for me outside church.

"Sister Camille," the woman began, "I don't think you'll remember me. I'm Mrs. M."

"Of course, I do. You're Theresa's mother," I replied. In a quick flashback I could see the classroom with its more than sixty students and, with them, the pretty, energetic little girl.

"How is she?" I asked. "What is she doing?"

The father looked away. His wife answered:

"She's dying."

In a few minutes I knew the outline of their daughter's life. Bright, independent, she married too young, divorced soon after, barely out of her teens. Stigmatized and rebellious, she stopped attending church. Professionally successful and financially secure, she had spent the last dozen years living with a divorced man whom she loved. Now she was dying without faith or sacraments.

"Will you please come to see Theresa?"

"When?"

"Now."

I got to Theresa's luxurious apartment a little before 10 p.m. (Before Vatican II I would have been home in my own convent bed.) Her parents let me in and I met the man who cared for her and whose own heart was breaking then.

They led me into a beautiful bedroom. Theresa, 35, appeared a skeleton, sitting up in bed, her hair all gone, large dark eyes alert with resentment.

"I don't remember you," she said.

I told her it was all right. I remembered her, I said, her spirit, her bouncing curls and talkativeness. I told her how often I wonder about my students, now grown-up, and how deeply sorry I was to discover her as she was then.

We talked a bit, she, softening somewhat as we did. I asked her if she would consider allowing a priest come to anoint her.

"I don't believe in God," she countered.

"What matters," I replied "is that God believes in you. There's no way to explain your suffering or all the years you felt outside the church; but God is as close as your own heart, understanding what no else ever could. God never gives up on us."

She let me pray aloud at her bedside, putting her bony hand on mine. In the end, she consented to see a priest. I promised her Ed Doherty, her parents' parish priest and my friend. He as a special gift for dealing with dying people and those who grieve for them.

He agreed to go. The next morning, very early, he phoned me.

"Camille," he said, "I want you to know that you gave Theresa the last rites."

He had arranged to visit her, but death got there first.

He offered the Mass of Resurrection for Theresa and, a few weeks later, a private Mass for her relatives in my convent. Together we two, who are fiercely devoted to world peace, helped bring peace to one small family who loved a daughter named Theresa.

Sometimes I have the feeling that my life is a parade ground for excellent people — for prophets and philosophers, for common folk with common sense.

I don't lightly claim friendship, but I am grateful for the example and generous sharing of Daniel Berrigan — first through his writings and example of public stands; more recently as a friend to my local community and as one who prays with us and gives us his time several times a year.

In addition to the many friends we have, in and out of communities, there are so many who have inspired me by their writing and preaching. Joan Chittister, a Benedictine, is one. Long before I ever met her I read a description she gave at a Leadership Conference of Women Religious (LCWR) meeting of the role of religious in these changing times: "to be a warm and caring presence in the many worlds through which she walks." That's like my ring motto, "He went about doing good." It's a goal I can live with.

I continue to be moved by Dorothy Day's compassion for the poor and tough stand against injustice; by Dom Helder Camara's cheerful witness for the poor and victims of unjust societies.

My concern for the church is that its sins of sexism and clericalism will catch up with it — like toxic wastes that pollute the waters — and return to poison its potential to carry Christ to the world. I fear this pope for his one-size-fits-all agenda. I distrust him for activating the SCRIS inquiry into religious life and I resent his heavy-handedness in the instance of Agnes Mary Mansour and his disrespect for Theresa Kane and the U.S. religious she represented as head of the LCWR.

On the other hand, I applaud his condemnation of the arms race. I appreciate his insistence on a more equitable distribution of the world's resources.

I worry about his uneasiness with speculative theology and his pre-conciliar style of resolving internal controversy. And, having registered so many direct observations, I know he is only a temporary resident of the Vatican, a short-term steward of the papacy.

I claim the church as my birthright and have no intention of retiring like some petulant or intimidated child from the struggle to enrich it. I hope always, with God's grace, to remain on the inside, exercising my mature responsibility for it, in collaboration and consultation with others who share my love and are sensitive to the need to share the pain of the pilgrim.

If I have come to any firm conclusions in my lifetime, one at least must be that it is an act of irresponsibility, perhaps a downright sin, to allow myself to be limited by the limitations of others.

With only one life to live and a final judgment to anticipate, the least we owe ourselves is the diligence to excise from our consciousness shallow justifications for inappropriate or cowardly behavior. Inappropriate at least, for any of us who have taken to heart the words God spoke through Isaiah:

"I have loved thee with an everlasting love; therefore, have I drawn thee, calling thee by name. You are mine."

Riding the City Bus from Pittsburgh

Maureen Fiedler

Maureen Fiedler is a co-director of the Quixote Center, a national Catholic-based justice center, where she works principally for Central American liberation from U.S. domination and for the rights of women in church and society. She also serves as National Coordinator of Catholics for the Equal Rights Amendment. In January of 1984, she completed a transfer from an earlier community to the Sisters of Loretto.

I remember well my own first, faltering steps toward a new path in "religious life." I didn't think of them then as part of "renewal" but simply as a response to an urgent call.

It was April, 1968. I was teaching high school social studies in Pittsburgh. A news flash had just announced the assassination of Dr. Martin Luther King. The black community in Pittsburgh, as in many U.S. cities, responded with anger. Not a few rioted. Flames from buildings burning in the Hill District, one of the largest black ghettoes in the city, could be seen for miles. The nation was stunned. I was in a state that moved from shock and outrage to deep sadness.

I had long admired King as a contemporary Moses leading his people to freedom, a present-day prophet jarring the consciences of the complacent, a contemporary Christ who suffered and ultimately died that others might live. The day he was buried, I sat before the TV set in silence as the meaning of his martyrdom seeped deeply into my being. I felt I was witnessing the events of Calvary being replayed in our own time. And in the midst of my sadness, I sensed a strange new sense of call and empowerment. Many years later, I recognized that day as a "contemplative" experience.

Looking back, I realize that King's death led me to a personal "resurrection." I felt challenged to *act* for racial justice in ways that I had not dared move before. I knew deep inside that I could not live peacefully with myself if King's death remained merely an event to be commemorated, or even just an occasion for contemplation. The death of King called me to *act* for justice, to put my body where my words had been. I understood just a bit of what it means for new life to come forth from death.

A few days after the King funeral, the opportunity for action came. One of my students approached me after class. As chance would have it, she was the only white student in the city who belonged to the NAACP. (The Catholic high school where I taught was 100 percent white!) My views on racial justice were no secret to my students; she knew that I longed to be more directly involved in the black community.

"I know a woman in the NAACP in the Hill District who wants to start a tutoring program for children on weekends," she told me. "She needs high school tutors. Maybe you can help." I knew the call instantly, and I had to respond.

But there were obstacles, serious obstacles. Even in 1968, my religious community, then the Sisters of Mercy of Erie, Pa., had not advanced as far as some. New ministries, even "on the side," were not yet seriously discussed. When they were, the "needs of our schools" were emphasized by community superiors. Moreover, I knew that both my local superior and the high school principal were likely to oppose such a program. And although we could now "sign out" for places around town "on our own recognizance" rather than asking for formal permission as before, the practice was new and "experimental." The coming special general chapter in the summer of 1968 could either legitimate such practices or wipe them out.

Moreover, the local superior had an eagle eye for the activities of underlings like myself, only in temporary vows at the time. If I were gone to parts unknown for too long, questions might be asked that would put an end to the whole enterprise before it had even had a chance to get started. Discovery of such a project might jeopardize my renewal of vows, even my membership in the community. Nonetheless, I was determined to answer what I felt deeply was a call from the Spirit and risk whatever I had to risk. I could not live with my conscience if I remained inactive on this front any longer.

I set up an appointment with Gladys Harper, the woman who wanted to start a tutoring program.

When the day of the meeting finally arrived, I stared at the "sign out" book for a long time wondering how to describe my destination. I finally wrote "town," hoping that its vagueness would not raise any questions.

Gladys and I laid plans for a pilot program on Saturday mornings that would last for the final four weeks of the school year. I agreed to find tutors and she would round up students who needed special attention and instruction.

Within a week, I had identified a small group of students who were academically qualified and sympathetic to the black struggle for civil rights. Because I knew the principal would block such a program, I discussed plans with them privately. For the next four Saturdays, I met them on a street corner in downtown Pittsburgh and took the bus to the Hill District. Together we launched a program that was to last two more years.

As far as I know, neither the local superior nor the principal·knew what I was doing that first month. By summer the special general chapter had legitimated all the practices I needed to keep it going. I celebrated those decisions as real steps forward.

Why This Decision Was a Watershed in My Life

In retrospect, that incident still stands out for me as a turning point in the way I have chosen to live religious life. It illustrates several dimensions of my emerging understanding of renewal in women's communities in the late 1960s. First, it was a concrete step toward solidarity with the poor and oppressed. I had moved from talking about blacks and the poor to acting upon my concerns. I had no idea what "solidarity" or real struggle meant, but I had started a journey that I sensed was a gospel direction in this time.

Second, I had made a decision to put the needs of people ahead of community law and custom. That choice seemed right, not unlike curing people on the Sabbath. But that dimension of the choice was most difficult because it set me on a course that was not pleasing to those in power in my community. And psychic need for approval from the powerful had to be discarded, at least for the time being. As I look back, I wonder just how much risk there was, but I was truly convinced at the time that the worst could happen.

Third, the choice was a result of societal contemplation. I had long reflected on King's life and work and had come to see the struggle for racial justice as a contemporary version of the gospel movements from slavery to freedom. Unknowingly, I had begun to embrace what I later understood as "liberation theology" and "noisy contemplation."

Fourth, I began to drop false barriers that had separated the "spiritual" from the "social" or "political" in my life. Like other sisters, I had been taught that religious should not be "worldly," a concept practiced in ways that separated us from struggles for justice, or even news about them. I had long wondered how we could live the Mercy tradition of service to the poor when it was clear that the social structures which caused poverty and reinforced racism had to be changed by actions that were systemic or "political" and thus "worldly." In time, I rejected "otherwordly" concepts of religous life and came to believe that authentic spirituality in this age needed a societal-political dimension.

Most important, the time of decision typifies what renewal meant for me at its core: the freedom to walk and struggle with the oppressed in response to a call that might come from many places: the gospel, the documents of the church and the community — but most strongly from the oppressed and needy themselves. Renewal for me was not primarily freedom *from* anything; it was freedom *for* others. It meant living as an adult Christian woman, responding to the call of the Spirit even if that involved major changes in community lifestyles and ministries.

Renewal: A Journey

The year 1968 may have been a watershed, but it cannot be understood as a dividing line separating the "renewed" from the "unrenewed." Rather it was a significant moment in a *process* that continues into the present and beyond. Where it will lead God only knows.

In fact, as I look back on that first Saturday morning when I boarded a bus for the inner city, I realize how little I understood of the journey I was beginning. It's a journey that has taken me far beyond the black community deeply into social movements for women's rights, peace and Third World liberation. It has even uprooted me from the Sisters of Mercy of Erie and led me to a new home with the Sisters of Loretto.

The journey has had its share of misunderstandings, controversy and problems — some of which were caused by my own inadequacies. The journey has been less like driving on a superhighway than bumping along in an old stagecoach in which the ride is uncomfortable, the dangers unpredictable, the road unmarked, and progress always slower than one wants. Nonetheless, the journey has been good, the call is strong and growing, and the commitment ever deeper.

The Early Days

If renewal for me meant freedom for service of the oppressed, the most troublesome aspects of life in the early days were those practices that made such service impossible.

I wasn't around for too many of those early days, having entered in 1962 just as Vatican II began. But religious life in the early to mid-1960s was still hardened into rigid practices. Life was tightly scheduled and regimented. Permissions were necessary for everything from going out the front door to reading books other than the Bible. Ministries were assigned. Prayers were conducted on schedule. Silence made up a good portion of the day.

Later, when I pursued graduate studies in political science, I realized how closely religious life resembled totalitarian societies in which every aspect of life was determined by authority. It was liveable as long as it was not questioned fundamentally, and as long as its premises were accepted as sacred and God-given. But once the structure was seen as repressive of individuals and as irrelevant to the modern world, the foundation was threatened and no amount of patchwork could save it.

Not that the old system did not have its positive experiences. Many of us were grateful for the days and months of the canonical year that relieved us of heavy teaching and study schedules and allowed time for prayer. We deeply sensed being a part of the mission of the church and the tradition of Mercy. Often, the very practices we did not like brought us novices together in common cause that poked fun at the absurdities.

But, as the needs of ministry in the contemporary world came more sharply into focus in the mid to late 1960s, the practices that hindered freedom to serve chafed most strongly. Denial of access to news on TV, radio, and even the front page of the daily paper, disturbed me greatly because it kept me apart from the social currents I sensed I would have to understand to minister effectively. When that denial was carried over into the year I began teaching high school social studies, it became intolerable. More than once I found a daily paper and read it anyway.

We were "protected" from many of the controversies then beginning to stir in the church — even though we would have to deal with them ourselves in the not too distant future. I can remember being denied permission to read Mary Perkins Ryan's *Are Catholic Schools the Answer?* even though it addressed questions vital to the future of our whole ministry as a community.

Before I understood what "justice ministry" could mean, I simply wanted to be an effective teacher. But regulations worked against the fullest giving even in that traditional ministry. Bedtimes were scheduled, and it was hard to add more than a half hour to the time for preparing classes even if the next day looked like a disaster. We were not permitted to attend high school basketball games in spite of the fact that students begged us to come. "Sister, we just don't do that" was the most common phrase for "holding the line" against change in those days of upheaval.

As time went on, however, and the Catholic publications to which we did have access began to discuss the civil rights movement and the fledgling anti-Vietnam movement, I began to think about new ministries of justice and a new "religious" lifestyle to go with them. I can remember sharing with a sister-novice as early as 1964 my "radical reflection" that the Sermon on the Mount's call to "feed the hungry" had to mean far more in our own time than handing a sandwich out the convent back door to a homeless person. It had implications for government poverty programs, aid to the Third World, racist structures that kept minorities hungrier than the rest of us. A sense of *structural* and *systemic* injustice had found its way into my prayer. As I pondered these realities, I began to read Vatican II's *Church in the Modern World* and Cardinal Suenen's book, *The Nun in the World*. Gradually, I questioned the whole structure and foundations of religious life as I had known it. I began to think about fundamental changes and talk about them with friends.

These were not conversations welcomed by my superiors. When I offered suggestions about participating in sympathy marches at the time of Selma, or even about going to the local parish for the Easter Vigil, I was met with the old answers: "We can do more by staying home and praying," or "We don't go out late in the evening, sister." Ultimately, my persistence in making such suggestions cost me an extra six months in the novitiate! The charge: I had a "critical mind." It was some years before I interpreted that as a compliment.

Why I hung on in those early years I'm not sure, except that I had a strong sense of being called to this life, and I did have hopes for change. "Doing time" for an extra six months in the novitiate (which I later realized was not a bad preparation for the risks of justice ministry) kept me quiet for a while, but it did not change my mind on the issues. It only made me think about them more deeply and await an opportunity to break forth and act.

Meanwhile, I questioned other parts of the old structure. Separation from my family was especially painful to me in the early years because it was so painful for my parents. I had no good answer for my mother's question: "Why should consecration to God separate you from those who raised you and love you deeply?" I decided she was right, and later pushed hard for freedom to visit families.

The habit had been an early object of fascination and romanticizing. But living inside it was another story. Not only was it sometimes highly impractical, it projected an image that I soon discovered was not me. Nuns were expected to be quiet, prayerful in traditional ways, good with children, or even much like children themselves. They were not commonly regarded as persons with whom to discuss "real" problems, and — God help us — they knew nothing about sexuality. Since no one ever accused me of being quiet, since I prayed in non-traditional ways, since I did not feel called to work with children, and since I had an interest in the "real" problems of people and society, I found myself in an identity crisis with the nun image. Moreover, I began to see that that image would severely hinder anyone who tried to be an agent of social change.

As if this were not enough, the habit often put us in a privileged position. Sometimes bus drivers refused to let us pay fare. One time I watched with amazement as a Pittsburgh policeman stopped traffic in all directions at a five-way intersection to let me drive through a red light! Older women on buses offered us seats even though we were far more able to stand than they. I wondered how in the world this fit with our call to serve. When I raised the question, I was often told that people were simply paying respect to the habit, or the Church, or Christ or something. But I had entered this life to serve and had no desire to be a symbol for "respect."

Later, I came to believe that solidarity with the poor included leaving aside symbols of class, even *ecclesiastical* class. As I grew to become a feminist, and especially as I watched Iranian women struggle against wearing the chador, I came to understand the habit as a means of controlling the behavior of women. There is no returning to it.

Summer 1968:
The Special General Chapter

Summer, 1968 was a time of celebration. The floodgates of change were opened at last and the freedom I had yearned for seemed just around the corner. I could now continue my part in the Hill District tutoring program; rules began to respect the adulthood of the sisters; the habit was becoming more wearable even if it was still identifiable with its black dress and veil. Hints that one might be asked about one's preference for ministries began circulating. Conversations talked about new styles of community, personal budgeting, moving into entirely new apostolates.

The spring and summer of 1968 introduced me to an important skill:

political organizing. Those of us who wanted fundamental change in community structures held late night meetings in basements, developed phone networks to keep allies informed, and learned the importance of setting agendas, preparing proposals in advance, and determining who would speak most effectively for our point of view. Little did I know then how valuable that experience would be for later work.

But more than that, the early days of religious life were indispensable to my personal sense of renewal because they allowed me to feel powerless in the face of structures that stifled my personality and kept me from the works I most wanted to pursue. That personal experience left me with a natural empathy for other oppressed peoples who yearn for self-determination and the right to determine their own identities, destinies and priorities.

At the same time, I learned my first lessons in risk and solidarity with others as we took our chances in the early years of struggle for change. They are lessons for which I am deeply grateful today.

After the Watershed Year

In the years after 1968, I set my sights on educational preparation for justice ministry, deciding that political science might offer valuable background and skills. Both Martin Luther King and the anti-Vietnam war movement reinforced my growing belief that strategies for justice and peace were inescapably political.

Moreover, I was coming to understand that politics dealt with power: domination and subordination. These power equations were at the core of what had to change, if justice were to become real: whether it was white domination of blacks, male domination of women, or superpower domination of small nations. Jesus' choice, I realized, was to side with those who had no power. He never chose to opt out of the political. Indeed, in the contemporary world that would mean abandoning the work of justice.

In the summer of 1970, just before graduate school, I came to know another experience of powerlessness firsthand. I worked in Petersfield, South Carolina, where I came face to face with rural, Southern poverty and discrimination. Ramshackle housing, malnourished children, the isolation of the black community, illiteracy, and the non-caring of most of the area left me with memories that will never go away.

In September of 1970 I enrolled in graduate school at Georgetown University in Washington, embarking on study in political science. With the reality of Vietnam and my own growing awareness of the Third World, I opted for international relations as an early field of study and comparative international politics later on. Ironically, the best graduate professor I had in those years was Jeane Kirkpatrick, U.S. ambassador to the United States in the Reagan administration. Her lucid lectures taught me a great deal about methodology, but never convinced me to follow her value system in politics. I am in deep disagreement with her policy ideas about Central America and most of the world.

Georgetown was a conservative campus politically, but no university was immune from the anti-Vietnam war activity sweeping the country. That debate and the concrete decisions I faced (to demonstrate or not to demonstrate) led me to reflect seriously on U.S. foreign policy and its value assumptions. I discovered a regular Sunday peace liturgy in an underground crypt on campus, where these concerns were discussed in the light of the gospel. There was something real about that worship with its link to life issues. I began to sense the power of an activist laity since most of my co-worshippers were families from the area who were convinced of the need to act for peace. In that community I worked through many questions about the use of force and economic domination of other lands by larger powers.

Like thousands of others, I participated in anti-war marches, protested the arrest of the Berrigans and their companions, asnd let congress know my views. But more important, I made my first real contacts with the "political left" in the United States and found my initial discomfort short-lived. When I began to hear their concerns and analysis, I realized that I had common interests with many of them even if mine grew from the gospel and theirs came from various schools of Marxist philosophy. My formal study of Marxism in political philosophy courses added a valuable dimension to my understanding of global political realities, and gave me the foundation I needed to understand liberation theology.

Becoming a Conscious Feminist

As the Vietnam war ground to a conclusion, I plowed into my dissertation which dealt with women in U.S. politics. That led me to yet another world: the movement for women's liberation. I read avidly, sensing the parallels between forms of racial and sexual oppression: stereotyping, poverty, subordination. It was not long before I began questioning women's traditional role in the church.

My personal faith had never been dependent on the sinlessness of the church as an institution. Indeed, I had always been taught, even in the early years, that priests, bishops and even the pope could sin and make mistakes. It made sense to me that some of these might be *institutional* sins, like sexism. So questioning the church itself, like questioning my community earlier, did not shake my basic religious faith. It simply made me realize that *any* institution, be it government, business, university, or church, was subject to challenge on the justice of its structures and practices.

At the First Women's Ordination Conference in Detroit in November, 1975, I saw injustice toward women in the church put into historical, theological and political perspective. I discovered that others believed as I did: Women had been denied the dignity and equality they deserved as baptized persons and the institutional church was clearly called to change its historic patterns of discrimination. Work to change those patterns was basic justice ministry.

By then, I had come to name myself a feminist. I began to see women's oppression in the light of the gospel, and came to believe deeply that the call to love one another — the core of the message of Jesus — could never be compatible with treating some persons as inferiors, with assigning them arbitrary roles based on physical characteristics. The Spirit was hindered when preconceived biases limited women from following whatever call they heard, including a call to priestly ministry.

But the women's movement in the church questioned more than women's roles. It critiqued the priesthood as an institution and church structures as we know them: clericalism, hierarchy, compulsory celibacy. Those elements of church structure that make it an authoritarian political institution no longer seemed compatible with the gospel, if they ever were. Like the structures of women's communities in the 1960s, they cry out for changes that reflect the gospel's call to equality and lead to new models of decision-making. Changing unjust patterns of domination and submission in the institutional church became part of the women's movement and part of my own ministry.

In the summer of 1975, I made my first directed retreat. It was only six days — but six days that moved my life along rapidly in the direction I had already begun to walk. I prayed long hours over questions of living simply and resolved that I would simply have to change patterns of my lifestyle that kept me too middle class. That resolution has gone through varying stages of intensity and struggle. I am rarely satisfied with my level of simplicity, but am convinced that that road is essential to authentic solidarity.

After my retreat I searched for a spiritual director who could help me, and I came upon a Jesuit who has been a wonderful friend ever since, Bill Callahan. He encouraged me in the direction of living simply as much by his own example as by his words. But more than that, he told me after several months about a new enterprise he and two friends were starting called the Quixote Center. It would, he said, be a place to "dream impossible dreams," to take risks for the gospel, to work on issues that others did not touch. Among those issues would be the equality of women in the church and civil society. Priests for Equality, which he founded, was just getting off the ground and it seemed very good. I thought about it for a couple of weeks, and finally said "yes." Another step in the dark!

Problems Emerge with my Community

I was no sooner on staff than trouble developed with my community. Since 1968 we had elected very progressive leadership, but after one and a half terms, the community president resigned. It became known that she planned to leave the community and it was rumored she would marry a priest. In a community with many elderly voting sisters, that was enough to produce a backlash election and a staunch conservative was elected about the time I opted to go to the Quixote Center.

All was fine (to my initial surprise) until the center decided to make ministry to gay and lesbian Catholics one of its issues. In the interest of being forthright, I informed the community leadership of this added issue. Within weeks, I received a letter which informed me that I no longer had permission to work at the center and should find another ministry. Since there had been no dialogue or even an inkling that anything was wrong, the letter took me by surprise.

Offers for dialogue on the issue were ignored. Letters from those directly involved in the ministry had little effect. Only when I told the community I had a contract with the center that in good conscience I could not break did the new community president go to the bishop (!) and on *his* advice give me permission to continue.

I was appalled and hurt. I could scarcely believe that any woman in community, even one who was not a feminist, would go to a bishop to seek advice on an internal matter. Moreover, I could feel the restrictiveness of the early days closing in on me again. I had thought those days were over. I was wrong. Gradually, I began thinking about other alternatives: leaving completely, transferring to another community, splitting off from my present community with friends to form a new structure.

For about a year, I and a group of about 20 friends who feared the community would move backwards under the new leadership, explored the last of these options. We called ourselves the Community of Hope. After months of discussion we presented our vision of religious life to the community at large. We articulated our clear preferences and forthrightly (perhaps too bluntly) rejected certain practices of the past. We expected opposition and hoped for dialogue, but we were not prepared for the open hostility that greeted us. Hopes for reconciliation were dashed.

The Community of Hope began to explore other alternatives. After months more of discussion we realized we were held together more by our opposition to the current trends in the community than by any common vision of the future that we were all willing to try. Sadly, we began to go our separate ways with some sisters leaving altogether, others transferring to new communities and still others sticking it out until change might come.

For me there could be no more sticking it out. Not only was I saddened by what had happened to the Community of Hope, I knew I needed to be about my work at the Quixote Center, and I sensed official disapproval of that ministry would continue. Within a year my name was quietly dropped from the list of ministries altogether and I began to get letters from community leadership suggesting I look for something new. The atmosphere of those days did not look promising for fruitful dialogue, so I asked for and received a leave of absence. Later when I was denied further leaves, I sought and received exclaustration.

A New Home with Loretto

In those years I tried to sort through my life, its directions and call. Justice work was by then a given. The Quixote Center was a true religious community for me, and I wondered if I needed another. I thought about leaving religious life entirely, but that seemed as if it would distance me from a tradition I had come to value. I sensed that women's communities were vital to new life in the church, often on the cutting edge of prophecy and change. I wanted to be part of a women's community challenging the church from within ecclesial structures. I began to look for a community where justice ministry was a priority, feminism was respected, and individual freedom valued.

After a search of several months, I found the Sisters of Loretto. In the course of four years, I came to know community members across the country. I was impressed with the extraordinary quality of dialogue at their assemblies and their deep respect for differing points of view. Justice issues were important considerations on the community agenda. And feminism, although far from universally accepted, was a respected philosophy. Most important, the community placed great value on the individual person, stressing "priority of persons over institutions." I felt very welcomed as I grew to know the members and co-members. On January 29, 1984, Loretto and I formalized the friendship that had been growing from the beginning at a liturgy in the "Catholic feminist tradition" in Washington, D.C. It was a great party!

Formally leaving the Sisters of Mercy of Erie has not meant leaving friends. My Mercy friends will always be a part of my life. There are even signs the tensions and problems that troubled them and pushed me to find a new community are being resolved and gradually healed under new leadership. I am sure we will visit often and recall the old days just as before.

Moreover, my decision has not meant leaving the Mercy tradition. In fact, my choice to become part of Loretto put me deeply in touch with both traditions: the Mercy tradition of service to the poor and to women, the Loretto tradition of the pioneer and the cutting edge. I hope to combine the two traditions, pioneering in the service of women and the poor.

The Quixote Center

My years at the Quixote Center have brought me into the mainstream of action for justice, both in the church and in civil society. They have been wonderful years where analysis of structural injustices is done in the light of the gospel, where strategies are explored freely, and where community has strengthened willingness to risk. Indeed, the Quixote Center has been every bit as integral to my experience of renewal and religious community as has Mercy or Loretto. Women such as Dolly Pomerleau, one of my center colleagues, are every bit as much "sister" to me as are my sisters in Loretto. The center has provided me with an immediate and challenging community base for the ministry of justice.

The center began life by challenging the church on its treatment of women. We never limited the type of activity we would undertake. The activity depended on "what the issue needed." Our methods spanned the gamut: from scholarly studies about Catholic attitudes on equality, to organizing in favor of the Equal Rights Amendment at the 1976 Call to Action Conference, to calling a press conference and organizing demonstrations when the Vatican issued its infamous declaration against the ordination of women to the priesthood.

Most difficult of all was my participation in the protest at the Shrine of the Immaculate Conception during Pope John Paul II's visit to the U.S. in October, 1979. Since dialogue with him during his trip was impossible and the pain of discrimination felt by Catholic women somehow had to be expressed, the witness seemed necessary. With a group of 40, I helped plan the action (standing with blue armbands as the pope spoke) and carry it out. Twelve more decided to join us on the spot, making a total of 52. Rarely have I been so gripped with fear as that morning in the shrine. I still count it as an action far more difficult than any demonstration or act of civil disobedience for civil causes. But rarely have I felt so empowered to act as when I heard Theresa Kane's memorable. if unexpected, words calling for women to be equals in all ministries of our church. Those words helped me to my feet; together we stood for all Catholic women.

The Struggle for the
Equal Rights Amendment

As intriguing as church politics seemed, I longed to be involved in civil politics as well. The Equal Rights Amendment badly needed a Catholic effort in 1977-78, and I enlisted in the struggle. Again, it was a road that led where I knew not. Within months I found myself fundraising and organizing in Illinois, lobbying recalcitrant legislators, and speaking to the media.

As the years wore on, I was called upon to articulate the message of women's equality in the light of the gospel and church teaching. I spoke to groups throughout the United States. Wherever I went, I met Catholic women who told me how sexism had alienated them from the church. I heard the stories of women who told of wife-beating, rape, incest, poverty, wage discrimination, the trap of marriage to an authoritarian husband. The need for equality was patently evident.

My work for the ERA covered a range of conventional political activities from grassroots organizing to lobbying. But as the 1982 deadline neared, I became convinced that the struggle needed a more powerful witness. At first that meant small acts of symbolic civil disobedience. In May and June of 1982, it meant fasting for 37 days in Springfield, Illinois with seven other women.

The goal of our fast was never that of the Irish hunger strikes: to fast to the death unless demands are met. Rather, it was an intensely spiritual witness that would make women's "hunger for justice" visible in our own bodies. We hoped that a daily witness in the capitol rotunda might even move recalcitrant legislators.

The fast was risky, public and tension-producing in the extreme. The internal dynamics of the group were not always reassuring. But the fast was another step in my ongoing journey of renewal. Those long days without food forced me to cope with anxieties and tensions I have never known before. The deprivation was real and the risks frightening at times, especially when my low potassium level sent me to the hospital for an electrocardiogram.

But prayer came easily in those days, and I began to understand why prayer and fasting come as a recommended biblical package. Those days led me to ponder anew the realities of hunger, famine and poverty in our world — those forms of fasting that are involuntary and too often inescapable.

It was good to experience that long hunger voluntarily. Working for justice has an uncanny way of resurrecting and renewing venerable traditions. Practices like fasting that were once undertaken for personal spiritual reasons are now done for societal reasons: to witness to the need for justice, to be in solidarity with the poor.

In the end, we fasters had to cope with defeat, but women from across the country told us that we left them with hope for the future. They were convinced by the fast that women's rights are worth significant sacrifice as we continue to struggle for the time when equality is ours.

Central America

At the conclusion of the ERA struggle in 1982, I took a welcome seven-month sabbatical. At the end of that time in February, 1983, I was able to fulfill a dream and visit Central America, specifically Nicaragua. The Quixote Center had been working on Cental American issues for several years and I had longed to be a part of that struggle, in addition to my work for women's rights. The cause of the poor of the Third World had been close to my heart since early years.

In Nicaragua, I lived in *barrios* (neighborhoods) where I experienced *campesino* life firsthand. I began to understand why the Sandinista revolution was welcomed by the poor. People told me of improved health care, parents who could read thanks to the Literacy Crusade, subsidized food prices for basic commodities, important strides in women's rights. But most of all I sensed a deep personal pride among these people — a sense that they had created a revolution they owned and directed. Many felt empowered for the first time in their lives.

I worshipped with people who *lived* liberation theology every day, and who had lived it through the long and violent revolution that overthrew the dictator Somoza. I was moved by the largesse and lack of vengeance among the Nicaraguan people. They were gracious to U.S. citizens despite our country's aggression against their land; they spent resources trying to rehabilitate even Somoza's former "guardia" who had killed and tortured so many; they granted amnesties even to those who joined counter-revolutionaries. I resolved to do what I could in the United States to stop our attempts to overthrow that revolution so precious to the poor.

In December 1983 and January 1984, I was part of a women's delegation visiting Honduras, Nicaragua and El Salvador. El Salvador especially left me with memories of terror: I talked with Mothers of the Disappeared, whose sons and daughters had been murdered by the security forces, women political prisoners who were pregnant because they had been gang-raped by the soldiers who captured them, refugees who had no homes and no hope, and human rights activists who showed us photographs of human carnage wrought every day by that country's government. Even more than before, I resolved to oppose U.S. foreign policy in Central America with every ounce of energy at my command.

Sorting It Out

That city bus to Pittsburgh's Hill District has taken me to places like Springfield, Illinois and Managua, Nicaragua and refugee camps in El Salvador. It may yet take me other places. It was the first step in response to a call heard in the early years, a basic call to work for justice. It has not been a static call; it has changed and grown over the years.

In 1968, renewal meant a basic freedom to serve the poor and oppressed. But my understanding of who the poor and oppressed are and who or what is oppressing them has grown far beyond the ideas I held in 1968.

My understanding of poor and oppressed peoples now includes far more than racial and ethnic minorities in the United States. It includes Third World people exploited by powerful nations and multinational corporations. It includes women in any culture or country, especially women suffering at the hands of patriarchal religious structures and teachings. It includes gays and lesbians, the disabled, older people, and many others.

Similarly, my understanding of *who* or *what* is oppressive has expanded. No longer is it only structures of racial segregation or those who enforce them, but *all* structures of domination designed to keep others in submission. I have come to understand that the primordial model for such oppression is the traditional male-female relationship. From this model have come hierarchical systems that operate on orders from above rather than consensus and dialogue among equals. This includes the hierarchical Roman Catholic Church as well as corporate structures, governments, and militaries. The call to renew and change such structures has led many women's communities — some borrowing from the Quaker tradition — to experiment with new consensus-building, freedom-respecting structures, at the cutting edge of feminist political experience. Being a part of such experiments has meant a renewal that reaches well beyond personal change to new collective realities.

Finally, my understanding of service has moved far beyond where it was in 1968. In the late 1960s, I tended to think of service as doing for others, offering others one's talents and gifts and knowledge. Over time, I began to understand solidarity as the pre-eminent form of Christian service in our day. For this, I am especially thankful to Betty Campbell, a Sister of Mercy, and to Peter Hinde, a Carmelite, of Tabor House in the days when it was in Washington, D.C. I often listened to them talk about "accompanying the poor" on their journey in Central America without determining the course for them. More than that, I watched how they lived that belief. I found that same message echoed in Gustavo Gutierrez' *Theology of Liberation*. In Nicaragua, I heard firsthand what it meant when people said: Go back to North America and do whatever you can, risk whatever you must, to stop U.S. aggression against this revolution we cherish so much. "We need you walking *with us* among your own people."

And I have begun to learn just a bit of what this solidarity means. It is more than just reading, writing, giving workshops. Sometimes, it involves suffering, fasting, jail, and ultimately a willingness to give life itself. Even more difficult, it can involve loss of reputation and misunderstanding from friends and family. Somehow that all rings true with what Jesus did. And as I learn more about risk, I am grateful for the community support of Loretto and Quixote that makes it all imaginable.

Renewal for me has meant far more than dispensing with restrictive schedules and leaving aside the traditional habit. It has meant a search for the truly radical (gospel-rooted) foundations of religious life itself. It has meant embracing the historic and prophetic role of religious communities in the church: challenging institutions and structures in civil society and the church itself, calling people to the service of the poor, taking the lead in risk when the gospel demands it.

That very process has led me to re-think religious life as a category. If indeed we are called to be non-classist in our living and our language, any notion of religious life as a higher state is out of place. A calling to prophetic ministry in community it may be — but a calling no better than anyone else's. Terms like "religious woman" or even "religious life" which imply that other people or lifestyles are irreligious or non-religious have become inappropriate. The search for words that express common sisterhood in struggle rather than separations is important and continuing.

Paradox

As life moves forward on this track, I find myself in a paradoxical situation. On the one hand, I revel in the freedom to develop new forms of communal worship, new styles of living and working, new levels of solidarity. At the same time, I find myself plunged ever deeper into the Christian tradition of death and resurrection, the symbolism of eucharist, and the ultimate meaning of incarnation — Jesus becoming one of us with the greatest act of solidarity in history. In the midst of that tradition, I search for the few scraps of history left by "Woman Church" — the early forms of feminism that surely emerged in various stages of the church only to be squelched, ignored or declared anathema. But I will not yield the Catholic tradition to anyone. Despite the pain the church causes in the lives of women, I stoutly refuse to leave the institution or its tradition. Nor will I let it be defined and shaped only by the hierarchy. Rather, I claim my own right to participate in developing it — for myself and for all those who will come after me. This is basic to my growing sense of an "integenerational ethic" of women who, like myself, do not have physical offspring.

In many settings I find myself a bridge person: articulating a religious belief in liberation to secular friends (often for the first time in their lives), and explaining feminism, ecumenism, or structural changes on behalf of the poor to Christians (often for the first time in their lives!). It is a stretching position and not always a comfortable one. But it is part of the journey.

Finally, renewal has led me to re-think the core structure of religious life that remained after the 1960s: the vows, community, canonical approval. Poverty has come to mean a choice to live as simply as possible in solidarity with the poor. Obedience is faithfulness to the call of renewal: the call to build justice and peace. Celibacy is a vow for which I have no new meaning: I know only that its living has been good even if I do not quite understand why.

Other questions remain to be explored fully. Do women's communities still wish to restrict themselves to those with the three vows? Are we at the point of admitting others to *full* membership? How do we learn from new realities, like the base communities of Latin America, in shaping the future of our church?

With present signs emanating from Rome, the question of canonical status becomes a persistent one. Can we survive without it? Can we survive *with* it?

How will all these trends and discussions affect that reality we have heretofore called religious life? There are no easy answers, only strong subjects for discussion among those who value church, faith, community, and the gospel tradition.

Hard questions and choices have led me on a journey that has been good. I am never sure what is around the next bend in the road but I know I wouldn't want to travel in any other direction. I just wonder once in a while where that city bus from Pittsburgh will stop next.

Reaping the Fruits of Redemption

Elizabeth Carroll

Elizabeth Carroll (formerly Sister M. Thomas Aquinas) has been president, vice-president and member of the policy board of her own congregation, the Pittsburgh Sisters of Mercy; president of the Federation of Sisters of Mercy of the Americas; president of the Leadership Conference of Women Religious, and U.S. delegate to the International Union of Superiors General. She holds a doctorate in medieval history from the Catholic University of America and has received five honorary degrees in humane letters, literature and law. She is a member of El Equipo para la Promocion de la Mujer of CINCOS (Social Justice Center for the Diocese of Chimbote) in Peru.

In the last month of 1983 — celebrated in the Catholic world as the 1950th anniversary of the redemption by Jesus Christ of all humankind — I begin this reflection on my life as a woman religious before and after the renewal of our congregations. I hesitate to speak of "after renewal" because the decisive moment of renewal, that is of appropriating the fruits of Jesus' redemption for all the women of the world, is just beginning. And certainly, for women religious, there can, in a profound sense, be no "after renewal." Renewal continues, as faith and freedom challenge us to plunge more deeply into the mystery of God's love and its meaning for women, and thus to change the church and the world.

A Wager on Faith

God's call to discipleship of Christ in religious life came to me as a summons, unwanted and persistent, in a way that I came to recognize as the "Hound of Heaven." Entering the Sisters of Mercy in 1935 provided me no joyous romantic high. I approached religious life with a kind of reluctant acceptance of what I thought God was asking of me — if there were a God! What appealed to me was that therein I could achieve one of my life goals: to serve a cause larger than myself which would benefit others, especially the poor. What bothered me, and still does to some extent, was whether I would have the faith necessary for such a life.

Caught in the Great Depression, I shared the cynicism of my fellow university graduates as we scoffed at "the rights and privileges thereunto appertaining." I flinched at the memory of my father's humiliation of having to ask for deferment of tuition payment, and felt the pain of his disappointment and disapproval as I gave up my substitute teaching position to enter the convent.

On the day I entered, I told myself I did not expect to be happy. Yet, as I looked at the peaceful faces of the old sisters, I convinced myself that "maybe 10 years from now I will be glad of this decision." The years 1935 to 1964 framed my incorporation into a way of life which I did accept, which nourished me.

In the earliest days my non-sensate tendencies enabled me to ignore the statues and other symbols of our religious heritage, often rendered in poor art forms, but some of the negativisms of instruction and prayer disturbed me. I rebelled (silently, of course) at the idea that I had to change totally, for I liked a lot of things about myself. I remember my dismay, the first few days, to find the sisters praying after dinner each day, "in sin did my mother conceive me" (Psalm 51). I gained the courage to join them only when I saw that one of the sisters whom I most admired was calmly reciting the words. This was one thing, I decided, I would have to grow into, and, through that growth, find meaning! The faith did come, if often only "sufficient for the day." (With my growing sense of the immense social sin in which we are born and to which we contribute, even these words of the psalm have become meaningful.)

From the beginning, I enjoyed my companions and found that most sisters were wonderful persons who made great friends. These friendships, forged in simple fun, in prayer, and in hard work together toward common goals, were deep, lasting and rewarding, a precious by-product that in the truest reality constitutes community. Also my assignment of study and teaching proved satisfying. The regular schedule of mass, reciting the psalms three times a day, reading treatises on the spiritual life, meditating on the life of Jesus gradually permeated my being and brought a certain peace of the "rightness" of religious life for me. As young people of a later generation of religious life would say, "It fit me."

The virtue of humility especially attracted and mystified me. I read everything I could find and sought understanding of the absurd and even cruel instances of humiliation which works like that of Rodriguez glorified. Fortunately I had a wise mistress of novices who apparently did not share the conviction that contrived humiliation was the only way to humility. What this pursuit gave me, in fact, was at least a partial cure for my native bashfulness.

My concept of God began to change. From God as the supreme poker player who held all the trumps, I began to find the God who cared, the God who, because of merciful love, gave us Jesus. Jesus became my life task, and eventually my freedom. God's presence within me as Holy Spirit, the very Spirit to whom Jesus had responded, filled me with reverence for myself. I gradually grew in the conviction of the power for good which this presence afforded me, if only I would not block it. This spiritual conviction has become the bedrock of my life. It enabled me, by the time I pronounced my perpetual vows, to utter words of total surrender to God's will in a voice of conviction and power. For my family, the change in the timbre of my voice convinced them that I knew what I was doing.

"Total Institution"

Among these vows, in the spirituality which had prevailed since the Counter-Reformation, obedience took precedence. Obedience determined at what task, level and place we were to work, where and how we lived with what companions and superiors. In other words, obedience established "the supreme" which dominated our lives. It required the generosity to offer one's life as a kind of blank check that somebody else would fill in, with the confident expectation that, with God's grace, the religious could handle the consequences. Life in community responded to bells. A wall-saying assured us, "The sound of the bell is the voice of God."

The obedience inherent in common prayer, private spiritual reading and devotions, which occupied almost three hours every day, both required stamina and afforded support. Presence was obligatory at mass and office (the choral recitation of the psalms). Often, even though we prayed in English, we did not understand the allusions nor appreciate the deeply human emotions of these wondrously poetic prayers. Our attention was largely on form, the rhythm, the pitch, the choral division; and our satisfaction came from the integration of the group effort and the beauty of the performance. It was largely up to the individual initiative to find meaning in the psalms. Formation in prayer depended mainly on the good example of our sisters. As a result of this schedule I, at least, developed a superego that guaranteed fidelity to prayer.

The prayers, however, that rooted my life in Christ and in dependence on the Holy Spirit were meditating on the gospels, spiritual reading, and retreats, preached regularly by Jesuits. Many of these were extremely formative of my spirituality and my desire to be whole-hearted in my gift of self to the Lord. Others provided only an exercise in patience and penance. For good or for ill, that was the system, and I for one did not rebel against it. I never even asked myself why only men gave our retreats.

Obedience also regulated the application of the vow of poverty. Though the individual might and was encouraged to develop poverty of spirit, the essence of the vow was in the permission granted or withheld by the superior for receiving, spending, or giving even the smallest of things.

This interpretation of poverty as dependence made somewhat difficult the attainment of simplicity that the vow of poverty was meant to foster. In fact, the need for permission encouraged a kind of irresponsibility in many of us and often resulted in a study of the superior's moods, personality, taste, and the cultivating of a manner that would achieve the desired results, a state of mind certainly contrary to simplicity!

Moreoever, a detachment of poverty from the reality of being poor allowed the growing prosperity of the Catholic population in the 1940s to affect, unconsciously, the life-style of religious. As Catholics moved to the suburbs, so did Catholic schools and Catholic religious. For "their sisters" these Catholics and their pastors wanted beautiful convents. "Nothing is too good for the sisters." Unfortunately, many of us came to feel the same way. Yet because convents and cars were furnished by the pastor, his wishes often dominated both superiors and sisters.

What we also did not realize was that dependence, unless continually willed to achieve a greater good, destroys human personality growth. Suppressed anger provokes self-depreciation, and readily gives rise to envy, hostility or depression. That some religious women tended to be childish or emotionally immature is therefore not nearly so surprising as that most were strong women. They had to become strong to survive "the system" with integrity.

Instruction on the vow of chastity took for granted the non-availability of marriage and sexual relations, and centered on rules of modesty derived from cloistral customs, such as custody of the eyes, silence, and controlled listening and reading. It insinuated a suspicion of all close relationships under the term "particular friendships." As a matter of fact, our associations were almost entirely with other women.

Survivals of cloister prevented attendance at night meetings, at plays, films, concerts and other recreational pursuits unless they took place in the convent. Access to newspapers, radio and television were strictly controlled. Though such restrictions had their drawbacks, they did foster an ability to concentrate on our particular tasks. We were responsible for doing *well* only what was assigned to us.

The immediate demands of our tasks, all assumed to be of equal importance, from being on time for common prayer to controlling a class of eighth-graders, together with this cloistered atmosphere, impeded our comprehension of society and of ourselves and these same eighth-graders within it. We somehow abstracted ourselves physically and mentally, and therefore spiritually, from the events and conflicting ideals which were struggling to shape the world beyond us. Somehow, the fixed truths of our religious heritage were to flow from us and implant themselves in those whom we taught. Only gradually did we learn about "readiness," and not for years did we apply the concept of "readiness" to the economic, social, and political situations of our students. In our teaching we did not realize adequately that we were not challenging young people to criticize the system that would develop into a monster of oppression to the poor. We taught obedience, conformity, and the competitiveness necessary to get ahead.

Rules limiting visitors and visiting, regulating minute aspects of daily routines, controlling access to news and books, inculcating obedience as the overriding value constituted us, as Guzman helped us to realize, a "total institution," in a category similar to that of prisoners and mental patients. The assault on human personality should have been ruinous. What of course prevented its worst effects were the grace of God and the generous love which so many brought to the life.

These were the years when the Catholic school system was expanding, almost exploding. And just as the individual sister adjusted to the fixed and demanding sequence of work, prayer, and "recreation," without much thought of their own preferences, so the congregations of women religous adjusted to the growing demands of bishops and pastors for teachers. Superiors of women religious assumed the full responsibility for filling a seemingly unlimited need for teaching personnel in the diocese.

The often joyous spirit of self-sacrifice with which young sisters, unprepared for teaching, worked at controlling and teaching large classes of children provided a remarkable witness to the power of a highly idealistic and controlled formative environment. Few persons thought of the injustice being done either to the students or to the teachers. But a heavy price was being exacted. Parents began to be disillusioned with the Catholic school system, particularly as costs rose to pay needed lay teachers. For the sisters, five full days of teaching, in addition to the regular prayer-and-community life, college classes on Saturday, teaching catechism in distant missions on Sunday, left little time for preparing work, correcting papers, study, or personal interests. Many were the jokes of people falling asleep at meditation or even while awaiting Holy Communion at the altar rail. Many the laughs about dinners burned as the young sisters prepared the main meal of the day before class and with hurried trips to the school kitchen during their teaching hours. Fatigue weighed on us all, depleting physical, mental and emotional resources.

Though my apostolic work differed from that of most of my sisters, the same pressures were present. When higher studies demanded time, a reluctant superior gave permission to remain up after the allotted hour, provided I could tell myself that I hadn't wasted a moment all day. Actually that justification was not hard to make. For years the rhythm of teaching college history classes, then supervising in the dormitory till midnight, and the 5:30 a.m. rising made morning prayer something of an endurance test.

For 11 years I served as college dean, when our administrative officers consisted only of a president, dean, registrar and treasurer. This work entailed long hours in the office, planning and counseling, speeches to be given, meetings attended and chaired, and the same demanding schedule of community exercises. I can still remember my fatigue as I went to chapel each night to "make up" for a vespers or matins or night prayer, or all three.

Yet, I delight also to recall the exhilaration of those years, the wondrous dependence on God I had to develop in order to cope with the many rich personalities of faculty and students, to attract enough money to make a good education possible for economically poor women, and especially to find ways to educate better the sisters of our diocese and beyond.

When I ask myself why I fared well under this regimen, I answer: the grace of God; a strong sense of duty; an ease of conformity to regulations that do not offend major principles of which I am conscious, and a good, but not brilliantly creative, intellect. Moreover, living always at the motherhouse, I escaped life in the small convent. Also I received a challenging education and was assigned to a vital apostolate which continued to offer me new challenging experiences.

"Young Women Shall Prophesy"

It was the education of sisters that most educated me. I had the good fortune to be dean when Sister Mary Emil Penet began the breakthrough project of Sister Formation. Although I was not part of the original Everett workshop, I soon after joined the University of Milwaukee summer school faculty for sister-formation. Undoubtedly this experience was critical, enabling me to work closely with fine people like Sister Annette Walters and Sister Emmanuel Collens and many others. Reading the *Sister Formation Bulletin* in which Sister Ritamary Bradley introduced us to the rich spiritual insights of French theologians of the 1950s writing articles for it, teaching and speaking launched me into a new world of hope and vision, the prophetic rather than the passive, static stance.

Our novitiates were filled with wonderfully gifted and alive young women; psychology was encouraged to exert its powerful and healthful influence; educational curricula embraced theology, philosophy, science, the arts, literature, politics, economics, sociology and history, all uniting to effect a deeper understanding of God's love in creating the world and calling us to help to convert it to justice and love and peace.

Through the Sister Formation Conference women religious became conscious of their basically unjust approach to their pupils and to each other by sending young sisters to teach without the basic academic work required of all teachers, and without the foundational intellectual and spiritual preparation for a mature religious life. Sisters became conscious of the killing schedules they undertook, and of the shoddy teaching this often made inevitable. Their attempts to remedy this situation met with some support, but more often with indifference even from bishops and pastors.

The injustice of an ecclesiastical system which built large parish complexes, expended huge amounts of time and money on the education of candidates for the priesthood, and begrudged sisters even the time to prepare themselves personally and professionally for their lifelong service to the church, provided a kind of reality therapy for many women religious.

The dream of Sister Formation, to provide all women religious in the country with an integrated spiritual, academic and professional preparation adequate to the demands of our complex society, was never fully realized in the disciplined way it had been planned. The colleges which Sister Formation spawned have since been dismantled. Most of the women who were in our novitiates then have left religious life. What happened?

To some extent Sister Formation fell victim to the great cultural changes of the early 1960s, identified variously as the "hippie" phenomenon, the generation gap, or the youth revolution which convulsed American family and social life. Novices were no exception to the spirit of probing ways of behaving long held sacrosanct. Stimulated by the better education they were receiving, they did the unbelievable. They asked,

"Why?" And we, who had accepted traditions as almost a divine order, found few humanly (or divinely) reasonable answers to justify much that we did. Moreover, the well-thought-out Sister Formation curriculum was something imposed on the young, and therefore, in their eyes, to be resisted. We were trying to store old wine in new wineskins. The assault on structures had begun, not out of ill will, but from a desire really to find the way to serve God best in our highly sophisticated world.

Misunderstandings and conflicts undermined leadership. In fact, the intellectual and personal quarrels in the Sister Formation Conference foreshadowed divisions in the post-Vatican II church and world. The attempt to contain theology within a framework of scholastic philosophy ran counter to the rich intellectual challenge of the Hebraic concept of meeting God in the history of a people, which new biblical studies were revealing. The New Testament offered much more evidence of the value of personal freedom and dependence on the Holy Spirit than had been apparent in the structures approved for religious life. Undoubtedly one of the reasons for the partial collapse of the Sister Formation Conference was the nervous insistence of the Roman Congregation for Religious that the Conference cease to be even partially autonomous, and that it become dependent upon the Conference of Major Superiors of Women. Not only personalities, but two world systems were in conflict, a conflict that still divides the church.

And yet the influence of Sister Formation on the church in the United States is massive and continuing, in the women who remain in religious life as well as many lay leaders in our educational and health systems, in pastoral ministry and work in the public sphere. Through the *Bulletin*, and its educational initiatives, especially through the new vision imparted to apostolic goals, Sister Formation challenged mediocrity in religious life and service, and, at the same time, introduced a humanizing self-respect, respect for the God-given talents of others, and a concern for loving relationships. Most of all, Sister Formation lives in the fact that it developed a biblically and theologically literate population, ready for the new teachings of the Second Vatican Council.

After 10 years of teaching history, another 11 years as dean and a year as president of Mount Mercy (now Carlow College), I was elected major superior of the Sisters of Mercy of Pittsburgh in 1964.

The Service of Love

1964 was a crucial year in which to be elected a major superior. The structures of religious life were still intact, but the strains on persons trying to live within those structures were becoming apparent. I remember a phone call I received from a much-loved superior of a local house shortly after I was elected. She pleaded with me to insist that hours for watching TV be strictly monitored so that the same rules would be observed in all houses. I had never lived in a small convent and had little concept of the closed world it created, but I found that I could make no such promise.

As I began the beautiful task of visiting every house and of talking to each sister in the congregation, I became more convinced something was wrong with the way we were living religious life, and it was not the sisters themselves, nor the superiors, but some of the assumptions that permeated canon law and the theology of religious life. Our mutual relations depended on inadequate bases. Accordingly, at the first meeting of local superiors, I told them that their main task was not to see that the rules were kept, but to establish a climate wherein mutual love could flourish.

Religious life through the centuries had been thought of as a "school of perfection." Through legalisms, the original concept, "perfection of charity," disappeared into the perfection of obedience to the least commands, the perfection of promptness, of cleanliness, of silence, of performance of duties, etc. The great commandment of Jesus that we love one another as he loved us had not been deliberately repudiated. Instead it had fallen from priority of rank. Persons were judged by "observance" and superiors disliked exceptions.

One of the customs that regulated community living was "seniority," the right of precedence by date of profession, observed in chapel, dining room, recreation and some house duties. Convinced that seniority distorted the spirit of communion which we sought, and mindful of Jesus' remonstrances with his disciples against a desire for precedence, our council decided to eliminate the ordering effects of seniority from our customs. I well remember the indignation of one sister, the senior in her house, who pouted, "All my life I've waited for this position, and now you take it from me." How hard is the loss of our idols!

Our effort to create communities where charity would flourish meant that the general council (five of us) spent endless hours and solid weeks working on assignments to apostolates and living units, a process that was irreverently referred to as "filling slots." In the continually growing pressure for more Catholic schools, more sisters in those schools, and the newly-awakened realization of our need to prepare sisters adequately before assignment to schools and other works, our first concerns were "apostolic needs," and the assignment of the sister best fitted professionally for each position. Then followed the hard work of discerning, for over 500 sisters, what was best, taking into consideration their aging, health, the particular physical environment and the human relationships involved. Certainly that process of trying to give a human face to life-determining obediences was the hardest work, the greatest burden on conscience that I have ever assumed. Yet we all took it for granted this was the way to govern a religious congregation.

The other element which made the system work was the constant reinforcement of a spirituality generously and even gaily embraced by most sisters. This spirituality evoked love of God and love of human beings in the service of a continuous self-discipline, hard work, and conformity to conventual custom.

The aura of "office" gave me the privilege of sharing deeply many a sister's beauty of soul, depth of relationship with God, struggles with and acceptance of life's hurts. Most convincing to me of the validity of our religious life was the discovery, again and again, of how, as sisters aged, they seemed to "fall into God." On the other hand, from almost the beginning of my term of office, I faced the unexpected obligation of counseling and assisting sisters who requested a dispensation from vows. The pain of these sessions sprang not only from what I then perceived as infidelity to God, but also my deep convictions of bondedness with one another that we assumed by profession. Only gradually in these situations did I learn to trust the personal integrity of the sister and the merciful providence of God.

All these interviews with sisters animated my search for ways to make our lives more meaningful, more able to extend God's reign of love to a world whose brief breath of great-heartedness in Pope John XXIII and John Kennedy, was soon to be convulsed in ever growing waves of violence. Imagination and creativity became values, and freedom-of-spirit a new found treasure to be guarded even when it challenged and seemed to disrupt the climate of charity we wished so intensely to see prevail in a disciplined observance.

To find the truth in all this simmering conflict of what was important in life-in-community, we allowed sacred scripture to play a more important role in our lives than before. The passages which spoke God's love most eloquently became the heart of our prayer, now enriched with artistry woven into liturgical and para-liturgical forms.

The publication of the documents of Vatican II gave new direction to all the instincts, questions, and restlessness operating under the surface of a very uniform life. For religious, chapter four of *Lumen Gentium* constituted a crisis. "The Universal Call to Holiness" overturned a theology of religious life that had prevailed for 1500 years. Wonderful in its fundamental insight, it was nevertheless devastating to many religious who had built their whole sense of vocation on the belief that they, as a "chosen people," had received a higher call to a more perfect life, the life of perfection. How hard I worked to present "the universal call to holiness" in a positive way, and at the same time challenge the sisters to an appreciation of their particular call!

The documents of Vatican II on the liturgy and sacred scripture, *Lumen Gentium and Gaudium et Spes,* provided inspiration that gradually would have influenced our lives, I am sure, but the document that made Vatican II real for us religious was Pope Paul VI's *Ecclesiae Sanctae*. This letter mandated special chapters (legislative assemblies) for all religious within three years. The document specified a goal and a methodology. All constitutions, books of customs, and regulations were to be restudied in the light of the gospel, the charism of the founder, and the needs of the times. In undertaking this study superiors and representatives to the chapters were to listen to every sister.

The respect for each sister, implicit in the process of soliciting recommendations for the chapters and listening to each speaker carefully before making decisions, produced far-flung results. Primarily it altered the concept of superiorship, of giving orders and securing compliance. It enabled those of us in positions of authority to examine what Jesus meant by "I am in the midst of you as one who serves." Authority became for us enablement of our sisters, the setting free of ideas, talents, qualities of personality that could be put at the service of others. We learned how much richer and more just were the decisions reached through joint discussion and debate. We learned to appreciate the giftedness of each sister, and how important it was for God's reign that she serve in that ministry for which God's gifts had equipped her. These were glorious years, though often painful, of watching people come alive. My greatest joy still is to realize the growth in personal maturity, in faith-filled generosity, and in loving ministry that most of our sisters manifest.

In our chapter decrees the element most decisive for change was the section on "person:"

> If we are to convince others of the dignity of their personhood and of their divine vocation, we must be deeply convinced of these truths in our own lives.

The dignity of each person and expectations of responsible action of the members strongly influenced changes in congregational government!

> Decentralization of general government frees the local mission to make decisions which arise from their own communal needs and their apostolic situations . . . Whenever possible, members of the community must be consulted before decisions are made which affect their lives in a fundamental way . . . Moreover, delegation of authority in all possible areas and in an adult manner is a concomitant of desirable community and the common good.

This decentralization is regarded as in no way opposed to obedience as response to authority. The power of making decisions is a necessary function of authority guided by the principles of collegiality and subsidiarity. Authority as leadership and service in community is preferable to that of government dependent on command.

Key to such positions was the realization of the close connection between responsibility and freedom. In a few words, we removed the deadening practice of requiring permission for every single act, such as using the telephone, receiving a visitor, or spending a little money. While it is true that freedom may stimulate individualism and egoism, it very often fosters a spirit of mutual respect and self-sharing love and availability that makes the concept of community vital.

Such chapter decisions were made possible only through a clear affirmation of belief in the power of prayer and trust in the Holy Spirit, attitudes we stated were "essential for the discernment of spirits necessary to achieve the delicate spiritual balance" that greater contact with the world would entail.

Concern for the world provoked the greatest struggle. Even though we were a community of well-educated persons, our life-style had almost dictated a smallness of perception, a concentration of energies on given tasks, rather than a broad attempt to understand what the world needs from us in order to promote God's reign. With limited knowledge of political and economic reality, accustomed to dealing in situations that we controlled and (except for our hospitals) with a Catholic population, we found it very difficult to articulate our concern for the world — and even more difficult to live it. We had to learn to cultivate the habit of listening to the secular world, or respecting the wisdom of the world, and the breath of the Spirit within it.

Only gradually, by pondering the words we had written and learning better the needs of our society were we able to articulate in our choices of ministry and manner of ministering, and then only on a small scale, the concern for the poor, the alienated, those unjustly discriminated against, especially through racism.

For me and for most of the delegates, I believe, the special chapter was a thrilling experience of intense prayer, extremely committed thought and hard work. We found a new way of working together, with disagreements and tears and the wonderful joy of reaching agreement. In a series of actions which completely altered almost all the accidentals of our life together, we learned trust in the Holy Spirit of God and in one another, gratitude for the personal and communal gifts that we had discovered, active love and a hope that made all the efforts a joy. In the end, we had almost total unanimity from the delegates on the final decisions.

Unfortunately, less than 10 percent of the congregation immediately shared in this excitement, struggle and agreement. The problem was one of implementation. Many were the sisters who, for a variety of personal reasons, resented the disruption of a life-style they associated with their fidelity to religious vows. Nor was every assumption of freedom prudent and lovingly considerate of other persons. Nonetheless, the regular chapter of 1970, which reelected me with a larger council, left intact the decisions of the special chapter and furthered their implementation.

As an unsettling aftermath of the special chapter, many wonderful sisters kept repeating that the new *Decrees* were "words, words, words." It was obviously necessary to examine the truth of this judgment. Consequently, we decided upon a fully participative chapter for 1974, a process in which every physically able sister would contribute to the formulation of positions, discuss the recommendations and vote upon them. In this process, often painful, time-consuming and frustrating, where the hurts of the previous repressive system often became highly visible, we again reached a solid consensus of approval of what the special chapter had done.

Examining young people for admission to the congregation or to vows in these years no longer took the form of fixed questions and standard answers, but involved a mind-and-feeling expansion of human possibilities, of wondrous aspirations of the human soul to serve God and people in self-giving just as reckless as had been our "blank check" concept of obedience.

Facing the Conflicts

The years of my service in authority within our congregation were also years of national involvement: through the Sister Formation Conference (SFC) where I served as national chairperson from 1969-70, as president of the newly founded Federation of the Sisters of Mercy (1965-68), as president of the Leadership Conference of Women Religious (1971-72), and delegate to the International Union of Superiors General (1967, 1970, 1973).

As president of the SFC I first attended meetings of the executive council of the Conference of Major Superiors of Women (CMSW). During the period mandated for renewal chapters, this group, overshadowed by the active presence of the representative from the Sacred Congregation for Religious (SCRIS), was struggling with the fears of the winds of change set free in the previous presidency of Sister Mary Luke Tobin.

A sociologist, Sister Marie Augusta Neal, had provided a major investigative work, the Sisters' Survey, which over 150,000 sisters in the United States completed. Her findings, together with the teachings of Vatican II, served to unleash new concepts of what religious life could and should be, and contributed immensely to the creativity and ferment of special chapters all over the country. At the same time fears of disaster among some leaders provoked an "old guard" mentality.

In 1967 I was one of four delegates to the newly conceived International Union of Superiors General. Under the leadership of Sister Mary Luke Tobin, we Americans learned how to influence an international meeting. The meeting also served to expand my confidence that not only United States sisters were great women, very able to learn. A representative of the Congregation for Religious , Archbishop Paul Philippe, presided at the plenary session each day. He insisted upon his desire to "listen," and did so, even though it was from the presiding chair, and with some hesitation. Nevertheless, the point was not lost on delegates from Africa, the Near and Far East, Europe or Latin America, when, after the United States delegation voted contrary to his stated position, he asked individually for our reasons. After a few days of thought, he reversed his own position. The body came alive. When on the last day, a press release, beautifully translated into all our languages, failed to convey the spirit of the meeting as we had experienced it, the body voted overwhelmingly to reject it, to change travel plans, and to prepare our own documents. Such an amazing meeting that was!

At this time the controversy over the Immaculate Heart of Mary Sisters (IHM) in California erupted. Both Sister Elizabeth Ann and Sister Humiliata (Anita Caspary) had been early and fervent contributors to SFC, and I knew and admired their congregation. It is important to understand some of the dynamics of this struggle in order to gain perspective on events today. With unique creativity and intelligence these IHM Sisters saw more readily than many of us the implications of trying to live as religious in the church in the modern world. They made decisions that soon, in one form or another, became standard in California as well as throughout the United States. Within their community, however, was one sister who was a close friend of the cardinal of Los Angeles. Through her he received a fear-filled and distorted picture of the congregational proposals. The cardinal insisted on the right to veto certain decisions of the IHM chapter. When dialogue failed between the cardinal and the officers of the congregation, the dispute reached the Congregation for Religious, and a canonical investigation ensued.

At this juncture, a resolution of support for the IHM Sisters was proposed at a CMSW meeting. Sister Angelita Myerscough and I were among the most active debaters to support the sisters. Just as our arguments were apparently convincing the delegates, the representative from SCRIS entered the debate with a warning against support of the resolution. For those days this was indeed a heavy! Nonetheless the debate continued. Despite our best efforts, the vote failed by a fraction of one point to achieve the two-thirds required. The persecution of the IHM congregation by SCRIS followed. It eventually split the membership, required dispensation from vows of all who supported the chapter decisions, and destroyed the unique vitality of their congregation. The IHM Sisters of California were the scapegoat of the renewal movement of women religious.

At the same meeting as our debate, Sister Angelita was elected president of CMSW. I was elected vice-president with right of succession to the presidency. A major contributing factor, in my case, was the fact that I had presented a resolution on behalf of Region IV against the abuses being suffered by religious congregations of women as a result of the policies and actions of SCRIS. The resolution was passed and we were elected. Thus began an often hopeful, often painful series of dialogues with the Congregation for Religious and the apostolic delegate over ecclesiastical structures and our new bylaws and name, the Leadership Conference of Women Religious (LCWR).

Through the responsibility of presiding over LCWR I came to realize the tremendous power of group-shared prayer both in deepening our dependence upon God and uniting us in a spirit of loving cooperation and search for truth and justice. The leadership's work might roughly be divided into three spheres: internal organization of the conference; relationships with the hierarchy both in the United States and in Rome; and the promotion of gospel values of mutual respect, friendship, search for truth, and the practice of social justice among our members. In this latter endeavor we worked informally with a large group of men religious superiors under the playful name of the "Loose Association."

In opposition to this effort arose *Consortium Perfectae Caritatis*, a group whose vision limited renewal to the literal application of *Perfectae Caritatis*, Vatican II's document on the religious life, diminished the application of *Ecclesiae Sanctae*, and denied the applicability of other documents, particularly *Gaudium et Spes*, to women religious. This group, and particularly its point of view, attracted those sisters in every congregation who feared the radical changes being inaugurated by general chapters. Because many members of SCRIS and many bishops in the United States strongly supported the consortium, division was sown in every congregation. Our efforts to deal with the leaders of the consortium failed. Dates and places for meeting at the convenience of the consortium were set, but only once did officers of the conference and the consortium meet, and then real dialogue was not possible. (The consortium gradually dimished in numbers, and its point of view was embraced by the Institute of Religious Life, a coalition of bishops, men and women religious, and wealthy Catholic laity who support a passive, conservative role for sisters).

This whole experience, painful in the divisions in the body of religious life and of the church, had the positive advantage of testing continually the renewal, and of teaching women religious how to live and try to deal justly and lovingly with diversity. The controversy, inherently a matter of interpreting the second and third chapters of Lumen Gentium and Gaudium et Spes, came to be symbolized by women religious in the habit. Around these issues we officers made repeated visits to SCRIS, dialogued with a largely antagonistic group of bishops and unsuccessfully sought an opportunity to meet with the pope.

When my term of office expired in 1974, after a few months spent in pastoral work in a poor section of the mountain area in Pennsylvania, I had the good fortune to work at the Center of Concern in Washington, D.C. Because our constituency embraced many religious congregations of women, I continued to interact in workshops, planning sessions, and reflection groups with these women as we pursued issues of ministry and justice: a clear outcome of our renewal. Among the justice issues we readily came to recognize the women's issue as an analytical tool and a challenge in itself. With testimony, quite unappreciated by the hierarchy, at the Bicentennial Hearings of the American Bishops, and, later, with my keynote address at the First Women's Ordination Conference, I helped launch the struggle for full ministry for women in the Catholic church. In 1977 the Congregation for the Doctrine of the Faith responded to these fledgling efforts with its Declaration on the Question of the Admission of Women to the Ministerial Priesthood. The poor quality of this document (see Swidler, Women Priests, Paulist Press, 1977) has left the church without a solid theological defense of its position toward women, thereby causing it to depend on disciplinary measures, such as the promise required of new bishops not to ordain a woman and the canonical penalties against women celebrating the eucharist.

After four years at the Center of Concern, I was reelected to the council of my congregation. 1978 was very different from 1968! A new peace, a mature peace, built not on uniformity and rigid obedience but on acceptance of a very human diversity, resulted from the mutual respect and love we had adopted as unitive values. The Sisters of Mercy offered a beautiful testimony to these positive achievements of renewal in 1981 when over 90 percent of us (almost one-tenth of all U.S. Mercies) came to Pittsburgh to celebrate the 150th anniversary of our foundation. Against a backdrop of polite hostility that had existed in institutional form from 1929 to 1965, and of separatism lasting still longer, the experience of joyous recognition of identity, of spirit and mission was unforgettable. As a crowning achievement of the process of reuniting, each sister received a copy of the new *Core Constitution* that a group of us had produced in the previous year to capture the essence of our renewal. At the same meeting the Federation (17 independent congregations and the Union with nine provinces) approved a process, MERCY FUTURES, which will continue our efforts to become a single body.

I found good relations prevailed between congregations that had changed little and those that had changed much, and we could cooperate generously with one another in projects such as world peace, opposition to the arms race and nuclear weapons, the war on poverty, and to some extent even the women's issue. Above all, I found a great concern for ministry. Our sisters were gradually beginning to respond to the methods of discernment that took seriously "the signs of the times" and the working of the Holy Spirit within each person, as well as official approval. There seemed less fear of responsibility, more desire to be an evangelical presence in people's lives, a willingness to work for and with the very poor. Through missioning services, our hospitals cultivated in all the staff a sense of ministry to the sick and established pastoral and social service departments to humanize the intensely technical preoccupations of modern medicine.

Certainly all was not perfect in our congregations. Although departures became much less frequent, the number of applicants to religious congregations of women dwindled. New problems of an aging population faced us. As ministry gained in importance in our lives, and as ministries varied in their demands on time, community became a value that required much effort, perseverance and creativity. Abandonment of large institutions and properties affected our sense of group prestige. Nevertheless, the growth in spiritual depth, the intensity of involvement in needed ministries, the sense of self-worth and of strong community friendships, all contributed to render us grateful that Vatican II, *Ecclesiae Sanctae*, and our own renewal efforts had enabled our self-gift to be used so freely to benefit others.

Euphoria never lasts long for women in the church. Storm signals from Rome were already appearing before I left for our mission in Peru in 1982. Accordingly, in response to the repressive climate which was appearing in the church, I accepted membership on the first national board of the Association for the Rights of Catholics in the Church (ARCC). Then, in quick succession came canon 590 of the new code of ecclesiastical law, the harsh and precipitous treatment of Sister Agnes Mary Mansour, the insistence that the Sisters of Mercy of the Union forbid all tubal ligations in their hospitals, the study of American religious life imposed upon the bishops, and the *Osservatore Romano* assertion that religious life is "in crisis," a crisis that will be overcome when religious renew their vows into the hands of the Holy Father and each one accepts him as first superior.

How do we keep faith with a church that ignores our herculean efforts to obey Pope Paul VI's *Ecclesiae Sanctae*, to give a greater gospel orientation to our lives, and instead seeks to impose *Essential Elements of Religious Life* and devise a law like canon 590 that changes vows we regard as sacred, and under the guise of loyalty to the pope plants an element of division within every congregation between sisters and their superiors, as well as one another?

The answer seems to be that we keep faith with the Holy Spirit of God and with one another. We are called to a more mature perception of what is divine and what is human in the church. We will calmly persist in the truth we have discovered about ourselves: that we are not merely roles, but persons, the image of God, gifted with intellect, freedom, love, and a mission; that our misson is to do all that we can to assure that the fruits of Christ's redemption are available to all humankind, including women.

The Truth Shall Make You Free

Ritamary Bradley

*Ritamary Bradley, a member of the Sisters For Christian Community,
is professor of English at St. Ambrose College, where she has taught since
1965. She is co-founder and co-editor of* Mystics Quarterly, *founded in
1975 as the* 14th-Century English Mystics Newsletter. *She founded the*
Sister Formation Bulletin *and edited it from 1954-1964. She was assistant to Sister Annette Walters during her terms as executive secretary of
the Sister Formation Conference.*

Renewal in the church, and specifically within religious life, came to
mean: being free from . . . in order to be free to . . .

Filling in the empty spaces in that experience is a process and a challenge extending over many years — in fact, something never finished.
Let it be known, of course, that being free is pain as well as comfort;
darkness as well as light. It is risk, but also trust. It is a value in itself.

For me, growth in freedom was initiated and mediated explicitly by
the church — by her members, her servant-pastors, her theologians and
scholars, her spiritual guides, her traditions, her sacraments. This growth
was crowned by meeting sisterhood and finding family also in a world
heretofore called "secular."

Let me begin with some anecdotes. There were voices everywhere in
the 1960s, and I was eagerly listening.

It was during the chapter of affairs of a traditional religious community
in the late 1960s. Many currents of change were in the air and on the
agenda. At the beginning of a recess from one of the sessions, mother
general said: "When we all come back, we will sit on the same chairs as
we had during this session." Then the gentlest of the sisters from the
ranks (as we then said with our military imagery), as naturally and
inoffensively as one could imagine, suggested: "No, I think we should all
sit where we think best when we return."

During that same recess there was another straw in the wind, forecast-
ing what might lie ahead. The place was the convent refectory. Sisters
who were not elected or who were not *ex-officio* members of the chapter
were tense, fearful, and uncertain about what was being decided behind
closed doors, for those decisions would profoundly alter their own lives.
There was a long-standing, but never examined, rule of secrecy covering
the proceedings of those sessions. No chapter member was ever to discuss
what transpired. Only the official report would be available to non-mem-
bers, and that only many weeks later. But on this day, after the startling

interchange about the chairs, another member of that same chapter, sensing the all-too-common distress and anxiety about the secret sessions, said that since the secrecy rule was cruel, irrational, unnatural, and immoral, she would conscientiously set it aside and speak about what was in progress in the chapter assembly. There was relief among the listeners. This was a shocking shift in procedure; but the walls did not collapse, nor did ecclesiastical authority come charging in to punish the offender. In fact, from that moment on it seemed quite appropriate that whatever was decided should be decided openly and with as much participation as feasible from all whose lives were to be affected by the proceedings.

There was a long way to go from that moment to a time of decisions by consensus among equals, but the barrier was down: Ballots had become less important; listening to the last and the least had been a breakthrough. Could one now move from this slightly modified army model of community government to a community model among sisters? What could we learn from Jesus sitting, in no special place of rank, among his apostle-friends at table, pouring out his eucharistic prayer?

There was nothing insular about the events in that community chapter. A similar dynamic was at work in the church as a whole, freeing the women religious (the most shackled of all church members) from the constraints of old forms. Women religious — even more acutely than women in society in general — suffered from the long tradition which taught the natural superiority of the male and the insurmountable inferiority of the female. But that tradition was not without some inconsistencies. For example, although sisters read in the *Encyclical on Catholic Education* (Pius XI, 1930): "There is not in nature itself . . . anything to suggest that there can, or ought to be, intermingling, much less equality, in the training of the two sexes," many of those same sisters were themselves products of coeducational schools and were often even teaching in such schools.

Having studied this text, the women religious could not help observing that the bishops of the United States did not apply it universally to the schools in their dioceses. Without confronting the teaching at the theoretical level, they regularly approved mixed-sex schools for pastoral (and perhaps for economic) reasons. The position of Pius XI has, of course, given way in the intervening years to statements of later popes and of the Second Vatican Council affirming the equality of the sexes and speaking against discrimination based on gender. In the interval, too, it is now recognized that the belief in a "special nature" for women grew out of 19th-century theories of biological determinism — the same theoretical base that justified inequality and separate education for American blacks and other minorities.

The question of the position of women occasionally surfaced during the years when the Sister Formation Conference provided forums for discussing the preparation of sisters for serving and surviving in a changing world. The earliest mention of the question that I recall was at a regional conference (1955-56 series) when Monsignor J.D. Conway, a canonist and a writer, called on the sisters to confront and reject the theory of woman's inequality as an assumption damaging to the pursuit of their mission. Here are his remarks, as printed in the Fordham University Press proceedings of that year:

> When I first prepared this paper, I expressed this appeal in the rabble-rousing language of an agitator, calling on you, as women of God, to shake off your shackles and proclaim your equality, in things spiritual and intellectual, with earth's supreme creature, man. But some of the sisters who looked it over were afraid that you might let . . . the inflammatory redness of my revolutionary words cast a tinge of pink on your Sister Formation program . . . So I will tone down my words and hope that they will not lose their effectiveness when spoken softly.

> As long as sisters are content to accept the proposition that women are inferior to men, the stronger sex will be content to accept their own estimate of themselves. The bishops and priests are not committed to any program of keeping religious women "in their place," but they are not going to constantly urge you to accept equality. I would suggest that you study Catholic theology and philosophy on this subject and see if some of your ingrained attitudes are not simply tradition and custom, unwarranted by modern circumstance. Our Holy Father (Pius XII) has shown that he is not unmindful of woman's role in the modern world.

Other canonists were also reflecting on the changing positions of sisters. Among these was Cardinal Arcadio Larraona, at that time secretary of the Congregation for Religious. When he visited the United States in 1962, I asked him to discuss whether vocation is to be ascribed to a public acknowledgment by the representatives of the church and canonical communities, or whether it consists in the action of the Holy Spirit in the heart of the called. He said that it was a difficult question. This reply was refreshing, for a narrow-minded perspective generally made answers to complex questions pat and simple. For example, a superior at a meeting of the then Conference of Major Superiors of Women asked a representative from Rome how long a sister could be away from her community before she should be dismissed. He told her exactly — how many weeks and how many written notices were required. Apparently no questions had to be raised as to why the person was away, what knowledge she had of these canonical rules, whether she was in need of help or money, or whether she was caught in a dilemma of conflicting responsibilities. The long journey of conscience and discernment was reduced to the rules of a child's game.

However, among moral theologians, too, a dynamic was in motion which would affect the lives of sisters. Francis McHenry, a Benedictine, had a clear view of some of the difficulties inherent in reducing complex moral obligations to "the will of God" fully manifested in rules and under superiors who applied those rules. He wrote in an issue of the Irish publication, *The Furrow:*

> A subtle voluntarism would seem to be the besetting sin of a great number of moral theologians. Obedience to the law itself is too often regarded

as an ordinance of the will rather than of intellect as Saint Thomas
would have it. Ockham and Suarez have done their work well! The
influence of their voluntarism is a fruitful source of scruples in convents
where "the will of God" is often run to the death.[1]

Similar changes in theology and in biblical and liturgical studies promoted long overdue "freedom to do" among sisters. There were, in addition, crucial events which interacted with these changing thought-cur-
rents. My own experience of nearly a quarter of a century, shared with
Sister Annette Walters, CSJ/SFCC, who was also active in The Sister
Formation Conference bears this out.[2]

In 1962, Cardinal Richard Cushing of Boston sent us to several Latin
American countries under the sponsorship of what was then the Latin
American Bureau of the National Catholic Welfare Conference (now the
National Conference of Catholic Bishops). Our specific goal was to help
sisters break down the artificial barriers separating them and keeping
them from working together as one. Mother Rose Elizabeth, CSC, then
president of Dunbarton College, borrowed lay clothing for us to wear in
countries where habits were illegal or where other obstacles to religious
garb might arise. Maryknoll sisters taught us Spanish.

First we visited Cardinal Juan Landazuri Ricketts, archbishop of Lima
and primate of Peru. He received us graciously, but said he was preoccupied with a document he had in his hand — a letter that had just
arrived from Pope John XXIII. The letter was an appeal calling on the
bishops of Peru to reflect that their responsibilities in their own country
and throughout Latin America were not only religious, in the restricted
spiritual sense, but were also religious in the sense of including concern
for the social, economic, and intellectual problems of that continent. The
document recommended that this immense mission be approached
through the active collaboration of bishops, along with the laity, including
religious, both men and women. The cardinal asked us to return in two
days and to meet with him, with the apostolic nuncio, Archbishop Romolo
Carboni, and with several bishops from throughout Peru.

We met on the day appointed in the austere surroundings of the seminary. My notes say that with the challenge of the papal letter before us
we talked — as brothers and sisters in Christ — of prayer, of poverty,
and of freedom. After the dialogue we were taken to the seminary library,
where the great doors were unlocked and swung open, and we were
invited to enter. "To my knowledge," said the cardinal, "no woman has
ever set foot beyond these library doors before."

Before Catholic sisters had fully achieved a working collaboration,
requests came from the Anglican sisterhooods for dialogue. Mother Ruth,
foundress of the Order of the Holy Spirit, had appealed over many years
to the hierarchies of both faith communions for permission to bring this
dialogue about. As a result, Sister Annette and I visited the Anglican
convent at Morningside Heights in New York City one bleak December
day in the 1960s. "You have come at last," the sisters kept repeating,
looking on us as emissaries of a larger community.

The first conference of sisters open to the Anglicans was on "Education for Human Rights," in which they took an active part. Next they joined us in collaboration with the Jewish community in a common effort for "freedom from bigotry," a bigotry which most of us had drunk in unawares with our religious cultural history. With the help of Rabbi Marc Tanenbaum, we reflected together on the timely message of Cardinal Francis Spellman: "By every means at our disposal we must wage war on the old suspicions and prejudices and bigotry which have set brother against brother (*sic*) and have spawned a brood of evils threatening the very existence of society."

This cooperation with the Anglican sisterhoods later reached overseas in the early 1970s. The Episcopal church funded Sister Annette so that she could go to England to speak at Christ Church, Oxford — a sanctuary seldom, if ever, entered by Catholics since the Reformation for a lecture. I accompanied Sister Annette and thus, in preparation for the conference at Oxford, we were able to spend time in a large number of Anglican religious houses, of both men and women.

Our conversations and the letters which followed focused on the theme of ecumenism. The Anglican sisters had long been inspired by the great apostle of unity, Abbè Paul Couturier. His "invisible monastery" was a movement whereby Anglican and Roman Catholic religious found a way to be united with one another in a new bond. The aim of the invisible monastery was to advance the fulfillment of Christ's prayer — "that all may be one" — through prayer and work. Person-to-person contacts were encouraged where possible. For example, the Sisters of the (Anglican) House of Prayer in Burnham, England, wrote that "Abbe Couturier asked us to correspond with his niece, a Sister of the Dames of Nazareth in France; and that was only the beginning of our touches with you (Roman Catholic sisters)." This spiritual ecumenism looked ahead in hope to some external expression of unity in the future. "Who knows," wrote a Sister of the Order of the Paraclete, Whitby, translating from a French letter, "whether one day the Holy Spirit will not permit this 'invisible monastery' to become visible . . . a direct reminder of the great mystery which should be vital to every Christian."

Like American sisters, the Anglican religious were wrestling with the problem of how to become transformed religious for the contemporary world. Mother Dorothea, of the Sisters of the Church, who had a house in the Liverpool slums, explained how her community was trying to achieve this: "For some time we had been wanting to do some other work in Australia besides that of running schools for the well-to-do. So we closed the school, and we are now established in the district of Glebe, with one sister working full-time in a laundry (getting danger money because of the germs and fleas); one as a part-time orderly in a small hospital, a third as a part-time kitchen hand in another hospital, where she is a fellow-worker with unmarried pregnant girls. A fourth stays at home. . . . It is not easy to take on the idea that one's aim is to be without status, to be among those who could not achieve if they wanted to."

During one church unity week this little community — supplied with sleeping bags and a contribution to the supper — stayed overnight with a Roman Catholic sisterhood. Together they shared the ideal that they were followers of the saviour "who entered the warp and woof, into the depths of mankind." Theirs was a freedom that passed through the valley of pain.

These and other sisters were moving out of a narrow ascetical tradition, with its "convent mystique" of regulation and dependence, into a world that demanded a mature conscience. The emerging influences on all of us were from within the church primarily. But there were also ecumenical and secular influences. We were now in touch with a community of rationality and moral insight on a broad scale. To this community belonged the disciples of Gandhi, teaching on non-violence, and Martin Luther King, devising strategies against racism in the American tradition, and, in his later years, brave initiatives (along with the Berrigans) for global peace. Contact with this world community of conscience, of moral insight, of inspiration was indeed "the world" — but not in the sense of a danger to holiness or as an opposite of "the convent."

Confirming guidance for discernment came from Vatican II: "With the help of the Holy Spirit, it is the task of the entire people of God, especially pastors and theologians, to hear, distinguish, and interpret the many voices of our age, and to judge them in the light of the Divine Word."[3] New roads to truth have been opened, the council documents affirmed, "thanks to the experience of past ages, the progress of the human sciences, and the treasures hidden in the various forms of human culture."[4] A narrow form of convent life was no longer possible. One laywoman wrote to me: "What need have I of the convent mystique? And how does it serve those who subscribe to it? It is like trying to long-distance run in a gunnysack. Not likely to produce Olympic champions." But sisters were becoming free — this time of a gunnysack.

For my part I returned to the work of education, filled in, where possible, with scholarship in medieval studies. (That field had been for me the back door to theology, from which women had been banned.) Now that I was free of the artificial rituals of the convent regime, I also found time to serve in the Christian community and in the civic community in new ways. As a religious sister I responded to invitations to be part of religious emphasis week at the federal penitentiary. That effort was followed by years of correspondence with inmates who wanted to continue the dialogue. The only restrictions now on letter writing were those of time and ability to respond. I could also answer requests to give days of recollection, either in homes where women gathered, or in parishes where all could come; to Lutheran groups as well as to Catholics.

Once I answered a call to bury the dead — to speak and pray at a funeral parlor and at the graveside of one whose family had been torn apart by religious difficulties. That night I had a call from the pastor of the parish where the deceased had lived. The priest was not calling to reclaim his turf, but rather wanted to inquire if there was anything more the parish could do for the bereaved family. It had been overlooked that the eldest son was permanently in a wheelchair, and his contact with churches had been therefore cut off. (In spite of that, when Sister Annette and I had visited him over the years, we had always found him active in causes for peace and the rights of the handicapped — and women.)

On the civic level I could also respond. Principal among such efforts was a rocky stint of service on the Civil Rights Commission in Davenport, Iowa, to which I was appointed by the city's first woman mayor. Fair hiring practices for women and minorities, and equitable use of federal monies for housing for the poor were the main issues. During my term as chair of the commission, a federal legal case over the housing conflict was launched, so that housing for the poor could have priority over new tennis courts for the affluent. An out-of-court settlement affected the use of a block grant of nearly $2 million, put in place a citizens advisory committee, and set a precedent for other cases. Understandably, I was not reappointed by the man who succeeded as mayor of the city.

Other sisters and their associates in Catholic, Jewish, and Protestant faith communities began doing on a continuous scale what I had been able to do only sporadically. An outstanding example is the Institute of Women Today, which, under the leadership of Sister Margaret Traxler, established nationwide programs for women prisoners, offering them a chance to learn trades for self-support and helping them develop as persons through the arts and humanities. Some sisters moved into depressed areas to advance neighborhood renewal programs or to offer educational and social assistance. Other sisters made their influence widely felt in civic and political areas. They touched on peace and justice issues everywhere.

But there were, I found, far-reaching justice issues in the educational field, too. The first one I encountered centered on one Sister Catherine. She earned her degree in theology after the graduate schools finally opened their theology departments to women. She paid her expenses by working after hours in a Jewish hospital. Male seminarians taking the same classes had a free ride for their education from the generosity of the Catholic laity. Catherine's first teaching appointment after her graduation was in an all-male college. Theology was required, but the college did not want the students to dislike religion and hence theology classes were seldom on a par academically with other courses. Then Catherine came — with her reading lists, her tests, her discussion groups, her dynamic intermingling of faith and academic progress. First there was grumbling. Then a large segment of young men who were in the peace movement but far from the church came her way. Some others, who had long ago quit confessing their sins in the confessional, came to be counseled. If a student's work was falling behind because of an alcoholic mother, Catherine might go to the home after hours and prepare a meal as a step towards bettering the situation.

But an all-male faculty committee decided that after one year Catherine must go. Reason: "Lack of rapport with students." The story hit the newspapers throughout the state. Students demonstrated on a large scale. When the public and the media asked questions, a talking head with a white collar appeared on television to explain: The students — those hundreds who were demonstrating — did not really want Catherine as a teacher. They were just gallantly "coming to the rescue of a maiden in distress."

I wept for Catherine. I grieved for the sexism that produced this charade. No longer did the jokes about prostitutes, about smart young college men finding their manhood in casual sexual encounters, and the malicious ridicule of ladies with fat legs seem merely immature. Evil lay at the root of such sexism.

The next time the victim was my longtime associate, Sister Annette Walters. She needed time off from teaching to complete a study of the psychology of conscience and moral development and to write a book about the subject. Help for the project was offered by Yale University, and interest had already surfaced in the audience of an international conference of the Religious Education Association, to whom Annette had presented her preliminary paper. The book would have brought together a lifetime of clinical experience, scholarship, publication, religious dedication, and teaching by the woman who had first introduced into a Catholic college a psychology program fully in touch with the human sciences. Perhaps it was mind-boggling for a sexist group to grasp the dimensions of what a woman had to offer. In any event Annette was set aside so that a man who wanted to pursue his first graduate degree after 16 years of college teaching might have preference. He was judged to be more valuable to the college. By this time I was thoroughly in sympathy with the movement for women's equality and the battle against the sin of sexism in church and society.

One way of dealing in part with that sexism was by support of women's studies programs that were taking shape. I taught one of the earliest courses in women in literature. That course was the occasion for rediscovering Dame Julian of Norwich, a 14th-century recluse and the first known woman writer in English letters. I learned and re-learned much from Julian. I pondered the contemplative lesson that we are sisters and brothers and co-Christians in the family of God and that we are called to a city of peace where Jesus is the center, to a feast where Jesus is present and brings joy, where his face is music. With a professor of English from the University of Iowa, Valerie Lagorio, I helped launch a newsletter that grew into a journal on studies in mysticism. Like myself, Professor Lagorio lamented the neglect of the Christian scholarship that relates to spirituality and sought a way to bring the scholarship of the "world" into contact with the religious tradition.

Julian freed me from much of the ill-fitting clothing that a male-centered church had designed for women. For example, in a male culture, the model repeatedly proposed for women religious was that of spiritual motherhood. Now as a sister I had renounced both marriage and motherhood, and I could not see a reason for re-introducing these sublime states symbolically into my kind of life, with which they were inconsistent. Furthermore, I had observed — both in the animal and human world — that motherhood was a function best completed as soon as possible and not prolonged beyond childhood without necessity. Over-mothered children may be psychologically crippled; and women who identify totally with their mothering role may become both stunted and possessive.

No developed adult needs to be mothered — except by God. Julian best explains how the motherhood of the best of human mothers participates only faintly in the mothering aspect of God. In fact, Christ himself is the perfect mother — bearing us to eternal life, nurturing us, teaching us, depriving us lovingly, leading us from the breast, to the taking of drink, to strong meat, as the scriptural symbolism suggests. Jesus is the archetypal mother; and all of us participate both in childhood and in the maturing process, in harmony with what we know of these states from the human sciences and from experience. But only some women participate in motherhood, while men and women alike have Jesus throughout life as their mother. Even Augustine, despite his degrading anti-woman bias, grasped the mothering function of Christ.

Helped by Julian's theology, I reformulated my belief that the woman religious can best be "sister" to men and women alike. "Sister" is an appropriate gender-related role, but it is not limited or time-bound. (Are sisters in their 90s still expected to be "spiritual mothers" and to define themselves by a special nature based on motherhood?) Sisterhood, by contrast, emphasizes equality and is unencumbered by the cultural baggage of inferiority that has unfortunately attached to the position of the woman who was a wife.

When I visited England again, it was to go to Norwich, to the church where Julian prayed, to the chapel rebuilt on the spot where Julian had written on the theology of love. Here was a place "where prayer has been valid," as T.S. Eliot said of such places of silence. (Sister Annette Walters had died since my previous journey to England but the memory of her ecumenical mission was very much alive. I heard of it from the Sisters of the Love of God at Fairacres and from Dean Donald Allchin of Canterbury.)

In Julian's chapel in the company of Valerie Lagorio, I prayed that "all may be one." Rev. Robert Llewelyn, director of activities at the Julian shrine, invited us to his flat nearby on King's Street to talk — over strawberries and cream. I felt reluctant to consume the very best of his resources, wondering what he would prepare for himself when we were gone. But none of the truly essential traditions of religious life forms seem ever to disappear. For, as if it were a repetition of the legendary marvels told of hermits of old, a visitor appeared at the door, bringing a gift of a new supply of strawberries, as plump, ripe, and luscious as the ones we were sharing. Back at the convent of All Hallows, Valerie and I talked with the Anglican sisters there — of their prayer, their parish visiting, their house of hospitality, and of the scholarship of a young Lutheran ordinand who had just finished a study of Julian's theology, after two years residing at Norwich.

All around me I saw dedicated sisters, many of whom, at an earlier time, would have been strained and sleepless during these August days, waiting for a mission assignment to be given out — and held in secret until the designated moment. Now I saw instead, not fear and anxiety, but open-hearted risk — in mature, marvelous women ready to plunge into situations where they could share gifts of love and affirm Christian community. At that moment they were out on the shore of the Atlantic, peacefully at prayer — not pressured to "get in their devotions," as in the past. They were free of the burdensome regulations which had been so counterproductive over the preceding decades.

Such regulations had not always existed in religious houses, of course, even in my own memory. I recalled that during my novitiate days there was a sister in her 80s who used the one telephone in that area of the convent to carry on a conversation that went on again and again: "Hello, Biddy," it began; and then took various directions. "Oh, I'm sorry. He's in jail again? There's not enough food for the children? . . . She can't help because she broke her hip? . . . No, I'm sorry. No, we can't come over. None of us can come . . . You see, we don't practice charity any more. That went out when the rule came back from Rome."

My religious upbringing had been in an era when prayer and charity were integrated into daily living. I grew up in Iowa, nurtured, in part, by tales my father James told of the Irish Bradleys who had settled in Pennsylvania. (Later, in libraries in Pennsylvania convents, I looked up the names of Bradleys who were associated with the missionary work of Prince Gallitzin in those parts.) On the high altar of the church in Stuart, Iowa, my birthplace, there was a small brass plate with the names of Martha and Andrew Muldoon, who had shared the wealth they had wrested from the land, in corn, grain and coal, by giving this gift of a marble altar. They were my grandparents. My mother Alice sang hymns — full of faith and courage — learned from her mother Martha, who was a convert from the song-rich tradition of Methodism.

In the Depression years I often spent the school vacations in Granger, Iowa, in the parish of Monsignor Luigi Ligutti, for whom my aunt was a housekeeper. At his table, where we all prayed and shared meals together, there were often guests from distant places around the world. They came to Granger to see what this Italian immigrant was doing to help people grow and preserve their own food. These marvelous guests, for whom my aunt and I cooked, talked earnestly of hunger in other parts of the world and of the technical means of relieving it. The means began at the simplest level. Under the rectory there was a small dirt cellar, which remained warm in winter and cool in summer. Ligutti would bring in fruits and grains asking, "How would you can this — dry it, preserve it in some way?" The children of Martha Muldoon knew this lore, learned from pioneer women, from Irish and German immigrants. The dirt cellar housed one sample of each kind of food, one sample of each form of preservation, all handled with the simplest methods and the most ordinary ingredients. Long after, Ligutti became the first permanent observer for the Vatican for the Food and Agriculture Organization of the United Nations. But for my part, on that spot in Granger, with its flood of world figures concerned with hunger, I glimpsed a view of a suffering world which could be lovingly healed by technical progress.

In the history books I first learned the other side of the official church — its twisted politics and unjust use of power. But though Ligutti went to the seat of church power, Rome, he did not change. In fact, when the work that Sister Annette and I were fostering was in jeopardy in the 1960s, Ligutti flew from Rome to Washington, D.C. to help us. He took us to the Mayflower for lunch and told us how matters were shaping up in the Vatican. "If Ottaviani comes into power," he cautioned, "take for shelter." As it turned out, even without Ottaviani in power, we felt the heavy hand of Rome disrupting what had been built.

First, Archbishop Paul Philippe, O.P., at that time secretary of the Holy Office, summoned Annette Walters and me to an Inquisition-like session, in Cincinnati, for three hours, in the middle of the night. We had been summarily called to the meeting with no hint as to what was at stake. Philippe alternately wheedled and harassed us and ended by saying that Rome found no fault — in fact, much to praise — in our work and writings. Yet shortly after, he issued a formal rescript effectively suppressing the Sister Formation Conference — a grass-roots, democratic group — under the guise of "elevating" it. It was made a commission of the Conference of Major Superiors, a group established by Rome. This latter organization remained under the direction of Bernard Ransing, C.S.C., who urged centralization of all sisters' groups, with the promise that Rome would then "protect" them from their bishops.

Meantime, I continued to reflect on the changing forms and ageless traditions of religious life. Back home I lived in the house which Sister Annette and I had set up for the benefit of sisters in transition. What is a religious community, I continually asked myself. I came again to think of it once more as a gathering of people whose closeness of spirit is rooted in common religious and human experiences. They bond together to stress or to carry out those parts of the gospel that need attention or are blatantly neglected at any point in history. I found that for me the Sisters For Christian Community, as shaped by Sister Lillanna Kopp, verified that definition: the profile of the community grew out of Christ's eucharistic prayer, "that all may be one." The Second Vatican Council, its theologians, and the experiences of Christians were pointing the way to responses to that prayer: in the search for ecumenism, the struggle for equality between the sexes, the battle for justice and peace in society, and above all the dream of a church where community superseded hierarchical arrangements.

My affiliation with this new community led me to its international assemblies. At one of these, in Narragansett, Rhode Island, I was stirred to write a little of what I had come to understand — in a freer context than at an earlier time — of the place of sisters.

My editorship of the *Sister Formation Bulletin,* then going worldwide to 11,000 subscribers, came to an end. I was informed that I could not reside in the houses of the Sisters of Humility, my community at that time. Later I learned of a rescript processed through the Sacred Congregation of Religious, giving me a "leave of absense," which I neither wished for nor sought. The request had been completed without my knowledge, and the reason given for the petition was "conscience." These circumstances left me, at one time, in St. Paul, Minnesota, knocking on doors, without a source of funds, a suitcase in my hand, seeking out "room vacancy" signs. Fortunately, I received a grant to attend the University of Minnesota and an offer of support from the father of one of the sisters in the Humility community. Annette in the meantime was subjected to systematic character assassination.

David Riesman, Harvard sociologist, who had long assisted the Sister Formation Conference, said of the chain of events: "This disturbance is being described as a little squabble among nuns. It reminds me of the fact that the problems raised by Luther were dismissed at the time as a little squabble among monks."

Thus, as in numberless other times in the history of women religious, the whim of male authority changed the direction of countless lives.

Such were my reflections as I sat by the ocean at Narragansett. The sisters around me were sitting where they pleased: agile ones on high rocks, older ones in solitude and in a safer zone. There were dangerous loose rocks on that shore, but beyond all was the limitless ocean, full of symbolism for poetry and faith alike.

So I wrote these lines, limited indeed, not literary, but ones which I feel free to share, just as they are. With them I bring this sketch of a journey into freedom to a close.

Song of the Seaweed

If humankind decomposes today, it will be because Christians have not been what they are called to be: "You are the salt of the earth. . . ."

But humankind will not decompose if it hears the words of Christ, "I am the living water. If anyone among you thirst, you should come to me and drink."

This is the song of the seaweed.

The seaweed is not the living water. The seaweed preserves and makes palatable the food that people eat. And if they eat food — take in delightedly the goods of the earth — they will also desire to drink.

And the desire to drink leads to the living waters where no one will ever thirst again.

Sisters are a special kind of seaweed. Sometimes they live in colonies. They seem without roots.

They depend on the sea. Their place is determined by the winding of the waters. Sometimes they appear desolate. Sometimes they are alone.

In modern times under the touch of technology the salt gives way to seaweed. Seaweed averts decomposition of goods and keeps variety on loaded shelves in supermarkets. It can be medicinal. It can purify where the air is cloying. It can arrest decay. But if seaweed strands are corrupted they can become pond scum.

Moses was seaweed, when he stood before the full flood of the Lord's being and brought back only the radiance on his own human face. And the people said: "Let not God speak to us, lest we die. Do thou speak to us." . . . Mary was seaweed, when without reproach she laid bare the fears of her human heart saying: "Where have you been? Thy father and I have sought thee sorrowing."

Seaweed is rootless. When struck by the sun it can transform water into the fruit of a living vine.

"We are seaweed," say the sisters. "If we abide not by the living water, we die . . . like the branch sliced by the sharp blade from the vine.

"We are seaweed, lodged between the shimmer of the sunlit water and the thirst to be slaked on the shore."

> "Blessed is the one who trusts in the Lord,
>   Whose trust is ever in the Lord.
> Such a one is like a tree planted by living water,
>   That sends out its roots by the stream
>   And does not fear when heat comes,
>   For its leaves remain green.
> And it is not anxious in the year of drought,
> For it does not cease to bear fruit." (Jeremiah 17:7-8)

Notes

1. Francis McHenry, O.S.B., "Sister Formation," *The Furrow,* October, 1963, p. 12.

2. See Annette Walters, "Religious Life, Yesterday and Tomorrow," *New Catholic World,* March-April, 1972, pp. 74-77.

3. "The Church in the Modern World," in *The Documents of Vatican II,* New York: Guild Press, 1966, Section 44, p. 246.

4. Ibid.

Go East New Nun

Pascaline Coff

*Pascaline Coff has been a Benedictine sister for 33 years. After serving
her monastic community in formation and leadership roles, she founded
a monastic ashram in Sand Springs, Oklahoma, and is currently its
director. She also serves as executive secretary for the A.I.M. (Aide Inter
Monasteres) North American Board for East-West Dialogue. She holds
a Ph.D. in theology from St. Mary's Notre Dame.*

Times were changing quickly for those who had entered stable, traditional monastic communities in the 1940s and early 1950s.

More than the walls (at Clyde, Missouri, they were three feet thick)
were crumbling. The Clyde community, the Benedictines of Perpetual
Adoration, from its inception had been dedicated to the eucharist and
had remained faithful to its founders and their spirit. Benediction of the
Blessed Sacrament was solemnly offered twice daily at the motherhouse
and at each dependent priory, with perpetual adoration in all the houses
of the congregation. This opportunity for total dedication to Christ in the
eucharist in a monastic life-style brought me to Clyde in 1949.

Already in the 1950s, valiant efforts were being made to update religious education in our motherhouse. Theologians Charles Davis and Bernard Cooke were among the early ones to impart deeper understanding
of eucharist and adoration. Christ's presence in the host, they pointed
out, was for the sake of an even greater presence within the heart.

When Sister Matthias Igoe and I were sent to get our doctorates in
theology at St. Mary's College at Notre Dame in 1957, we were described
by other students as "holy cards," since this was our first extended time
outside of the monastic enclosure. The two of us could not attend our
theology class picnics when priests were present, but we never missed
out on the good food, because friends brought an abundance of it to our
doorstep afterward. A theologically convincing letter saying Sister Matthias and I should be allowed to attend the picnics was sent by the dean
to the head of our congregation in Clyde. Back came a masterpiece, a
marvelously worded response buttressed with biblical quotes, informing
the school administration we were to keep semi-cloister in our rooms
during picnics.

We owe our scholastic progress to the late Cardinal John P. Cody, who
was vicar of our diocese at the time. His insistence caused the Congregation of Benedictines of Perpetual Adoration to close their famous dairy
farm (after sending off a papal baby bull to Castelgondolfo) and began
sending sisters for higher studies. At St. Mary's Sister Matthias and I

gleaned much from this last time that St. Thomas' *Summa* would be used as *the* text book. Vatican II was in the wings.

That same year Carroll Stuhlmueller, a Passionist just completing his own doctoral studies, came to teach scripture in the theology program at St. Mary's. He urged us to explore the new theology of eucharist with our sisters back home and to do so within the experience of perpetual adoration. The new eucharistic theology concentrated on Jesus giving himself as food for our journey, a mode of presence that emphasized his leading us into the future. This theological exploration later resulted in the change from a five-foot monstrance in some of the priories to a small one-foot chalice-monstrance, a change which caused some laity and religious to feel that Christ was being dethroned and displaced by other interests.

In 1959 soon after graduation from St. Mary's, I was given the responsibility of the novices at the central novitiate at Clyde, a sacred trust for six years. Besides theology and monastic history, the novices began to hear about Vatican II and the great hope flowing from Rome. The purpose of the council, Good Pope John had said in his opening words to the fathers of the council and to all men and women, was: "to devote all our energies and thoughts to the renewal of ourselves and the flocks committed to us, so that there may radiate before all men the lovable features of Jesus Christ, who shines in our hearts 'that God's splendor may be revealed' (2 Cor. 4:6)."[1]

Signs of conflict were beginning. Clyde — as well as many other communities — had recently experienced its largest group of novices, 21. Men were walking on the moon. Then Pope John died, Kennedy was shot, and droves of young people began to leave other religious communities. There was smoke but not yet fire as our monastic structures seemed impervious to the quaking that had begun throughout the world.

In 1963, the *Constitution on the Sacred Liturgy* was promulgated, the fruit of 50 years of pastoral liturgical experience in Europe and America. It brought fresh and overdue theological insights. One of these was especially relevant for those whose lives were devoted to eucharistic adoration: the rediscovery of the dynamic presences of Jesus Christ in our midst! Godfrey Diekmann, the Benedictine liturgist who was a long-time friend of the sisters at Clyde, pointed out to us that the new theology was moving away from a rather static understanding of the presence of Christ confined primarily to the eucharist. A more dynamic understanding was expressed in Vatican II's *Constitution on the Sacred Liturgy:*

> Christ is always present in his church, especially in her liturgical celebrations. He is present in the sacrifice of the mass not only in the person of the minister . . . but especially in the eucharistic species. He is present in the sacraments. He is present in his word, since it is he himself who speaks when the holy scriptures are read in church. He is present when the church prays and sings.[7]

The joys and pains of experimentation soon began with another women of the West. The decree provided treasures for many religious but gave no recognition to monastic life as it had been lived by Benedictine sisters for almost a century in America — a great omission repeated in the new code of canon law promulgated in November, 1983.

Just as the history of Vatican II is not the history of any one pope or bishop, so too renewal of religious life is not the story of any one religious or even one community but rather an intertwining of the Spirit in the dance of life and love throughout the world. A phenomenon both human and divine, the hope of renewal among religious in a given person or community is to enable the Lord of the dance to radiate the lovable features of Jesus ever more brightly before all men and women.

In six of the most difficult years for all religious (1968-1974), I was called by my community to be prioress general, and by other Benedictines to be chairperson of the American prioresses. Drawing on my experiences with the novices, postulants and aspirants and on theological training, the governing council and I tried to be sensitive to the Spirit and continue the updating that had begun as well as bring fresh insights. A "golden age" of building had preceded 1968. A new motherhouse and novitiate had been built in St. Louis, but between 1968 and 1974 our efforts were concentrated on the building up of persons, and not one building was erected. Priority was given to monastic prayer and spirituality. Spiritual direction was strongly encouraged, especially at the leadership level in the priories. Leadership training experts were invited to teach all members how best to propose new ideas and to support or critique those of others. Establishment of a formation team and a prioresses' council was a deliberate effort toward collegial leadership.

Beginnings were slow and difficult because many sisters required more preparation for change. Some sisters were selected to study spiritually in new settings. One spent nine months at a Cistercian monastery for in-service training; another spent time in the simplicity and poverty of an Indian reservation in the West. Meetings and sharing sessions wore thin some of the best words of the time: "relevant," "fulfillment," "grass roots," and "future thrust." The pyramid-shaped structure, in which only a few were trained and thought capable, gradually gave way as the gifts and potentials of each individual were made available for the good of the church and the community.

Composition of music for monastic liturgy was being encouraged and congregation liturgists for the first time toured other monastic houses. Later organists spearheaded a liturgy pilgrimage to Europe, in the company of American Benedictine sisters and monks. New artists began to emerge.

Small was becoming beautiful. Small primary groups, which provided an opportunity for deeper relationships, were welcomed in the priory at Clyde. Groupings of elderly, young and middle-aged sisters were brought together from all six priories to share life experiences. Chapter sessions were opened to non-delegates and to presidents of other Benedictine federations.

During these decades, Thomas Merton, the Trappist from Gethesemani, was having a profound but subtle influence on monastics. I had read his *Seven Storey Mountain* before entering the community. Book after book continued to flow out from Gethsemani with growing insights into the signs of the times. Gradually Merton's real gift emerged amidst much personal agony. He saw that the very structures created to enable a monastic to begin the spiritual journey later blocked full receptivity of the Spirit. To Merton the most essential of the vows (he also dubbed it the "most mysterious") was *conversio morum* — that is, the commitment to total inner transformation to become a new person. He regarded this as the end of monastic life and the most essential thing no matter where one attempts to "do" this.

Merton died in December of 1968, my first year as prioress. His impact on me and many others was immeasurable. In his prophetic "last discourse" in Bangkok, he said, "We can no longer rely on being supported by structures that may be destroyed at any moment by a political power or political force."[2]

Eventually the delicate and growing problem of perpetual adoration in its old form surfaced within our congregation. Great love and devotion, sacrifice and joy had been poured forth in millions of hours of perpetual adoration since the first five sisters came to Clyde from Rickenbach, Switzerland. All six priories of the congregation had had adoration around the clock, but numbers were dwindling, sisters were aging, newcomers were less numerous. New forms were tried. Adoration was tried on a congregational basis so each priory covered two nights a week and the entire week was covered by the whole. For some this new approach was the will of God, but for others it was a painful departure and the beginning of a spiritual landslide. Still, the Spirit was ever present and continued to dance in the hearts of all, and we remained strongly devoted to Christ in the eucharist and to each other in monastic community.

During the time I was chairperson of the Benedictine prioresses, monastic women were beginning to ask for equality. We petitioned Rome to allow sister-presidents instead of local bishops to preside at the elections of prioresses. American abbots were petitioned to allow prioresses, their the female counterparts, to be present at their annual retreat-workshop. And the male monastic musicians were asked to include Benedictine sisters in their regular gatherings. Only the third of these requests was granted immediately.

European Connections

In a Roman garden at midnight, Sister Joan Chittister and I faced four large dogs that barred the path to the main convent building. We had entered from the street with the key given by the hospitable Italian sisters in whose large convent we were staying during the 1973 Congress of Abbots. We had been invited by Abbot Rembert Weakland, O.S.B., primate of Benedictine throughout the world, to represent American

Benedictine sisters at this first congress where women were chosen to
be observers. "Aggregation" was on the agenda. It was a proposal by the
Benedictine abbots that would have taxed Benedictine women equally
with the men but would not have given them voting rights or even an
assurance of presence at major meetings! After Sister Joan responded to
the assemblage on behalf of U.S. Benedictines, a youthful, newly blessed
English abbot was heard to wisper to his colleagues: "I am scared of the
caliber of expertise I am hearing."

Enroute to Rome, Joan and I each visited the original European
motherhouses of our communities, Eichstatt and Maria Rickenbach. In
the Swiss Alps, we rode in the shiny red cable car that carried us together
with tons of crated apples up dizzying and fantastically beautiful green
slopes. This return to the sources from which the Clyde community had
come 100 years earlier was invigorating on many levels. Some of our
Clyde sisters, who had never been to Europe, but were clinging to "what
we always did," were anxious to retain our original charism of perpetual
adoration as it was carried out at Rickenbach. An indult of perpetual
exposition of the Blessed Sacrament given to our Clyde community in
1920 was celebrated annually with much gratitude and festivity on St.
Michael's Day. And yet here at Rickenbach the Swiss sisters were still
offering their formal adoration from a balcony at the rear of their chapel
without continual exposition. Later the whole matter of perpetual exposition became the source of much pain for us as the times brought unavoidable change.

Reflecting on renewal from those mountain heights, I wrote to the
sisters back home:

> During this 100th anniversary year it is a great joy to return to the
> spot of our original inspiration, and to breathe the same air and see
> the same sights which delighted and gave promise to the hearts of
> our holy founders. But the renewal of our religious life as a community
> cannot come about unless each one makes the personal effort to follow
> Christ as proposed by the gospel and to regard this as the supreme
> law of the community . . . The Spirit, the charisma, the heritage is
> alive in us today. Let us open our eyes to the deifying light and hear
> what the Spirit is saying . . . The changes attempted in our Congre-
> gation have brought with them many blessings, but not without the
> price of much pain. Nonetheless our Benedictine Rule and way of life,
> together with our devotion to Christ in his Sacrament of Love, have
> kept our heads above water. Let us continually remind ourselves that
> the religious life is intended above all to lead us to an imitation of
> Christ and union with God through the profession of our vows, and
> any changes made on behalf of contemporary needs will fail unless a
> renewal of spirit gives life to them. Such interior renewal must be
> accorded the leading role, and no one can do this for us. We must be
> open to the Spirit guiding and directing each of us and all of us together
> . . . (September, 1973).

The Storm of Renewal

In 1974, the chapter of elections was a very emptying experience for me. Actual lightning and thunder during the evening confirmed the storm I was feeling. The emptying was from so many angles at one time that I felt it had to be from the Lord himself.

In an article on monastic therapy, Merton describes Reza Arasteh's study of Sufi mystics, pointing up the need everyone has for the social self to die. He spoke of Rumi, the Sufi, at the heights of his career, for no justifiable reason, feeling as though the bottom had fallen out of his life.[3] Merton told the novices at Gethsemani the year of his own death about this same experience. Often, he said, we put all our blood and energy into being the best monk, the best novice, the best vice-president, etc., and then it happens! We find this all-out effort isn't enough! We can't understand what is happening to us and if we don't have help at such a time, we are liable to think it is a vocation crisis. But it isn't. It is rather a very profound existential crisis. In fact, it is what we came to the monastery for! According to Merton, what is happening is "a disintegration of the social and cultural self, the product of merely human history, and the reintegration of that self in Christ, in salvation history, in the mystery of redemption, in the pentecostal 'new creation'."[3]

But the process of disintegration and reintegration is one that involves a terrible interior solitude and an "existential moratorium," a crisis and an anguish that cannot be analyzed or intellectualized. Over and over Merton described the crisis as extremely severe, something like the dark night. With his delightful satire, he told the novices anyone who chanced to fall into the dark night of the soul today, would, if discovered, soon find himself getting shock treatments "which would effectively take care of any further disturbing development!"[4] Something like this disintegration process was happening to me. Transfiguration, renewal — where does it take place if not in this bit of clay which St. Paul assures us day by day falls away?

After the chapter of elections, I was called to serve as prioress of our convent in Kansas City. I was also asked to head a committee investigating the possibilities of a new small community. India loomed large as a possible source for a new monastic life-style for a small community. Driven by the weighty responsibility for others that came with being novice director and prioress, I felt the need to search intensely for a way of deepening my own inner life and to help others do the same. St. Benedict makes the responsibility of teaching the inner life dreadful enough but many former sisters and novices at Clyde had said explicitly they came to learn to pray. They always expected somebody would teach them and that maybe it would happen "tomorrow."

Thomas Merton said something similar, saying he always expected the "experience of God" to happen on the next feast. He frequently put up and took down altars on feasts and still found himself frustrated. He felt that within the monastic structure as he knew it at Gethsemani, the breakthough just didn't happen. Looking around, Merton turned to the East. The East, he felt, had a lot to offer westerners who are busy and unable to settle into contemplative atmosphere or work needed to experience God deeply. He found many busy monks like some of his companions,

surrounding the Dalai Lama, yet he also found many who had gone
deeply into the inner life.

A Look Toward the East

About this time the congregation publication, *Spirit & Life,* carried a
feature article on an English Benedictine monk who had gone to India
and started a Hindu-Christian ashram in Tamilnadu. Earlier, the French
Benedictine monk, Mayeul de Dreuille, had come to American monasteries showing colored slides of Africa, ashrams in India, and scenes from
the Bangkok Congress. He spoke about the effort to spread monasticism
in the East. The East had also been mentioned at our recent general
chapter but had remained in the background. Reviewing the chapter
tapes, I noted delegates said they felt the time was not right for establishing a foreign foundation. Instead, they said, the turn to the East could
be explored by sending one sister to Africa or India. One place mentioned
specifically was Shantivanam, the ashram in India of Father Bede Griffiths, the Benedictine from England. A letter to Bede brought me an
assuring reply: Women were included in the life of the ashram and several
sisters were there at the time. Costs would be minimal, $1 per day!

At a retreat in 1975 a delightful friend from formation days reentered
my life. I was invited to help give a retreat at Sacred Heart Priory in
Alabama, of which my friend, Sister Maurus Allen, was a member. She
had just returned from her father's funeral. Thus, when we went for a
long walk, we shared much heart-to-heart talk, including our ideas about
monastic life and its renewal.

Hearing of the possibility of a year in South India at the Hindu-Christian Ashram, Maurus began to dream enthusiastically. Both of us eventually submitted formal requests to our communities to make the pilgrimage together:

> for an intense prayer experience under the guidance of an English
> Benedictine scholar and master; for meditation and contemplative
> prayer. . . . It would be most profitable for the congregation to have
> someone actually experience contemplative prayer in a monastic set-
> ting in the Third World with the possibility of personal guidance and
> direction. . . . This experience would be more fruitful and important
> than academic hours in ongoing formation. Such an experience and
> consequent growth could be important even for the whole of American
> Benedictinism.

On the Feast of the Sacred Heart in June of 1976, the 200th birthday
of the United States and my own 25th anniversary of profession of vows,
Maurus and I boarded an Air India jet liner in New York for Bombay.
We had sought the advice of Benedictine monks at the international level
and had been given a number of reasons why it was not wise to pursue
the pilgrimage to Shantivanam, with suggestions that Japan or other
parts of the world would be more promising.

An uncle of one of the sisters insisted that the beach at St. Petersburg, Florida, would be cleaner! But somehow we knew this was to be our inner journey and we said to each other, "Are we going to let men run our lives forever? Why not go and see for ourselves since we have enough alternate places to go in India if 'Plan A' doesn't work out?"

After spending 10 days with the young and vibrant Indian Benedictine Sisters in Shanti Nilayam near Bangalore, we took a night train to the Hindu-Christian ashram that was to be our home for the next year. We spent the entire night sitting up on a plank that was supposed to be our berth. The berth's chain hook-up did not look promising. One plank hung on top of the other and a break in one link would have plunged the top sleeper down on top of the other, plank and all.

We arrived by bullock cart at Shantivanam at 5:45 a.m. on July 7. Bede, dressed in sannyasi orange, was waiting to greet us and to offer the eucharist Indian-style. Sitting cross-legged on the floor for mass and breakfast was not a major problem but finding that a rat had eaten a whole in my canvas suitcase (during a sermon on not storing your treasures where "moth and rust" can claim them) did cause us some alarm. The rat's booty: peanuts from the New York airport that I had forgotten about during the 10 days in bangalore.

Economically and socially, going to India seemed like a step backward. But interiority is India's gift. At the same time Western structures were no longer satisfying to many in the West. The result: A turn East to the religions of Asia and the tradition of spiritual, mystical wisdom which comes down through Hinduism, Buddhism, Taoism, Sufism, and other religions.

Shantivanam Ashram was like a crossroads of a million private lives with people from all over the world seeking and sharing. The Satsang (faith-sharing) each night after supper was especially invigorating. These sharings were reflections and sometimes a continuation of the afternoon classes on the Upanishads or the Bhagavad Gita in light of the gospel and the intensely hot Indian sun! Coconut trees afforded students welcome shade as they sat in the sand on straw mats, listening and taking notes, with the sacred Kavery River a few yards distant.

We two American Benedictine women participated in several seminars on East-West spirituality at Asirvanam Benedictine Monastery in Bangalore. Eastern and Western scholars from all over India were present. These sessions offered some of our greatest enrichment. A Buddhist-Vipassana meditation, conducted by Goenka at Igot Puri was also part of the year's unique learnings. We found several Hindu-Christian dialogues at the ashram and at the Jesuit seminary in Tirichiapalli to be helpful in understanding the present day Hindu mind and practice. The search for deeper levels of consciousness and the teaching about the self grew more intense and fascinating for me as the year unfolded. There was much in the Vedas that threw much more light on the deeds and words of Jesus:

What lies beyond life shines not to those who are childish, or careless, or deluded by wealth. To many it is not given to hear of the self; many though they hear it do not understand. Wise is (she) who can learn of it. Wonderful is (she) who when taught by a good teacher is able to understand. The truth of the self cannot be understood when taught by an ignorant (one), as the self is thought of in many ways. Unless taught by one who has known him in himself, he cannot be reached. He is higher than the highest thoughts, in truth above all thought. This sacred knowledge is not attained by reasoning; but it can be understood when taught by another."[5]

On my 50th birthday I received from Bede Sannyasi Diksa initiation into the state of *renunciate,* characteristic of Hindu monks. The tradition of renunciation underlines the profound link between the call to sannyasa and the call to the desert that was heard by the first Christian monks. The discovery of the mystery of non-duality at the very heart of human consciousness is regarded as an essential condition of genuine sannyasa. If it does not spring out of inner illumination and out of an awakening to the *aham asmi* (I am) in all its purity, then sannyasa is no more than one among many possible ways of living. It goes along with breaking "the knots of the heart"![6] I was given the name of Eka-hrydaya ananda (the bliss of one heart), carrying within me forevermore both the call and the response to the communion of East and West.

After visiting the major temples of South India as well as an all-Hindu ashram in North Kerala and other sacred places, Maurus and I traveled for 40 days in North India prior to leaving the country. The communion of East and West was deepening in us as we met more of the beautiful people of India and sang the Jesus prayer out over the waters of the Ganges. One sannyasini, a Tamilian from South India who had been living as a hermit on the banks of the Ganges near Rishikesh for eight years, took us both under her wing, brought us to her own sacred bathing spot in the Ganges and offered us her own towels with which to dry.

Eucharist was celebrated at dawn on the beach at that sacred place, home of the Indian sannaysis. An English monk, traveling with us, arranged for this profound experience on sands made sacred by thousands of years of silent adoration and chanted meditations. We three then prayed at Varanasi, the Hindu holy land, and meditated overlooking the Deer Park, where Buddha gave his first sermon. Native Sisters of Nazareth at Macoma took us to the famous Bodh Gaya where we sat under a "fifth generation" Bodhi tree by the ancient temple built near the sacred spot where Buddha was enlightened.

It was with some reluctance that the two of us took leave of an India that had shared herself with us so deeply, especially through the gifts that radiated through her people: interiority, hospitality and the reality of the self in cosmic dance and play. These gifts made the Christian Holy Land which we visited for 20 days enroute to America, call our hearts to ever deeper inner renewal and wonder.

A New Understanding

The year just passed had been beyond all expectations and yet there was no way to measure its impact on inner renewal. Like all growth it was slow and subtle, but the hunger had been fed, the thirst had been slaked. The East had thrown new light on the riches of the ecclesial and monastic traditions of the West. A new understanding now supported many former pactices, e.g. the use of mantras, and beads. Repetition and chanting were ways of focusing the mind and allowing one to go to deeper levels of consciousness, and even into prayer beyond words and imagery. Body, soul and spirit were more essentially interconnected than ever. Listening to the body and its sensations and responding wisely was more a part of discernment of spirits than one imagined. All the great scriptures of the world, including our own Christian scriptures, are written in symbolic language and need time, space and grace to burst open within the cave of each one's heart.

Called to share some of the treasures of the year with the sisters in each of the congregation's priories, I spoke at the same time with those who were interested in a new simplified monastic life-style. On Christmas, 1977, I made a formal proposal to "initiate in communion with the congregation and on behalf of it, a small community with a simplified monastic style of life, somewhere apart from the present structures and grounds, with sufficient freedom for birth and growth, life, death and resurrection."

The purpose was to expedite and make more efficacious the effort at "appropriate renewal" as urged by Vatican II in the areas of monastic life-style and the mode of eucharistic adoration. This was seen as a sign of hope and an expression of new life, not only within the congregation but among American Benedictine women. It was an effort "to clothe the openness of our congregation to experimental forms of living as agreed in the Spirit at our eighth general chapter" and to better "enable the deepening of relationship with the Lord, facilitating and sharing faith consciousness with a deeper sense of church as urged by the council, and social justice according to the signs of the times." Other parts of the proposal cited poverty and prayer as the "focal point of future religious life." They also called for creating and sharing contemplative settings and monastic atmosphere with all God's people: "to strive more deliberately to be a center of God's presence on earth where there is neither East nor West — but where East and West have embraced and to show forth Christ more clearly in the world day by day." Lastly, the effort was seen as a move to make "more possible the awesome and eminent task of rewriting our constitutions, since it was preferable to have them spring from life, rather than to force life into the mold later."

I am executive secretary for the A.I.M. (Aide Inter Monasteres) North American Board for East-West Dialogue. The board has recently begun a two-phased monastic hospitality program for Tibetan monks. With the coming of the Easterners into Western monasteries, dialogue, while only in preparatory stages, has begun. In a semi-private audience with the

Dalai Lama at Boulder, Colorado, we requested he send some of his
monks to our Western monasteries. The American Benedictine and Cistercian abbots, who were asked to host the Buddhists, pooled contributions to cover international air fare. The board, especially through the
labors of Abbot Lawrence Wagner, worked in conjunction with Tibet's
office in New York to arrange final details.

We cannot afford not to be knowledgeable about the East in our monasteries today. It is foolish not to take seriously the search of the young.
The present vocation crisis is very subtly linked with the East. Young
people are bypassing the monasteries and going down the street to zendos
and ashrams because what they are looking for is no longer offered.

With the presence of the Tibetan monks recently invited into American
monasteries a new light is being cast upon the present monastic crisis.
We do not have spiritual masters, those adept in teaching methods of
prayer from their own experience of God. We excel as professors, department
heads and even as pastors, but fall short when it comes to helping others
pray and recognize the Spirit within.

Our own small community was eventually established as a monastic
ashram in the Diocese of Tulsa, Oklahoma, near the town of Sand
Springs. Osage Monastery in the Forest of Peace was dedicated by Bishop
Eusebius J. Beltran of Tulsa on the Feast of Corpus Christi, June 8, 1980,
the sesquimillenium anniversary year of St. Benedict's birth! The community is made up of five Benedictine sisters, a young lay woman and a
Trappist monk. Contemplative prayer and its atmosphere are given priority at the ashram, a place of intense spiritual exercise. It is open to people
of all religions, and many have already made themselves at home in our
midst. A common house and 14 individual cabins make up the physical
surroundings nestled deeply in the green country of Eastern Oklahoma.
We draw on a blend of Eastern and Western spiritual sources for common
prayer, to which all are welcomed. Symbols of the world's great religions,
as well as American Indian religious art and architecture, are in evidence.
A sundance circle invites all to daily eucharist and the hours of the monastic office. Eastern *bhajans* are used at break of day to introduce meditation
and communal adoration before morning praise. The magnificat is
chanted after *satsang* to introduce the evening meditation and adoration.

Directed or private retreats are offered. Peace vigils, common fasts and
interdenominational Christian unity celebrations have all marked the
short history of our small community. "I see Osage Monastery as one of
the signs of a new age which is just beginning, but so far the churches
tend to stand outside this movement," Bede Griffiths wrote to us after
returning to India following his stay with us last fall.

Experiential learning goes infinitely deeper than books and courses.
Three years of small group living in a simplified monastic life-style with
an Eastern influence has been much more demanding and much more
rewarding than anticipated. Common rooms have kept the members in
touch with the poor and less fortunate. Liturgies, while not grand, have
been intimate. The sundance circle setting for prayer has been conducive
to including and interrelating with all present. The blend with the East

has been enlightening and a cause for continued awe. The impact on those who have come has been refreshing and rewarding. The enrichment has been mutual.

As in the beginning, the Spirit in our day is again brooding over the waters of the unconscious, bringing life, harmony, new consciousness and contemplative awareness. Therefore, we find ourselves in the birthing of a new age rather than in a movement. At this dawn of the 21st century we are welcoming the age of spirituality, of the feminine, of global and cosmic consciousness, of peace and justice, and of the Spirit in a new light. This intuitive age will see as never before the real mystic, hear the real prophet, and be the real fool and clown for Christ, truly playing before the Lord.

The well-tested Chinese theory of yin-yang, which holds that our race swings from the masculine to the feminine pole every 500 years, finds us at the "turning poing," having reached the rational, mechanistic, scientific, aggressive limits of our present patriarchal society.

I believe three factors have been and will continue to be vital in the progress of religious renewal: vibrant liturgy, East-West dialogue and the threat of nuclear war! All three are interrelated.

First, liturgy has been and is a much more powerful force for change in the religious renewal than has been evident. Through the constant flow of word and worship — and for the monastic this is literally so — the unconsciousness of all the people of God has been touched again and again. The word is "more powerful than any two-edged sword" and often cuts to uncomfortable depths. The word is sacrament, the rite is sacrament, the communion is sacrament. Themes chosen by the church have kept peace and justice, conversion and transformation ever before the faithful. Without deep adoration, without being Christ-bread broken for others, without knowing and recognizing his life, death, and resurrection within our very own lives, where can renewal take place? Many young people are being lost to the church for want of a meaningful context from which to receive her treasures. We have many structures that need to be revitalized, rejuvenated, and made more deeply radiant before Christ will be seen and known in our midst.

Second, dialogue, as "the art of spiritual communication," is vital to our entrance into the next century as a human family and as members of that Body whose conversation should be "intimate and familiar, full of faith, of charity and good works."[7] Dialogue with each other is all the more urgent for us so that dialogue with the East can no longer be ignored. Though so badly needed, dialogue is strange to us. But dialogue with the East is stranger still. The East is the other half of God's creation and his gift to the human family. The riches of Eastern spirituality are ancient and profound.

Wholesome integration of the feminine as in the East is essential for us in the West. We have learned about God in a totally patriarchal society, hence all our language about God is masculine. We need to discover the feminine dimension in God who is both feminine and masculine and yet neither. The unconditional love of a mother in the heart of God bursts through the daily word when we awake to it.

Eastern masters have come to the West and books and courses are being made available. The young are seeking deeply and finding methods of prayer and meditation taught by Eastern traditions far more satisfying. It has been verified that half of those in American zendos and ashrams today are former Catholics. The East can only help us better recognize our own dormant spiritual riches and recover them. Merton called this dialogue at depth "contemplative comunion."

Last, the arms race and the 44 wars the world is currently engaged in are a heightened cause for renewal. Early in the 5th century St. Benedict encouraged his monks to keep death before their eyes daily. The immediacy of the insane global situation is gradually dawning upon us so that eschatology is again coming into its own and the Parousia, while never before invisaged as a man-made blast, is being seriously addressed. That "he comes in the flash of a moment" is a profound upanishadic truth! Pope Paul VI often said if we want peace we must strive for justice. God's justice is not "an eye for an eye" but rather fidelity to promises. From the Old Testament it is evident that God always keeps promises and when people stand in the way God takes them into exile to bring them back to their center.

Religious renewal has been fanned into a great flame by the thousands of religious responding to the cry of the poor. We are awakening to a new understanding of the humanity of Jesus and the true place of Mary, his mother and ours. In fidelity to our promises, we religious, while fewei in number, are becoming more simple, more voluntarily impoverished, and more attuned to allowing the Spirit within to burn up everything that would impede the flash of his coming!

"You, O Lord, know me and you see me, you know that at heart I am with you" (Jeremiah 12, 3).

Notes

1. "Message to Humanity," *The Documents of Vatican II,* Walter M. Abbott, S.J., ed. New York: The American Press, 1966, p. 4-8.

2. Thomas Merton, "Marxism and Monastic Perspectives," *The Asian Journal of Thomas Merton.* New York: New Directions, 1975, p. 338.

3. Thomas Merton, "Final Integration: Toward a Monastic Therapy," *Monastic Studies,* Dec. 1968, P. 87-99. (cf. also tape: *The Mystic Life* #8, New York: Electronic Paperbacks, 1972).

4. Ibid., p. 98

5. *The Upanishads,* Robert Baldick, C.A. Jones, and Betty Radice, ed. Middlesex, England: Penguin Books, 1965, p. 58 (Katha Upanishad I. 2, 7-9).

6. Swami Abhishiktananda (Henri LeSaux), *The Further Shore.* Delhi: I.S.P.C.K., 1975. (A reading of the entire book, which also includes an introduction to the Upanishads by Abhishiktananda, is highly recommended.)

7. Archbishop John Quinn, "Dialogue and the Bishop's Pastoral Service to Religious," *Origins,* Dec. 1, 1983, Vol. 13, No. 25, p. 428.

Uprooting and Rerooting

Maureen McCormack

Maureen McCormack, Ph.D., psychologist and human resources consultant, is vice-chair of the Sisters of Loretto and serves on their executive committee. Her previous ministries include being a college dean of students, first coordinator of life development for her community, and management consultant to the U.S. Forest Service. The Institute of Women Today has presented her with a citation for work with women in prisons. She is past president of the board of directors of the Center for Communications Ministry Board of Directors and was recently appointed by the Leadership Conference of Women Religious as adviser to the Catholic Telecommunications Network of America Board.

Kathleen and I were standing in the postulant recreation room engaged in conversation. She was sharing with me the exciting news about her sister's pregnancy. I was only distractedly present to her. On my mind was the novitiate rule requiring conversation in groups of three or more. Kathleen seemed oblivious to the rule, so I was taking the responsibility upon myself to try to include someone else in our conversation.

A few days later, Kathleen was gone, having decided convent life was not for her. I always regretted having been less than totally present to her as she was sharing such important family news. I never saw her again.

This regulation and others like it, created for the few, worked against the deepening of friendships for the many. In those days, close personal relationships were not a high priority for the community nor for me. More attention was given to the development of a relationship with God, professional growth and service to others.

Now from my perspective of 30 years of community life, during 20 of which I widened my circle of friends within and beyond the community, I consider what I learned and experienced. I learned that structures can facilitate the deepening of relationships as well as hamper them. The traditional structures, however, were inadequate. Fresh structures and a variety of them were needed.

I resonate with Raymond Moody's belief that what matters in the end and what will continue into the next life are two things: What we have learned from our experiences, and the quality of our loving. Commitment to these goals requires an enormous investment of energy, the investment of a lifetime. There is no easy road to their attainment.

As religious women began to create their own path into the future rather than following age-old traditions, some who watched commented:

"They're all out there doing their own thing." The comment clearly had a negative ring. Still, it made sense to many of us to try on different styles of being together and with others until we found a new fit.

Our small living group took one day a month in the mountains sharing solitude and conversing about deeply-held values. Community prayer grew out of what we were becoming together and a clearer awareness of global needs. We wrote our faith autobiographies and shared them with one another. There were opportunities for extended periods of time together at retreat sites with input from our own sisters instead of from priests, shared vision about the next steps of the journey, fun, laughter, and a deepened sense of bonding, of being sisters to one another. In small self-selected groups we explored the role of interpersonal relationships in building a world community of justice and peace. There were programs created for individual communities to assist with communal growth and understanding of why we had come together.

Individual sisters networked with people in their geographic areas — with men, women, married, single, young, old, people of different religious beliefs and some with no denominational ties — to plan the building of a world community and to strategize for peace. There was heightened energy available for what we might do and be. The potential we envisioned for a religious community of women in our day expanded dramatically.

All this is not to say that everything moved forward without difficulties. The pain, struggle and setbacks experienced by people in other life-styles trying to build together were ours too.

I recall the pain I experienced when one of my living groups broke up. I was the only one without new plans. We had shared so much and now it was abruptly ending. It was an event not of my choosing. I had no control over it. I was not consulted.

Some events in life are like that. They are not our events. They are simply thrust upon us. They do not grow out of inner unfolding or appear as natural next steps. Rather, they enter our lives as a violent force — uprooting without care, disrupting the harmony and integration, leaving us to pick up the pieces and somehow move on to new growth.

Sometimes I can direct the movement of my life. At other times I must yield to the movements that refuse to take account of my limited desires, movements larger than the self that must go forward and take me with them.

All the movements of my life are one movement. My life is one whole life. The parts that have already been integrated reach out to heal those that do not resonate with the whole. Harmony will prevail because it is already present in such great abundance. If I am deeply rooted in the entirety of my life, then I can learn to accept the uprooting and rerooting of a part of it. It is one whole life.

The great unknown loomed large. But the unknown was not only darkness. It also contained possibilities for new growth. I wanted to be open to these even as I leaned into my pain.

I was weary from what had been too many tears. I know. Tomorrow there would be wonderful surprises. I had to learn to consent to the present and all that it held so that I would be ready.

I felt as though I were spending three days in the tomb, preparing for the resurrection. I knew it would take at least three days for full acceptance of death to be completed. I would try not to push it or ask for a new life before its time. New life must be allowed to grow for a time under the earth where I could not see it before it would be ready to break forth. I was beginning to understand!

My spirit was beginning to be at peace. Maybe it would even be possible for me to let go enough to move with the movement of my life. I felt tentative about this and wanted to be gentle with myself so the plant was not cut above the roots.

Time has its own way of healing, of softening the earth so that the roots were set free. I must be gently uprooted from where I am so that I can be where I need to be.

Difficulties began as we developed deep friendships outside the community and as some close relationships flowered in community subgroups. The former structures did not have formulas for dealing with such situations. They were set up to help us avoid precisely the complications we now experienced.

We had to find our own way, create a new path. It was not easy to balance various commitments, providing quality time for each project and relationship. Nor was it possible to avoid feelings of being left out, the pain of not being chosen, divisiveness and growing apart as some people's lives moved in contrasting directions.

We needed to respect each other's differing rhythms — sometimes for solitude, sometimes for communion. An awareness of just missing one another when these rhythms did not fit together was accompanied by disappointment and frustration.

Suspicions developed about community members who developed significant relationships with men. Questions such as "what do they do when they are alone together?" were in the air. Colorful imaginations filled in the blanks with worst-case scenarios. The label of "sisters dating" carried the message of inappropriate behavior. There were painful silences as people found they could not always talk about their differences.

Later, these same suspicions were directed toward sisters who had strong friendships with other women, both inside and outside the community. There were one-on-one conversations in low tones as people sought intimate sharing in the living group, while at the same time wanting to avoid exclusivity.

Married men who spent time with these newly-uncloistered women felt safe in the presence of the sisters' strong commitment to religious life. Their wives were not always so sure.

Early in this new era, I remember being part of a discussion about what we would do if we felt a man was becoming serious about any one of us — or we about them. We decided the first thing we needed to do was talk about our feelings with the one involved — and with others if we chose. We did talk — processing endlessly, over a period of years in some cases. Mistakes were made. Naivete diminished, but not without cost.

Out of all this struggle to find new patterns of relating, a rich network of people who are very special to one another is emerging. These people are free to develop nourishing relationships that enhance their commitments rather than destroy them. We are still in the midst of weaving this new thread into our lives. The pain and struggle are not over. At least we are talking to one another about what we are experiencing, and allowing people to work through their commitments. At least we are trusting people to know what it is to be faithful, and that their commitments are precious to them.

Our families had difficulty understanding or appreciating the religious renewal we were charting. In fact, from their perspectives, we had moved away from what was valuable about religious life, and they could not see evidence we were replacing time-honored traditions with anything worthwhile. When we were teaching children and praying in chapel, our life communicated a clearer message.

Now we were marching in the streets, going to jail, creating our own liturgies, designing our own jobs, living in Third World countries, becoming radicalized, challenging the institutional church and making headlines. We prayed in our rooms instead of the chapel, did our yoga, Tai Chi and Zen sitting, used a mantra and spontaneous prayer. We were fasting in order to highlight injustices, giving homilies in church, working in soup kitchens, learning about Christian socialism, demonstrating against the Vietnam war, counseling draft resisters and cheering the Berrigans. Some people were even calling us communists. We socialized with men, gave retreats, called ourselves feminists, held press conferences, promoted women's ordination, criticized the U.S. government, rejected our middle-class upbringing, wore jeans, gave workshops, associated with hippies and read questionable books and articles.

No wonder our families were confused and unsupportive. It seemed that no matter how often we tried to explain our new stance to them, it did not make sense. The same questions and comments came up over and over:

"Are there any sisters still teaching?"

"I thought only priests were allowed to do that?"

From the time that I was in second grade, I knew that I wanted to be a nun. I also knew that I wasn't going to join any of the congregations with which I was familiar. My child prayer went like this: "OK, God, if you want me to be a nun, you better find me an order." In the eighth grade, I met the Sisters of Loretto, and I knew they were it. There was one small obstacle. They wore a covered-wagon type of veil. I wasn't sure

I could carry all of that on my head and still move about. My adolescent prayer went like this: "OK, God, if you want me to be a Sister of Loretto, you had better do something about that headgear." Two years before I entered the Sisters of Loretto, their veil was simplified considerably. I breathed a sigh of relief and a prayer of thanksgiving.

After I had worn the religious habit for 12 years we began experimenting with various forms of modern dress. When I heard that one of my friends had been asked to gather information about simple hair styles, my startled response was: "You mean our hair is going to show?"

At first many of us inherited our wardrobes second-hand from relatives and friends or found exciting bargains in thrift shops. One of our senior sisters, who chose to retain the traditional habit, once commented: "I wouldn't mind telling you how nice you look if I didn't always have to hear the whole history of the garment."

Another sister confronted me angrily one day with: "Now you give me one good reason why you are wearing *that*." Later, I overheard her say: "Mark my word. They're on the way out." A third sister suffered excruciating pain as she yielded to pressure from within herself to adopt modern clothes rather than risk having her ideas judged outdated. She had worn the religious habit for some 50 years. I watched her age visibly through the decision process and felt a deep pain within myself that such a choice should cost so much.

Somehow we survived those early years of too much conversation about clothes, too much pain accompanying the transition and too much misunderstanding of what our purpose was.

A significant number of our Catholic laity were keenly disappointed when we shed the religious habit that they had grown to love. To them the habit was a valued symbol, a sign of our religious commitment, and a reminder of what religious communities of women had done through the centuries, particularly in schools and hospitals. To them we had clearly lost something.

My own appreciation of signs and symbols has not disappeared but has taken different forms. I may not have a sign except for this small ring, and sometimes a cross, but I am beginning to become a sign. I am becoming a sign of the times — a sign of life in these times where death and the forces of death too much abound. My sign stands for the building of an earthly city where there will be no more crying or weeping, where death shall be no more. My sign is moving me toward compassion for all people, peace-making, a sense of urgency about world community and love. My sign moves to the depths of me, cutting its message into my quick so that I will remember what I must be about. The gospel gives clarity and shape to the sign I am becoming. It does not comfort me but keeps a vision before me that gives direction to my life. I will never exhaust its possibilities.

The sign that you, my sisters, are, nourishes me. I see that we are pulling the same way. Our sign of sisterhood contains within it something powerful, something we can create together with our lives that

*I, you, cannot do alone. We will sign together on the dotted line —
indication of a commitment, that we can count on each other to get a
job done. Some of what we sign are blank checks. The amount — the
extent of our commitment — will be filled in later. We risk this because
we believe in each other and in what we are doing.*

*What is my sign? I am a sign. You are too. We are signs of all we
attempt, struggle for, build, all that is possible as our lives are gathered
into wholeness, into unity.*

The ways we influenced one another during the years of renewal had
the effect of escalating the rate of change we were experiencing. Our
annual assemblies provided a forum in which we explored and charted
our future direction. Our style of interaction became increasingly participative. Leadership was wisely shared. We scheduled skill-building
workshops for ourselves to learn more about communication and conflict
management.

Our reading added momentum to our transformation. In the early
years of renewal, we had access, through translations by our sisters, to
writings not yet available in English. The thinking of forward-looking
theologians was shared while their ideas were still germinating. Scripture
scholars were invited to discuss their latest findings with us. Because
we had our very own official auditor at the Vatican Council (Sister Mary
Luke Tobin), who informed us about changes as they were happening,
we set ourselves on the path to renewal in advance of decrees from Rome
to do the same. It was an exciting time to be a part of the church.

Instead of relying on the U.S. press for information about what was
happening in Central and South America, we learned first-hand from
our sisters in those regions about the systematic repression which existed.
We became more enlightened about the role the U.S. government was
playing in keeping repressive systems in place.

We involved ourselves in the political process as a way of working
within the system to change unjust structures and policies. We participated in political caucuses at the local level and elected delegates at state
conventions to carry our ideas to national forums. We put pressure on
congressional representatives through letters, telephone calls and visits
to their offices. We participated in boycotts, rallied community support
for urgent issues, engaged in a lawsuit over a justice matter, and encouraged sisters to run for political office.

Some of us chose a meatless diet when we learned how much of the
world's grain was used to fatten livestock so that we might enjoy a better
grade of meat, and that, as a result, impoverished nations were deprived
of grain needed for survival. We were horrified to discover that the U.S.,
which comprises six percent of the world's population, consumed two-
thirds of the world's resources.

We recognized the importance of keeping our bodies fit and our energy
levels high. We exercised, swam laps, ran or walked, played tennis and
went cross-country skiing.

It was difficult even for us to realize the extent to which we had adopted our traditional role and the amount of transformation later required. Some of the ways we viewed the world from our cloisters developed with great subtlety. I recall the generosity of the laity as they collected canned goods to give the sisters at Thanksgiving. The subtle message engrained in me over the years was: Many groups give to us. Our giving is in the form of services and prayers.

My complacency was jolted when the president of our congregation proposed establishing a "one percent fund" through which we would share our material goods with the poor. The fund has grown through the years to its present 10 percent of our financial resources used for immediate needs of the poor and to support long-range social change projects. We took a vow of poverty and lived comfortably. Too many others lived a kind of destitution that needed no vow to identify it.

One Saturday in March, 1973, I received a call from the Denver office of the American Friends Service Committee. The National Council of Churches was organizing a group to go to Wounded Knee, South Dakota, to serve as neutral interpositional teams, placing themselves between the FBI-federal marshal forces and the American Indian Movement (AIM) community in the little hamlet that had been seized 12 days earlier by AIM.

Even as our plans to drive there were being made, the picture at Wounded Knee was changing like a kaleidoscope. An FBI agent was shot in the wrist and there was fear of an FBI invasion to rout out the encamped Indians. The hope was that this neutral force would be able to prevent a massacre.

The Indians were prepared for a shoot-out. If it happened, we would be right in the middle. My fears began to mount. I had not come to die. I had only recently turned my sympathies to the Indian cause. But now I needed to come to terms with a more drastic possibility. The Indians were ready to die rather than surrender. Some suggested that if we really wanted to help, we join them in the front lines. But our commitment was to non-violence. The federal forces were announcing publicly that they would starve-freeze the Indians out. This caused the Indians to smile, as they have been cold and hungry most of their lives. "It is better to die on your feet than live on your knees," they said.

Wounded Knee is now a public memory. While my brief stay gave me a sense of the dogged determination of this oppressed people, I experienced disappointment that fear tactics and a show of force were chosen by both sides. Before I left, I copied a poignant message I found on a wall in the trading post, so that I would always remember:

!!NOTICE!!

We the people of this Land are
at the point of no return so this
will be your last chance white

man Larn to live with *us*
our suffer your own greetiness
and your sins to are people.

We will overcome are plight
We will be free once agian
Let know man stand — between
are, search for freedom.
Less he is willing to be chastied.

We only die once
so lets die here
Together!!

Wounded Knee

(again)

There is a deep yearning in the human spirit to be known. Being set apart as "other," being the recipient of well-intentioned deference can block this process.

Religious life as I experienced it in the old days had many structures that kept us anonymous. Most people called us "sister" without a personal name attached. At the time, it sounded as appropriate to me as to those who used it. It is only in retrospect that other reactions occur to me. It was a great boon for people who had a hard time remembering names. Conversely, it was not appropriate to respond with "Well, Mr." or "Ms." The fact that a dangling title was used to address us and would sound foolish if applied to other groups was a clear indication to me that I was in the group set apart.

There is a special significance to being called by name. In the Genesis story, when Adam and Eve named the animals, each received a name in keeping with its identity. So too with us. Our name is part of our personal identity. "Sister" doesn't suffice.

The religious habit played its own part in distancing us from others. I put it on with great joy, valuing its symbolism which consecrated us in God's service. I was at home in the habit as long as I was with sisters or Catholics for whom the habit was a familiar sight.

My worst experience beyond this comfortable setting was the first day I set foot on a Methodist-related university campus and felt the curious stares. I wished the ground could have opened up to swallow me. The climax came as I passed a group of students in the library and heard one of them say, "There it is." It! The word cut through me to the quick. I was less than anonymous. I was reduced to a thing.

I recall how readily I too have categorized people as "other." I lumped them together as prisoners, or Russians, or the enemy. Only after I began working with prison inmates did I recognize that my previous tendency to stereotype people kept them anonymous and distant. As long as I kept them in their proper category, I had no reason to get to know them as persons capable of deep feelings and clinging to treasured dreams. I was free to dismiss them, perhaps even subliminally picture them as less than persons. It was quite clear that they were different from me and not yet established that we shared the same humanity. With Russians, commonly called "the enemy," it is possible to do more than dismiss them as persons. It is possible to annihilate them.

I need to reflect more on what being separate, being set apart, signals to me. I do recognize its more positive dimensions — being unique in all the world, being special. And there is even some value in being anonymous. It can allow a person additional freedom to be oneself — free from the expectations of others, free to be unself-conscious.

Sisterhood, being sister to another, has taken on new meaning for me in the context of feminism. At the 1980 International Women's Conference in Copenhagen, I heard a British feminist say of Margaret Thatcher: "She may be a woman, but she is no sister." Everyone understood her meaning; no elaboration was needed.

The term sisterhood suggests bonding, being with and for other women, a solidarity, struggling and sharing together, throwing in one's lot with others. These were surely among the purposes and meanings of sister as applied to religious life before some of the meaning was distorted. As I regained my appreciation for the term in wider contexts, I experienced it in deeper ways with my own sisters and those of other religious congregations. A favorite card I received from one of our sisters last Christmas carried a quote from Emily Greene Balch: "We have a long, long way to go. So let us hasten along the road, the road of human tenderness and generosity. Groping, we may find one another's hands in the dark."

We are only too capable of placing barriers between one another without having them structured into our reality from outside. Barriers can widen the rift between women and men, rich and poor, religious and laity, people of different faiths, people from other parts of the world, people of diverse ideological and political persuasions.

More and more I experience religious life as part of all life. The sharp outlines we saw in the past are more blurred. We have freer access to one another across the borders. We can comfort one another more readily, be inspired and strengthened by our complementary commitments, and be enriched by our differences. Groping, we reach for one another's hands in the dark. We are on our way to the great unity. We are on the way to being people to one another worldwide, being sisters and brothers to all.

For a decade or more the structures of religious life were my daily bread and just what my spirit needed. During those years my inner fibers were strengthened. Regular discipline and the practice of meditation deepened my awareness. Friends tease me about the extreme piety with which I entered into life as a religious sister and how thoroughly cured I became later. Left to my own devices, who knows how long I would have continued these disciplines and routines? I was not an initiator.

But my spirit has always responded to what is fresh, new. My heart was made for adventure. So the changes in the structures of religious life allowed fresh breezes to enter my being and transform my spirit. Unbelievably breathtaking vistas opened to me both in my inner and outer worlds. In the language of the new imagery which entered my life, I experienced myself in a garden, where things that I was not aware of planting burst forth. Spaces enlarged themselves within me. I was reaching beyond any place I had been. Sometimes I was a small boat still afloat after venturing onto the high seas. A rainbow was arching. Then there was only rain.

There are images of streams that touch and transform, waters that nourish new experiences. Everything is holy, sacred. The streams reach everywhere, touching the pain, the abrasions, the hurts, the joys, the delights, the dullness, the sharp sword. Washed away are the pessimism, depression, the grasping, the narrow vision, the weariness. All is new. I am healed so that I might move to wholeness, move from preparation to beginning, move from unfolding to development to fulfillment. I am painting a picture and have finished the first part. I will present myself to be transformed.

The imagery persists. Now I am moving through the layers of the self into a narrow place. It closes around me, blesses me, anoints me and escorts me to the next level. Expanse, Opening. I am alone now. My body is charged with energy. A glow of light attracts and draws me. I am transparent again. The light becomes the entrance to the next level, directing my course to each new level of experience.

I am transported to depths, to a rich atmosphere of deep knowing. There are magnificently formed flowers in brilliant colors and deep hues, new aromas. I make a graceful descent. A sense of myself becoming. An announcement to this effect is made. Applause. I begin to unfold. There is a fountain inside me, commencing its flow, slowly at first, moving toward full spray. I am waiting for life to be born, darkness to be dispelled.

Tears of joy rise from inner wells. I embrace all the content of my life — what has been, what is and what is to come. I need it all. I will not change a single thing. All of it will be transformed if I am transformed.

I was to explore many diverse paths as the structures gave way to individual preferences. Discovery, rather than someone else selecting the means of growth, is what quickened my step and urged me forward.

When the requirement of 30 minutes of daily meditation was lifted, my own requirements lasted longer than the institution's. When I finally let the practice of meditation drop away, I experienced relief and freedom, as though a burden were lifted. I sensed that I would one day return to meditating but, for the time, I felt no need of it, no time for it and didn't seem to miss it.

Later, when I chose to reincorporate meditation into my life, I had a new kind of energy available for it. A new appreciation of its value was taking hold of me. I found that a one-hour period of meditation suited my spiritual needs better than the previously-required 30 minutes. This was quite a revelation. One of the benefits of a self-designed spiritual growth program was the possibility of just such discoveries. In some views of human nature, a requirement is necessary to ensure that people do a minimum. It is clearer to me now that our inner requirements have their own rhythms and our inner self knows what it needs. When certain practices which I treasured drop away, I am learning to trust it may be a natural part of the cycle.

One day I decided to test the extent of my inner need for quiet, solitude and stillness. I sat in meditation, open-ended relative to length of time, and was surprised at the end of it that four hours had elapsed. This gave me some glimpse of my insatiable spirit and how little I have attended to its desires.

For years I had heard others speak disparagingly of the dualisms which can be part of our lives — such as spiritual-secular. Such comments always seemed to enter the conversation when there was mention of taking time out for prayer, meditation. Since I valued these times apart, I was suspicious of talk about everything being one. Yet, these assessments of reality were coming from people whose views I respected, so I was reluctant to dismiss them entirely. I half wondered if there were routes to the integration for which I yearned other than the path I was on. It was only after I reached certain depth levels within myself that the lines of separation between the inner and the outer began to blur.

I am learning to incorporate a sense of the deep place into more of my active, outer life. An exciting awareness! A statement made by Sister Mary Daniel Turner: "The authenticity of our solitude is demonstrated in our capacity for communion when we are most engaged" strikes a deep chord in me. I understand more about dualisms. I discover that on days when I do not set aside any time for solitude and prayer I can be deeply present to the events of my day. All of life is becoming sacred. Many of the places in which I dwell are holy places. I experience sacredness filling my life through interactions with precious people. Still the pull, the invitation, the lure of the depths of me, beckon for me to enter, explore, remain for extended periods of time. I choose it all.

I can see beyond the surface of things. Sometimes I see clearly into the center of things, understand the unity of everything, the purpose of each, the wisdom deep inside everyone and everything. I am caught up in an ambience of reverence and awe. My spirit enlarges to incorporate more than before.

The place where I stand enables me to look forward as far as the eye can see, to embrace it with all its unknowns. I sense that the preliminaries of life are over. The reality of full, responsible, knowing life begins. There are some growing edges still ahead.

The imagery returns. I participate in an acceptance ceremony — deep grateful acceptance of the essence of each part of life and its contribution to the whole. Each person places a final link to complete the dance of life. As I face a new direction, I raise my head expectantly, open to the new. The image of a small bird becomes a herald of transformation for me. The bird smiles peacefully, even as it turns new corners.

I have experienced new images of connectedness with the communion of saints in recent years. Part of this relates to the death of my parents just three years apart. The rest stems from a book by Karl Rahner and Johann Metz.[3] The death event has the power to center me. It enables me to see life in its larger movements, to have a sense of destiny, wholeness. The new perspective and vision which my parents now experience are beacons for me as I continue my journey. My parents let go of life as we know it here. As I am learning to let go of them, all things are returned to me in new form.

My father's deep presence to me is richer than before. The church bells at his funeral call all of us to new life. My mother's appearances to me after her death connect with the appearances of Jesus after the resurrection. She has gone before us into Galilee.

It used to be that when the priest paused at mass to commemorate the dead, I could pray for the souls of those who had gone before us. Now I use the time to be present with precious people — known and unknown — who have lived and died. The bonds in the communion of saints are strengthened.

A significant portion of my ministry in the past 10 years has been devoted to conducting the Ira Progoff Intensive Journal workshops. With the help of such a powerful process for life transformation, people all over the country and in other parts of the world are developing more of their potential than they ever imagined was possible. The journal writing has had a marked effect on my own personal-spiritual unfolding.

The journal workshops I have given to women and men in prison during this same decade have left their imprint on my consciousness. As I sit in the presence of these experiences, letting them speak to my life, it strikes me that the people I met are very much like people everywhere, but the structures that encompass their lives and the atmosphere in which they breathe are decidedly different. One of the most painful deprivations is the loss of freedom. Is this system the best we can design for people who have broken, or are thought to have broken, society's laws? I think of all the creative energy in the world and how little of it is directed toward more humane systems of justice. A glimmer of hope appears as I recall that an international conference on prison abolition was held recently in Canada.

Vivid memories of my own experiences at the prisons surface. I see again the gun line inside a facility in Mississippi's poverty belt. Step over the line, and you risk being shot. There are the towering guard stations and the clanging and locking of doors behind us. Signs yellow with age in an Illinois prison forbid the doing of this, the doing of that. Inside, people lead lives of quiet desperation. Kerrie is trying to work through her anguish — on this, the third anniversary of her daughter's death — over having stood by while a boyfriend killed little Laura. Gary has the onset of an anxiety convulsion during a workshop as he recalls his mother's suicide and fears that he may be on the same path. The quest for decency and respect is evident in the smallest things. A woman asks for a cloth to dust the desks as a workshop is about to begin.

I am surprised that the women in the Nashville lifers club dress in their Sunday best for our workshop. "It makes us feel better," explains Betty. Usually one dull day is the same as another, with nothing to distinguish today from tomorrow. The days stretch into years and years into life. At a Michigan facility, journals are confiscated when it is discovered that the notebooks have metal spines. Almost everything is viewed as a potential weapon. The men and women in the workshop are disturbed about this violation of their privacy. In Texas, a small lockbox beside their beds in a large dormitory is the extent of privacy offered the inmates. I sense how much the women in a West Virginia facility need affirmation from me. I respond by giving it lavishly. Their lives have been so deprived. They are endearing themselves to me.

The wheels of bureaucracy can turn very slowly. A woman receives word from her parole board that she is to be released as soon as her papers are processed. What normally takes two or three weeks is at a standstill six weeks later, because of administrative turnover and papers buried on someone's desk. No staff person at the prison will call the headquarters to inquire about the reason for the delay. Meanwhile, dangling the hope of freedom before Marie day after day provides its own kind of torture. She has more than paid the debt to society.

In other circumstances, it is remarkable how quickly things can happen. Roger, one of the more humane wardens, is caught in the politics of superintendent-dumping. He has introduced new programs that are more life-giving for the inmates and is let go "for fiscal reasons." The one who replaces him is not qualified for the position and has a mental breakdown. My sensibilities are offended as the replacement sits at his desk cleaning his cigarette holder with a piece of toilet paper during our appointment.

A dream in which I was being toured through a prison, heard screams of someone being tortured and pretended not to hear, returns to haunt me. As I read about political prisoners in Brazil, the graphic portrayal of the tortures they endured is etched in my memory forever. An Indonesian woman in one of my journal workshops relives the horror she experienced as a child in a concentration camp when she watched her brother and sister have their heads chopped off. The depth and breadth of human suffering abound.

Peace efforts constitute one of the most misunderstood movements of our time. Proponents of disarmament are labeled naive and reckless with regard to national security concerns. Protests against nuclear buildup and proposals to convert nuclear plants to peacetime industry have been dubbed impractical. The term "peacenik" carries with it the low esteem with which peace activists were regarded. I remember my gentle father becoming enraged when I appeared at home with a peace symbol around my neck. For him, the symbol had been associated with violence, with young radicals destroying or defacing buildings and then painting the peace symbol on their work. It may also have represented his worst fears about what I was becoming.

Sisters have been active in the peace movement from the beginning. A chapter statement which the Sisters of Loretto issued in 1967 addressed itself to several social concerns including peace. Sisters were urged to take some responsible action in the move toward peace and work to hasten the end of the Vietnam war. A list of possible actions was developed. In the following year another peace statement, more controversial, was adopted by the chapter delegates.

It read:

The courage of a Sister of Loretto to act on her Christian conviction deserves the support of her sisters. A common application of the gospel to any public issue may never be reached by us, but respect for another's integrity and conscience is a value we affirm and pledge ourselves to preserve.[4]

In March of 1969, we had an opportunity to activate that support. Sister Joann Malone, S.L. became a member of the D.C. Nine, a group which ransacked the Washington office of Dow Chemical Company in protest of the company's manufacture of napalm for the Vietnam war. The reverberations of that action are still felt 15 years later in conservative St. Louis, where Joann was a high school teacher.

Our involvement in the search for international peace and the prevention of nuclear annihilation contained both educational and action components. Our Disarmament / Economic Conversion Task Force took creative leadership in educating us and suggesting constructive action. In recent years we have seen the peace movement mainstreamed. There is probably no other issue in our time as critical as the dismantling of nuclear stockpiles and the creation of alternatives to war to settle human differences.

I sit on the grass at Denver's state capitol with 30,000 other people, listening to John Denver and Judy Collins sing as part of a peace rally. I pull a blade of grass and focus my awareness on the good earth we are capable of destroying. Tears rise to the surface readily. I participate in the peaceful encirclement of Rocky Flats Nuclear Weapons Plant. Arms stretch out to meet arms stretched out for 17 miles around the facility. We are bonding with one another for peace and will not stop until it is accomplished.

An experience during the first years of renewal gave me a quick reading on how the process fits with the local church. I had brought an out-of-state team of two priests and one laywoman to our college campus to conduct a student retreat. The students responded very enthusiastically to the content and process of the retreat, as well as to those directing it. The experience kindled a new commitment to Christ and to Christianity in them.

It came to the attention of the local Ordinary that we had contracted with a rather unconventional retreat team for their services I was called before him to explain the situation and to receive his strong suggestion that we invite more traditional people to campus in the future. As I left, he pressed a rosary blessed by the Holy Father into my hand.

There is something about our current relationship with the institutional church that is not a good fit. In my worst moments, I wonder why we continue to bother, trying to make it better. As church, we are readier to criticize structures outside ourselves than our own internal systems. Yet, because our house is not in order, our effectiveness in wider circles is diminished.

The word that most often describes how I feel is "saddened." I am saddened because there is so much potential in the church that is underutilized. The creative forces that surface are quickly and effectively checked by a misguided preservative added to the heritage.

Fear and suspicion are everywhere. Fear prevents people on the lower steps of the hierarchy from speaking with forthrightness about what they experience. Fear prompts those at the top to tighten the controls. An atmosphere colored by suspicion does not contain healthy spaces where the Spirit can enter easily. Vatican authorities suspect that U.S. religious are not very "religious." U.S. religious suspects that the Vatican uses the press as a major source of information about them. Increased involvement in political and social issues by women religious has prompted the issuance of edicts.

Altercation with the institutional church runs deep in our congregational heritage. It took almost 100 years for the first rule of the Sisters of Loretto to be approved by the "official" church. Our archives document the steadfastness and courage of our sisters in story after story of harassment and interference.[5]

From time to time history raises up a fresh voice, such as John XXIII, exemplifying that church leadership need not be authoritarian or oppressive. The voice of Paul VI echoes through the chambers of the U.N. general assembly and down the corridors of history: "No more war. War never again." The U.S. bishops write a courageous peace pastoral. Individual bishops speak out against war and the machinery of war. Others are martyred in the cause of justice.

From where I stand, it does not seem necessary for "official" church leadership to be so heavy-handed in dealing with individuals and groups in the church. Instructions from Rome to Agnes Mary Mansour evidenced the invoking of a higher authority than was warranted by the circumstances of the case. The wisdom of the principle of subsidiarity, raised up by the Second Vatican Council, becomes apparent in its absence. An

opportunity for collegiality was present in response to Theresa Kane's greeting to John Paul II at the Shrine of the Immaculate Conception. Yet, repeated attempts on her part to initiate dialogue were thwarted. The dispersing of the California Immaculate Heart of Mary sisters seemed a brutal interference with the mission of a group which had contributed such richness to the church.
richness to the church.

I believe that the energies of those who are part of the Congregation for Religious and Secular Institutes could be spent more productively if they were released from the task of poring over constitutions from a far away land and making changes which appear reasonable from their very different context. Religious congregations contain sufficient diversity in their membership to steer a course between Scylla and Charybdis. Congregations also value the kind of resource they can be to one another as they search for the voice of the Spirit and respond to the demands and opportunities of the gospel.

If the canonical structure seems to fit too tightly, it may be time to explore alternative modes of presence to the church and world. This could appear to present a frightening prospect to some sisters. Individuals in our congregation have only haltingly raised the question. Other groups are proceeding with greater daring. If we do not free ourselves to explore options and discuss them openly with one another, we choose to remain enslaved by our own fears. The church deserves a better quality of minister than that.

The U.S. church of which we are a part is in a difficult period of its history. The best thinking and acting of all of us is being summoned as we make our way into the future. We move forward, trusting our own experience as we never have before, sharing that experience with one another with greater openness, and believing that God will continue to be deeply present to each of us and to the whole church. Our early sisters have placed deep roots in the earth. A sturdy trunk has been formed through centuries of rich traditions. Some pruning has been done. More may be needed. Then the time will come for a magnificent flowering, with strong and supple branches reaching everywhere, participating in the transformation of the earth. The tree will not be cut down.

Notes

1. Raymond A. Moody, Jr., *Life After Life,* New York: Bantam Books, 1976.
2. Frances Moore Lappe, *Diet for a Small Planet* New York: Ballantine Books, 1971.
3. Karl Rahner and Johann Baptist Metz, *The Courage to Pray* New York: Crossroad, 1981.
4. Helen Sanders, S.L., *More Than a Renewal* Nerinx, Kentucky: Sisters of Loretto, 1982, p. 184.
5. Florence Wolff, S.L., *From Generation to Generation* Louisville: General Printing Company, 1982.

New Priorities, New Potential

Caridad Inda

*Caridad Inda is executive director of the Spanish Education Develop-
ment Center, an agency serving low-income Hispanic families in
Washington, D.C. She has had extensive experience in international development projects and while in Honduras developed a methodology for
participatory research at institutional and community levels. She translated from Spanish to English the* Position Papers and Conclusions of
the Second General Conference of Latin American Bishops, Medellin,
Colombia, 1968, *published by the Latin American Bishops Conference,
and* A Theology of Liberation *by Gustavo Gutierrez, published by Orbis
Books. She is a member of the Congregation of the Humility of Mary and
the Sisters for Christian Community.*

The call to the religious life came to me in a foreign language within
a year of my arrival to the United States as a student in a small Iowa
college. It came clearly and unambiguously in terms my conservative
Mexican background made intelligible. I had been conditioned to respond
to discipline and order, to hierarchy and tradition, eager to follow, to
learn and to teach, which was the principal work of the community to
which I was being called.

Having been born and raised on the high dry mesa of Mexico City, I
found the lush Iowa countryside an alien land indeed, but in retrospect
it seems to stand as an allegorical representation of the potential of my
new life. It both provided and characterized the background for a new
experience — community life American-style on the one hand, and on
the other, teaching a foreign language and culture to youngsters from
relatively insular rural backgrounds. It was also my first opportunity to
experience parish life from the perspective of the North American religious in the pre-Vatican era. For me the most striking difference with
Mexican sisters was the public wearing of the habit. In Mexico, religious
are forbidden to wear their religious garb on the street, although, admit-
tedly, the purpose of the law is frustrated by the universal costume of
the religious — unmistakably nunly long black dresses, hair bound in
neat little chignons on the nape of the neck.

The United States sisterhood was a new world and I learned to speak
its language, to internalize its rationale, to become a part of the institutions it had created and continued to support. But as experience helped
me to acclimate, and increasing maturity opened dormant areas of my
consciousness and pulled me in other directions, I became more aware
of contradictions and incongruities. As my struggle with these tensions
mounted, Vatican II burst upon us.

The Second Vatican Council had direct and concrete implications for me. As a young religious I was teaching religion and other subjects in a parochial high school at the time the fathers of the church were deliberating in Rome. It was an exhilarating period as centuries of tradition were updated in a relatively short time. *Aggiornamento* was on. Community traditions were also updated. Input from the real world became acceptable. Strategies for experimentation were instituted; empirical evidence was generated and evaluated in the search for better ways to respond to the needs of those we had been organized to serve — in our case, children in poor parishes, orphans and the sick. In the North American church we were lucky to have not only easy access to documents but a strong sector within the religious communities who had the openness and courage to attempt to implement the concepts of those documents. Their example was a powerful force.

Renewal expressed itself in my life especially through the lives of religious women in my own and other communities who had dared explore beyond acceptable perimeters in search of appropriate ways to be church in the modern world, to be religious, to proclaim the gospel. It also came in the writings and example of Latin Americans who were raising their voices for justice and peace. I was galvanized by their perceiving these two terms as opposite sides of the same coin, linking them by a cause-effect relationship. If you want peace, work for justice.

A third emphasis of the call to renewal was a growing awareness of the systemic interactions that affected international affairs. Examination of the social and psychic impact of economic and political dependency made the need to eradicate dependency relationships in all our institutions urgent. What became clear at these various levels was that those who advocated liberating change and attempted to bring it about were generally held suspect and often had to pay a high price in their own personal lives for having challenged the status quo. If their efforts were unsuccessful, they were blamed for insubordination, disloyalty and pride and urged to mend their ways. If they succeeded, their accomplishments were held to be suspect, and by a variety of harassment techniques, they were "encouraged" out of the community setting and often out of the community.

I saw a distressing parallel between institutional change within the church and that among the community of nations. This was accentuated by the growing interest of the theological community to examine the psychic, social and religious dimensions of dependency. However, it has always been a source of great puzzlement to me that there has been so little reflection on the impact of the church as an international institution, and on the power relationships within its institutions and structures.

The sharpness of my concern for the issues of international relations — especially inter-American relations — was not rooted in unhappy personal experiences of belonging to an oppressed minority. The experience of belonging to a minority group has not been a painful one for me. Indeed, because I was blessed with excellent bilingual academic training in my early school days and because during my teaching days I had the opportunity for further study during the summers, thanks to a teaching fellowship awarded by St. Louis University, I was prepared to bridge language and cultural gaps. I have become in a very useful degree multilingual and multicultural. It is for this reason that I have been able to take part in the Latin American Justice and Peace debate not as a partisan but as an interpretive participant on both sides.

I have never felt co-opted because at the time I chose life in a North American religious community I was entirely unaware of the underlying rift. I had never considered giving up my culture, nor my Mexican citizenship — in fact, I did not until forced to do so to obtain a teaching certificate in the state of Montana. I was not then aware of the difference between the universality of the church (i.e., of all people) and the pull of national, class and cultural loyalties on religious institutions within nations. I do not consider myself co-opted now for I believe that the renewal has, at least conceptually, enabled us to make our choices in terms of justice/ peace rather than geopolitical considerations.

At the level of religious institution, the spirit of renewal favored decentralization and, in our community, allowed for the principle of self-determination. Although there was a high level of distrust in many circles regarding those of us who chose to experiment with diverse life and work styles, it nonetheless became possible to rent apartments, seek employment in other than church-related institutions and create communities and support systems that went beyond the members of the religious groups to which we were affiliated. This arrangement contrasted sharply with the traditional missioning procedure whereby in mid-August the general superior informed each sister where and at what she would be working for the coming school year.

The internal politics involved and the decision-making procedures did take into consideration, of course, community commitments and financial needs; but often, from the point of view of the subjects, it did not sufficiently take into consideration personality characteristics, personal choice, career paths, professional development and other needs. Sisters accepted these assignments and carried them out in a spirit of dedication and self-sacrifice. I am sure the work promoted the institutional progress of the church, but over the years it extracted a level of personal energy that was highly debilitating to the personalities of many of the participants. It became clear that there had to be a more humane and productive way to utilize the dedication and self-sacrifice of the religious.

In the new mode, the security of being assigned a job and a work place are gone. Instead, we are being offered the challenge to be responsible for our own support, to compete in the marketplace on an equal footing with other professionals and to be judged by the same standards. More important, we are given the opportunity to make an impact on people, causes and concerns that were totally inaccessible before.

The concept of self-determination in a religious community is still new to many persons. The stereotypic image of the good sister teaching in a parochial school, nursing in a Catholic hospital or caring for orphans in a Catholic institution is giving way to a much wider range of possibilities for action and commitment. In many cases, there is no going back, for it must be acknowledged that much change has been forced upon us. Rising costs and regulatory requirements together with shrinking memberships have forced many congregations to withdraw from traditional endeavors. This has been especially true for groups who focused on providing services to the poor. The schools in which we taught have been consolidated or have closed down.

Further, many religious believe that merely being able to support the cost of the services teaching sisters can provide does not give middle and upper class parishes an undeniable claim on them. Studies of the parochial system have raised questions about whether the results of Catholic education are commensurate with the resources expended to support it.

After several years of teaching in urban and rural Catholic schools, especially in the parochial system, I found it incompatible with justice to continue to support a system which drains an inordinate amount of the resources of the local community/parish (as much as 80 percent in some cases) to serve a relatively small group within that parish and that not too effectively. I also realized that I was not personally suited to the role of dispensing information about a language and culture that I loved to children who found it a bore. This, coupled with the pain of attempting to relate to young people whose motivation, principles of organization, habits of recreation and definition of respect differed enormously from mine, led me to seek other ways to make a contribution.

As I began to explore other avenues, I experienced in a new way how difficult it is for Catholics to accept the idea of a religious carrying on strictly professional duties in other than a Catholic institution. The freedom of choice allowed by the renewal of religious life has caused family tensions for me too. Persons brought up to internalize the image of the religious as habited and securely hidden from the wickedness of the world behind convent walls, find it difficult to accept the wholly new life-style. Hard as it was to become resigned to seeing their child only three days every three years, it is, I am afraid, even harder for my parents to understand how I can travel extensively, essentially choose my mission and live as a professional while maintaining the integrity of religious life. In their culture these activities are not acceptable for any adult woman, lay or religious, single or married.

Within the community itself there have been tensions regarding those of us whose diverse life and work styles do not conform to traditional patterns, and although no active pressure has been put on us to change, neither has there been great interest in sharing the insights derived from a different praxis. This indifference seems to derive in large part from an enduring dualistic vision of the sacred and profane. Dual membership, that is, in the Sisters For Christian Community as well as in my original community, has proven to be in many ways a bicultural experience for me. It has been an exercise in bridging two sets of priorities and preferences, attempting to understand and integrate the best of both and to move closer to the ideal towards which these two different paths lead.

With all its difficulties, the era of renewal and experimentation did, however, allow for a broader vision of the boundaries and opened professional development opportunities for a larger number of sisters. As a result, I chose to deepen my academic knowledge of international affairs, specializing in Latin American area studies.

My long-term interest in church affairs was deepened and broadened by several special opportunities for comprehensive study and reflection on the current Latin American reality. The Medellin Conference, which translated the Second Vatican Council thought and applied it to the Latin American area, had taken place in 1968. I was asked by the United States Catholic Conference to provide the official English translation. Translation work requires a line-by-line, word-by-word scrutiny of the documents and extensive reflection upon each paragraph as well as the total message.

Another opportunity came in the form of an invitation from Philip Scharper of Orbis Books to provide an English translation of Gustavo Gutierrez' seminal work *Una Teologia de Liberacion*. It was published in 1973. A third opportunity was the preparation of a doctoral dissertation on development thought in Latin America in the 1960s. These efforts allowed me to put into English thought and words important pieces of cross-cultural information and to formulate coherently insights gathered from a variety of places — among others Harvey Cox's *The Secular City*, the Sister Formation Bulletins, the works of Paulo Freire, Dennis Goulet, Andre Gunder Frank and Ivan Illich, as well as the encyclicals issued by Pope John XXIII. Above all, the experience of living in the "real world," mediated perhaps in some circles by the shield of a religious identity, immersed me in everywoman's praxis. The Washington area, where I have been based for the last 15 years, offers many opportunities for exploration.

Later, I found a job which provided extensive travel in Latin America throughout the latter part of the 1970s. It provided extraordinary opportunities for contacts with some of the major protagonists of change in important sectors of the Latin American church — Leonidas Proano, Hugo Assman, Dom Helder Camara, Paulo Freire, Oscar Arnulfo Romero, Gustavo Gutierrez — and many less well-known, but equally significant persons engaged in the struggle for liberation. They are deeply rooted in faithfulness to the gospel and the person of Christ the Liberator. Special among these are Julia Esquivel, Guatemalan theologian and poet who sings and suffers the captivity of her people in rich theological tones, Sisters Rose Dominic and Rose Timothy of Maryknoll, who minister to Peruvian women from all walks of life and inspire and support creativity and change, and Luz Beatriz Arellano, a School Sister of St. Francis now working in Nicaragua, who shared with me many of her insights and the warmth of her community during my eight-month assignment in Honduras in 1981.

The encompassing question is: Given this orientation, background and experience, how does one proceed? The contradictions are so clear, the needs so urgent, the resources so lacking! What are we, what am I doing, to support and enhance liberation and efforts toward change? This question is a powerful motivation to action.

There is also the constant and sometimes agonizing question: Where is it more important to work at this time — at the center of power, supporting and participating in efforts to make an impact on policy decisions, or on the periphery, attempting to ameliorate, if not heal, the effects of unjust and dependency-creating measures in an environment hostile to change and torn by violence?

For me, the very existence of these options recognizes the potential of self-determination to challenge responsible decision-making. One no longer depends on a "superior" to choose (and to lay in one's lap or on one's back, as the case may be) the strands with which to weave one's future; it is now a personal choice, a response to that living intention of God recognized many years ago as a vocation to service. This is not to say that the religious community and its corporate goals and commitments are not to be taken into consideration. It does mean that within the general objectives of the church to pursue peace and justice and the more particular charisma of each congregation to respond to the gospel imperatives here and now, it is theoretically as well as practically possible to have understanding and respect for the calling which each member has received and which is indeed gift and responsibility at every level.

The Power of Dialogue

Francis B. Rothluebber

Francis B. Rothluebber is a member of the School Sisters of St. Francis. She was engaged in the ministry of leadership in her community from 1966 to 1976. During that time she was an active member of the Leadership Conference of Women Religious and served as president of the conference in 1973. Currently a director and staff member of the Colombiere Meditation Center in Milwaukee, she has published a set of meditation tapes entitled From Meditation to Ministry *and is currently producing a new set on the feminine dimension of God.*

It is difficult to single out a beginning point for this personal story of renewal that also happens to be without an ending. It is difficult, indeed impossible, to separate the threads of this personal story from the interweaving of a community story. And it is even more difficult to focus on a particular emphasis in a story that encompasses significant changes in every dimension of one's life.

The focus of this particular journey back and through these renewal experiences is the life-giving power of dialogue. Several facets of the energizing power of dialogue occur here: the refining power of the meditative inner dialogue with one's life and the Source of Life, the freeing and growth of sharing with others in an atmosphere of trust, the clarifying power of dialogue in creative conflict, and the balancing of inner authority and outer authority.

The beginning of this focus is the experience of sitting early one morning in the fall of 1965 at the typewriter in the office of the Chicago Catholic Board. I was drafting an introduction to "Religious Life in the Church Today," the first of several position papers a network of committees was preparing for a total U.S. community small group discussion process. The School Sisters of St. Francis were scheduled to convene a general chapter in April, 1966. I had just reread what I had typed:

> The overemphasis on docility and on the obedience proper to children can stunt personal growth. The true person has established a reasonable self-identity which means she is capable of observing and evaluating, of reflection, of creative thinking, of personal decisions, of responsible long-term commitments. It means that she has the initiative to follow through with new patterns of action if necessary.

An image shot through me: a torrent of a driven river taking trees and rocks and underbrush along in its current.

The torrent broke loose with the discussion process. Seven thousand proposals were sent in for consideration at the general chapter. I was a delegate to the chapter and went to share what I had absorbed from the study of Vatican II documents which my work as director of high school religious education had demanded. But even more I wanted each member of the community free to experience what I had come to know. I had been trusted to develop a schedule that fit my responsibilities, to handle a car and a budget, to participate in the house events as I could. At the office I had been given a desk and the task of doing something creative about the teaching of religion in 105 high schools. The experience of the responsible freedom, the creativity, the fun and challenge of working with a core group of talented and dedicated women and men, the caring, the remarkable growth that happened in people and in the work through successes and mistakes gave me a vision of what a faith community could be. It also gave me a sense of what the beginning days of the community must have been.

The torrent broke loose in my own life, too. I believe that because I had written a history of the community, could carry responsibilities and was not considered too radical, the middle and more traditional delegates, without knowing much of my heart and mind, changed my life with a simple majority vote. On the same day four others were elected to the council. We inherited that very day the leadership of the international community, assumed the steering committee work of the chapter with its 7,000 synthesized proposals, were the provincial council for nearly 1,000 members who had as yet no specific U.S. province, and became the legal board of all the subsidiary corporations.

The work of the chapter of 1966 was incredible. Convening on weekends in the spring and fall and during intermittent weeks in the summer, the delegates produced *Response in Faith*, a composite of principles and directives that guided, inspired and wonderfully challenged our interpretation of our life for the next decade. *Response in Faith* came into being through the growing trust and hope the delegates experienced in the honest, often painful sharing of small group discussions, in the bonding of meaningful artistic prayer, in fatigue, silliness, and in tears.

The emphasis in this experimental rule grew out of the needs of a time of necessary transition. Some of the statements became part of our community bloodstream:

> Let us understand that only as full human persons living in relationship to Jesus Christ can we enter into any of the relationships of our life.

> Let us be, in him, truly sisters to one another . . . Let us share ever more completely . . . Let us listen in shared openness . . .

> We are a continuing response to Christ's call to share his mission in the world.

> Let us be free to move into his risen life with faith and hope in the future, knowing that he may require something of us tomorrow that he does not today.

> Let us so live that all persons see in us a community of dedicated women within the church, women who form a widening center of human

values and human progress toward the fullness of the humanity of Jesus Christ.

One of the major efforts of the chapter was to translate the principles into concrete directives. What were the authentic responsibilities and what was the appropriate level for the corresponding decisions? What fittingly belonged to personal, adult choices, to living groups, to provincial and generalate councils?

The five of us on the council or "the five" as we came to be known, since we could not retain the old titles and had not found appropriate new ones, took *Response in Faith* out to the community. We travelled from Montana to Mississippi, from New York to Colorado, to Honduras and Costa Rica, to Germany and Switzerland. We directed and participated in days and afternoons and evenings of reflection, invited questions, worked through anxieties, listened, prepared presentations, became angry, ached with those who were hurting, prayed together, and, when we could, celebrated.

I wonder how many times in those days I said, "Pentecosts are messy." I believe it was a little Pentecost. A powerful Wind was stirring in us and changing us. One vivid remembrance of that Wind happened in May of 1966. Previous Mother Generals had given a conference to each of the groups of sisters (300 or 400) who came to the motherhouse for retreat weeks during the summer. We decided to continue the tradition.

In preparation we did what quickly became our lifeline. We met to reflect, pray, discuss, be led by our dialogue. On this particular day we drove out to a retreat center in the country. We walked down the path to the creek, discovered May apples, sang Gelineau psalms, read scripture. Then we separated to study quietly the first part of *The Constitution on the Church in the Modern World*. When we returned, we had each been stunned by the very same section: Article 17 that begins, "Only in freedom can one direct oneself toward holiness." The notes we gathered called for a breakthrough from the slaveries of sterile patterns, of isolation, of authoritarianism into the freedom of life in the Spirit. A not-so-mild explosion followed as participants began to prefer tapes to conferences, challenged the retreat master, started to converse with each other.

The Pentecostal Wind touched another dimension of my life at the time. In an effort to stay physically energized, I began to practice yoga every morning. A door opened into a new dimension of my life. Bit by bit through the writings, first of the Benedictine Deschanet and gradually through other books and experiences, I was introduced to what I then described as Eastern-style meditation. I learned the power of interior dialogue. In spite of the little voice that judged it ridiculous to be sitting doing nothing when the whole community was falling apart, I learned with effort to quiet, to become more deeply present, to cross over into a symbol, to experience sinking into the Divine Source. The process changed my sense of spirituality, in fact my life. It was a beginning of developing a connection with all being, of waking to the hidden movement of the creating God, of a transformation of consciousness as I learned to respond in faith, in truth, and in compassion. It was a beginning and still is.

A new image struck us that first year during the time the three of us were in Central America. We made retreat in San Jose, Costa Rica, with the members of the community and with John Lefebvre from Cuernavaca. The rich reflective sharing focused on *Response in Faith* and *Perfectae Caritatis* as a call to a 20th-century gospel life. The image that struck us was the shell: Life in the shell dies when the shell is too rigid and constricting and life out of the shell prematurely becomes chaotic, form-less and disintegrates. The life and the shell need to change together.

Life in the shell was certainly too constricting in Latin America. For one thing the shell was too narrowly a European-U.S. shell being forced onto the Central American sisters. The life style, prayer style and institu-tional commitments did not fit the burning call to work in pastoral ministry in the growing basic communities, in nutrition and health ministry in the rural villages, to work in prisons, to create homes for the street orphans, to assist in community organization and in educational reor-ganizing.

On our jeep rides over the bridgeless rivers and up the mountain roads of the perpetual thin curves, we studied the Medellin papers and listened and questioned. To experience the residual oppression of a colonial spirituality that glorified suffering and resignation, to experience the oppressive burden of U.S. business ventures and the weight of a U.S. church mind was to acquire new eyes. We also acquired new ears as we listened to the Latin sisters and learned how we imprisoned them in assembly with our Roberts Rules of Order and caused them to feel like foreigners in their own country with an imposed way of life from prayer styles to food preparation. With all the positions of major responsibility filled by U.S. and European members, the possibility of change for these Latin sisters was fraught with doubt and fear. The first regional election of community leaders and an extensive study of institutional commit-ments and local needs brought hope. The life inside was deepening and the shell was beginning to change.

Two of us who went to Germany and Switzerland to share the develop-ments of *Response in Faith* with the members of the European province learned another significant dimension of dialogue: respect for the history and cultural traditions of others. European members were often frus-trated with the rapidity of change in the United States. They found that before they had a communication translated, disseminated, thoroughly studied and responded to, the new modification was already arriving from the U.S. Their deference to authority, their gracious hostessing, their — to us — more formal patterns of religious life made it difficult for all of us to sort out what was true collegiality and subsidiarity and what was simply a more casual, democratic U.S. approach or what was a reluctance to change. Here we learned the power of mutual questioning in trust and in concern for an authentic 20th-century religious life within the church. The changing life inside the shell needs its own time.

Those first years of renewal brought an avalanche of letters, telephone calls, meetings, days of reflection, requests for dispensation, and always questions — searching, protesting and affirming questions. Sometimes it was difficult to synchronize the changing structures and the deepening life. But the searching led to several basic convictions:

First, apostolic religious life is not static but a dynamic experience. It is life. Religious life is not a status one possesses but a becoming, a meaningful response to changing situations.

Second, the life we live does not have two "ends" or purposes, one of personal holiness and one of apostolic service. The evident need is to integrate the two dimensions into a community of contemplative, competent ministers at work within a world also in need of healing.

Third, the root meaning of life is relational. We become mature, we take life and grow as we understand and reach to love and respond in love. Friendships are an essential dimension of life.

Fourth, religious life is based on a respect for person. The power to relate to others and minister to them is dependent upon a measure of self-awareness, inner freedom, education, concern, responsibility, competence, joy, delight in the beautiful. Unless religious life is conducive to the growth of such persons and the deepening bond among them, it is meaningless.

Fifth, the community, like the church, is for the world, which is the human family. As part of that family and within it the community refuses to sit helplessly in front of misery, disease, ignorance, injustice and ugliness.

Sixth, all members are responsible for the quality of life within the community-in-ministry. The primary authority in religious life is fellowship authority. Centralizing authority is at the service of fellowship authority. This assistance is both coordinating and directional.

Seventh, the structures of religious life need to serve this developing life.

This listing of convictions reads rather smoothly. The actual experience of the living of them was not. But it seemed vitally important to risk letting any question be asked. One of my sentences from that era came back to haunt me often on the banners that were so popular then: "It is better to be creatively wrong than dead right."

Part of our dilemma at the time was the responsibility of balancing inner authority and outer authority, particularly the inner authority of community and the authority of the larger church. We desired to be faithful to the essential elements of an apostolic religious community. Part of the difficulty, however, was that women had had no input into the canon laws that defined and delineated those elements. Such laws could not provide for the manner in which adult women share responsibility, for the significance of consensus and the prayer-study process in their development, for the need to work outside church structures, for the right to just contracts, for the necessity of participating in social and economic developments — to name but a few aspects.

The power of dialogue to achieve a balance between the inner authority of the community and the authority of the Congregation for Religious in

Rome was challenged beginning in May, 1969. A letter from the apostolic delegate arrived in the mail.

> In its concern for the spiritual and temporal well-being of the institute of School Sisters of St. Francis, the Sacred Congregation for Religious and Secular Institutes has decided that it would be opportune to have an apostolic visitation of the community. It has, therefore, appointed the Reverend Benjamin Roebel, O.F.M. to the office of apostolic visitor.
>
> Father Roebel will be in contact with you regarding the details of the visitation. In the meantime you may notify the community of this development and urge all the sisters to extend the utmost cooperation to him so that his coming may be a source of great blessing for the community.

If I remember correctly, I shared the information with the others at the morning coffee break. Immediately the experience of the Immaculate Heart of Mary Sisters of Los Angeles (IHM) came to mind. We had at the time participated in the letter writing, had urged the (then) Conference of Major Superiors of Women (CMSW) leaders to make a position statement, had written articles, had met with the committee of bishops involved — all in an effort to seek clarification and understanding. We knew something of the possible outcomes of an apostolic visitation from the IHM event.

We gathered at the "farm," the old house several of us lived in at the edge of the city, to prepare the letter to the community. Our feelings ran the gamut: anxiety and fear for the future; anger that no reasons were given, no opportunity offered for discussion or involvement in the selection and that it was taken for granted that we would cover the expenses; apprehension over a possible sharper polarization in the community; and a sense of challenge to all of us to stand in our truth. What came to be named "the dialogue with Rome" began.

It began with the most sincere dialogue we could create, a prayerful reflection quietly alone and then together. We drafted a rough copy of the letter and decided to share it with all the members of the U.S. provincial teams before sending it to the community. During a June weekend we met with a canon lawyer and our public relations staff. Prayerful and heated discussions in small groups and in the total group helped refine and clarify the letter. We spent time, also, creating a design both in preparation and for the actual visitation. We decided to approach the visitation as we would any professional evaluation, using it to assess our strengths and weaknesses in the renewal process.

The general letters to the community had been a source of spirited exchange and bonding within the community. Although the language seems dated now, as far as we could sense from the response, this July 5, 1969 letter set a positive current moving through the community.

> Dear Sister,
>
> Tonight I come to share a question with you. We have received word

from the Apostolic Delegate, Archbishop Raimondi, that, at the request of the Congregation for Religious, Father Benjamin Roebel, O.F.M., is to conduct an apostolic visitation of our congregation. The question for us to consider is: "How shall we respond?"

As I type these words tonight so many of your faces come alive in this little circle of light. And I know that a great variety of responses will greet this announcement. We took the question to a discussion afternoon at Elkhorn and would like to share our thinking and reactions with you.

How shall we respond? First, by understanding the purpose of a visitation. It is a time of responsible review, a time of evaluating, a time when, together with the one conducting the review, we gather the facts about where we are, what progress has been made, what our strengths and weaknesses are. Evaluation and review are part of every healthy community, but particularly at a time like today when so many changes are being effected in religious life, there is a need for an ongoing study of the developments.

An apostolic visitation is a regular event. We understand it is an ordinary procedure and several reviews are underway at the present time. Unfortunately because of the present publicity concerning the IHM situation, the announcement at this time carries notes of investigation and fear. It is possible that some questions and occasional letters may have prompted this review, but it is equally possible that interest in some of the changes being effected in religious life would also suggest that the Congregation for Religious make several such progress studies.

We have been communicating with Archbishop Cousins and Father Roebel. Since we are already engaged in such a review through our provincial and general chapter work, it was decided that the present work continue through the first rounds. The plan now is to meet with Father Roebel through these summer weeks, sharing with him the experiences and the reasons for our renewal. The review proper will begin in mid-September.

How shall we respond? Secondly, by affirming the basic thrust and direction of our growth and development. We will continue to concern ourselves with the real issues, to live more honestly and more responsibly.

We are a graphic picture of the whole church today. The dramatic change of life within the church and within us is the result of the new emphasis, new insights, which are developing. There is no turning back nor could there be.

It seems to us that three major working ideas are moving us along the direction we have taken. First, a new awareness of the worth and dignity of the person. Each of us has the right to life, to greater life: to deepen our meaning, to evaluate our responsibilities to decide, to share our life, to serve, to love. The day of the faceless Sister is gone. Secondly, new understandings of the meaning of life within the church. The new emphasis in *Constitution on the Church* is transforming the hierarchical church into a people-of-God church. The Spirit dwells in the whole church. From thinking of the church primarily as the hierarchy, we are beginning more and more to think of the church as a gathering of those who are aware of Christ, who speak the continuing great *Yes* of Christ in sharing his death-resurrection life, who are bonded together by his Spirit into a dynamic life, living and working that all may come to a fuller, more meaningful, more human life. We as a religious congregation are simply striving to be a living definition of this new emphasis in the church. The day of waiting for all initiative and directives to come from superiors is gone. The third idea which is transforming our lives is the realization that the church is for the world. The whole of humanity is the Kingdom of God, in whom he lives and with whom he works, bringing all to fuller life and unity. And the People of God, the church, are in the midst, aware that Christ is the love and mercy of God made visible, praising and working, discovering and fostering the good in humanity, suffering and woking against injustice and for peace. The day of huddling together in religious life to save our souls is gone.

We cannot return to whatever in the old patterns led to depersonalized, institutional living, to artificial inhumanness, to authority-dominated living, to withdrawn, safe living. We may not betray our truth.

How shall we respond? By acknowledging that we are a sinful community. Our renewal is incomplete; our inadequacies glaring. It is easy to be hard, the new song says. It is easy to be so right, to be complacent, to snuggle down in our over-clean homes, to say we are concerned but there really isn't much we can do about injustices, misunderstandings, hunger, breaking families and broken young people, about riots or war or dishonesty, about our anemic parish life. We are still so unloving, so closed to others in community, so full of pretenses and masks.

Surely, in trying to discern what is of the Spirit, there is a rightful time to submit one's insights and manner of living for the refinement and evaluation of the community. In the same way there is a place for a religious congregation to submit its manner of living for consideration and help to those in the church who minister to the People of God, who can place the ever-large questions before us, who will be concerned that ours be a true expression of radical gospel living. We must be open to whatever is offered in competence and understanding and concern.

How shall we respond? By deepening our love of the church. Most of us are aware that, although some efforts are being made, many of the present structures in the church do not embody the new spirit and life in the church. Structural patterns are necessary for greater unifying and effectivenness. But some structures we now have are too autocratic and depersonalizing. For one thing, there is little opportunity for dialogue. Authentic dialogue is at the heart of renewal of structures. Only through honest interaction will adequate structures arise as old ones are replaced. If we really love the church and want to be a sign of Christ's love, it seems to me that we are responsible to do all in our power to effect a change in this minor structure of visitation, to make the experience a life-giving one. We are responsible to help make the structures serve love.

How shall we respond? By remembering that we are women. I believe that it is our serious responsibility to create a way of living religious life which is strongly and beautifully womanly. And further, it is our distinct responsibility to communicate the experience, the differences, and something of the quality of this life to those who are involved in directing the growth of religious life. We are women and as women we must bring to this time our power to love, to give life by persuasion rather than by violence, by concern rather than condemnation. But we must bring to it a woman's power of firmness and creativity.

Every now and then in the midst of the confusion and growth and transition and joy, I have the feeling that we are in the current of a rushing, Spirit-driven river that is sweeping us along to greater life. Great trees come crashing down; little old islands may hold for a while; but the river whirls on.

The Lord give you his peace and a prayerful hour near a swirling river.

Benjamin Roebel, congenial and scrupulously noncommittal, arrived for a planning session. It was quickly evident that he had no awareness of our size, history, or renewal experience as an international community. His directive for the review was a general "listen and report." In the months that followed, individuals, living groups, large gatherings made appointments or invited him to meet with them.

The visitation sharpened the polarity that already existed in the community. I realized at the November meeting of the International Union of Major Superiors (IUSG) in Rome that our community was a small cross-section of the world-wide experience of religious women. Sharp differences and tensions were emerging. These differences focused on the question of relationships with the Congregation for Religious, often strangely referred to as "the mind of Rome."

In the discussions at the IUSG meeting and in our own community, two widely divergent requests arose. One group spoke strongly for more specific directives from the Congregation for Religious and for sharper limits to experimentation. The second group maintained that religious women were responsible for the creative thinking and for the evaluation of experiences so necessary at a time when new patterns were developing. It was evident that there were two very different ideas of loyalty and obedience, two different ways of reacting or responding to change, two different ways of seeing the ministry of authority, in fact, two very different concepts of church and certainly of the essentials of religious life.

The theme of the IUSG conference reflected exactly the themes of our community's 1969 general chapter: the problem of the apostolate in a changing world and a changing thrust within the church, the impact of these changes on the structures of religious life, and the necessary re-thinking of the process of initial and continuing formation.

The statement of themes does not capture the high emotional tone of these months. Letters of condemnation and of support, lists of signatures, meetings of every kind filled the months.

Benjamin Roebel departed. In response to our request for a copy of the evaluation, he indicated he would make our request known to the Congregation for Religious. In April of 1970, I noted in a letter to the community that we had not been informed as yet that Father Roebel had submitted his report.

Be assured, of course, that if we receive any communication, it will
be shared with you. Perhaps the delay is good. It helps us to understand
more clearly that it is our responsibility to face the deeper questions:
Are we living the gospel life as Christ wants it at this time? Are we
really praying more deeply in our living? Are more of us becoming alive,
more loving, more creative, more reflective? Do we have the energy as
a community to be a good Samaritan to the overwhelming needs of the
human family? Whatever the report from the visitation, it can only be
a help to face these real questions. No review nor report can give us life.

The report on the apostolic visitation came in late August in the form
of a letter from Cardinal Antoniutti, prefect of the Congregation for Religious. The first part of the letter was a commendation for the dedicated
work of members of the community and for our sincere search for renewal.
The second part was a summary of the negative criticisms of developments
in the community given in an unfortunate scolding tone: "an exaggerated
cult of freedom," "nullify authority — by encouraging 'collegiality,' " "a
desire to be 'women of the world,' " "practices that are — a source of
scandal, such as late hours, indiscriminate visiting and worse," "regret-
table and unedifying division and tension." The concluding section called
upon us to clarify how "those who are responsible for the existing policy
of uncontrolled experimentation feel that the resulting life-style can be
reconciled with the religious life."

We were asked to make a copy of the letter available to the sisters of
the community so "they may give thought to it and express their minds
on it." It was to be discussed at the next general chapter and the observations of the chapter transmitted as soon as possible. There was little
time to get a balance after the letter was shared with the community.
Somehow almost immediately every television station, radio station, and
newspaper office in the Midwest and beyond had a copy of the letter from
Cardinal Antoniutti. For weeks it was as if psychological nuclear fission
had occurred.

Only the deep quiet of meditation times, the rich support we could give
each other, the many calls and letters from friends, from groups and
assemblies of religious women and men, made it possible to keep our
equilibrium.

At the closing of the cover letter we had sent with the letter from
Cardinal Antoniutti, I had written, "I have just come back from a walk.
A rush of wild, dark clouds against a deep-red evening sky. 'Always be
prepared to give reason for the hope that is in you.' " The community was
prepared indeed. A surge of energy carried us through the next months
of synthesizing all the responses to the statements of the letter, of the
work of the provincial committees and chapters in drafting working papers, and in the refining, paragraph by paragraph, the work of the general
chapter delegates. We were ready to present our comprehensive report:
the nine provincial summary syntheses of the community survey, the
paper relating *Response in Faith* to the documents of Vatican II, and the
reports of the retirement program, the financial developments, the apostolic work developments, and the major community experiences in life-
style and authority patterns of the past few years.

The general chapter directed that the report be presented directly by a group of four, representing leadership, chapter delegates and sisters in general. In March, 1971, we forwarded copies of all the materials together with a request for an appointment "in the near future."

We waited. U.S. provincial superiors of men's communities could request an appointment and receive it within two weeks. We waited for eight months. Finally with the assistance of the archdiocesan vicar for religious, we obtained an appointment for November, a week-long series of meetings with the staff of the Congregation for Religious.

Sister Augustine Scheele, Sister Alphonsa Puls, Sister Colman Keeley and I met with Archbishop Augustine Mayer and five other staff representatives of the Congregation for Religious around the longest, most formidable table ever created. The dialogue, after the first strained moments, was open and sincere, often direct and politely, mutually confrontational. Several areas needed further delineation. The dialogue was to be ongoing. The areas of further concern were: the need to emphasize the faith dimension of our life, the polarization of the community, our relationship with church authority, and authority patterns in the community. Henri Nouwen's sentence, "Dialogue is not a technique but a way of life," proved true for us. We continued to present and discuss during 1972 and 1973. Finally in January, 1974, we were able to present our revised *Response in Faith* with this sentence in the preface: "Authorization for the use of *Response in Faith* as our provisional constitution was given in November, 1966, and renewed in November, 1973."

One of the most difficult moments in the ongoing dialogue occurred at the time of the May, 1972, general chapter of elections. In the closing moments of our week-long discussion in Rome the previous November, we had been asked if there were any other points we wanted to bring forward. One that we felt needed attention was the experience of the apostolic visitation. What could have been a more positive experience had we been involved in planning for the review and in presenting a joint report became a source of mistrust and increased tension in the community and beyond it. We were promised that, in the future, preliminary consultation would definitely be included. But without any consultation, within a few months we received notification that an apostolic observer was being appointed to the May general chapter. At the opening session of the chapter, the delegates voted unanimously to "tolerate" the presence of the official observer at the opening session only. The observer withdrew. The statement of the reasons for the objection to seating the observer was signed by all the delegates and forwarded to Rome. No acknowledgment was ever received.

To engage in dialogue as a way of life is to realize the energy it takes to sustain it. "The cure depends on the wound being kept open," Kierkegaard wrote. Covering over what is not just nor true too quickly deepens the illness. Sustaining the dialogue is essential at a time of ongoing renewal. Within the church we face major shifts in the meaning of genuine authority according to the gospel, in justice toward women and the naming of sexism as sinful, and in living a spirituality that reverences full human life, the body and sexuality. All of these concerns impact on the presence of people of faith in the contemporary world with our unjust exploitation of people, our unjust distribution of goods of the earth, and our insane efforts to cure human ills with military weapons. It is the power of dialogue to keep the wound open until it is healed.

Great Tide of Returning

Margaret Ellen Traxler

Margaret Ellen Traxler has been a School Sister of Notre Dame from the Minnesota province for over 40 years. Currently she is director of the Institute of Women Today, a national organization of Jewish, Protestant and Catholic women, whose purpose is "to search for the religious and historical roots of woman's liberation." Helping to carry out the goals is a faculty of over 100 women representing the disciplines of law, psychology, theology and history. One of the main works is to set up programs for women in ten prisons and two jails. One of these jails is the largest in the country.

The years from 1917 to Vatican were an aberrant time for American sisters. In these years nuns were not following their gifts of pioneering and prophecy as in the days of their founders. This is a principal thesis of a forthcoming book, *The Yoke of Grace: American Nuns and Social Change,* by Dr. Margaret Susan Thompson, a historian at Syracuse University. Becoming interested in sisters because of a casual decision to include a lecture on them in a course on American women's history, Margaret Thompson was greatly impressed by the diversity, daring, professionalism and social commitment among 19th century sisters. She even found a precursor to the sister-lobbyists of today — Mother Katharine Drexel who, both before and after founding the Sisters of the Blessed Sacrament, exerted important influence over U.S. policy toward Native Americans. In many other ways, too, Thompson's research suggests clear continuity between post-Vatican II renewal efforts and the pacesetting and prophetic bases upon which American sisterhoods were originally founded.

I have lived 24 years in religious community before Vatican II and 17 years since, so it is a balance of time that helps me assess the changes to my life regarding relationships with my family, with ministry, and in my life of prayer.

Family

Without my family, I could not have persevered in the sisterhood. Ironically, the idea in the convent was to remove and separate the young girl from her family as soon as the postulancy began, even though the family was the nurturer of the vocation, and home is where it began.

My father died in 1960, well before a new openness to family had begun. I was teaching in North Dakota at the time and I was not present when he died. I was able to attend his funeral, but had to return to teaching duties on the same day that we buried him. That I could not take time to grieve with my family brought me years of pain and delayed the process of healing.

Once when I was in the novitiate, I had to go to St. Paul, about 90 miles away, for a regular appointment with an orthodontist. My father, knowing of the date and time, drove all the way into St. Paul so that he could see me for five minutes in the bus depot. This is the father that the holy rule decreed I could not see more than several times a year.

I never knew my father as an adult. I remember him as a perfect man, gentle, benign, humble, tall and so handsome that I looked away in pride when he appeared in the public school yard where, as president of the school board, he sometimes came on business.

In his later years, my father kept saying to my mother, "Haven't we had fun!" Now, I think of how they worked side-by-side as a country doctor and nurse, sometimes 18 hours a day. And his assessment was, "Mother, haven't we had fun!" It was my father who really understood me and cautioned my mother lest she discipline me too strictly. Often I heard him say in his gentle voice, "We mustn't break her spirit." This, it seems to me, represents the peaceful temper of his Swiss forebears and the more volatile spirit of my Irish mother.

Even though I left home in 1941, the rules that kept us in cloister and restricted our visits with our family are the reason why I never knew my father as an adult. I often wanted to discuss with him his ideas on a woman's right to make decisions over her own body. I wish I could have asked him about the ethics of such medical issues as tubal ligation, gene-splicing or the right to die. His opinion would be paramount with me because I remember him as a man who was a model of faith as well as professional integrity. The way he lived and the example he gave us gave credence to his studied and careful opinions.

My four sisters and I attended public school in our small town of Henderson, Minnesota, a place of trust and friendliness. After each of us completed the eighth grade, our parents sent us to a Catholic boarding school because they wanted us to have a grounding in our faith. As we look back, we all agree that our father and mother were our models of faith and how it is lived, even though, in their judgment, sisters were the true educators. In fact we did love the sisters but we now know that in those depression years, when the cash flow was meager, it was a hardship for our parents to send us to the academy, about 30 miles from home.

I recall a conversation between my parents about this. My three older sisters were already in high school and the question was whether to send my sister Kitty Jo and me. My father concluded the discussion by saying, "Well, Mother, let's send them all so we'll know that we did all we could to save their faith."

My mother was my first and last "blind lover." I recall that after the changes came about there were nine years in which I was able to visit her often and spend weekends with her. During this time we talked over the changing world, the changing church and current social issues. She was a woman of common sense and balance. Her name was Marie McCarthy-Fitzgerald and she married my father during World War I in San Antonio, Texas. They lived near the army base and had originally met at St. Joseph Hospital in St. Paul, Minnesota, where my father was an intern and mother a graduate nurse.

Mother was a natural leader and beyond her interests in the field of medicine, she was an artist. She read a book a day and played the piano long hours into the night. She was tender and affectionate. I have vivid memories of her coming into my bedroom where, finding me awake, she would rock me to sleep. That must have been during my pre-school years because I recall that in the first grade, we were asked to stand and give one sentence about ourselves. I stood up and gave my name. Then I added, "I'm all my mother has in this world," whereupon Eddie Schultz challenged, "Your ma got plenty of kids." Then I recall giving what I suppose was my first rebuttal, "No, Mother sings that song to me at night, so I know."

My mother never allowed my sisters and me to quarrel, not even argue. When people asked her, "How then will they learn to fight life's battles?" my mother would reply, "I don't know, but they will not learn by fighting with one another." My sisters and I have often blessed her wisdom in this. We feel that one result was our deep union with one another.

Each year my sisters and I spend a week together at the lake. They leave their families in charge of the husbands, and we sisters have our reunion. I call this "my second annual retreat." Last year my sister Pat said something that startled me. As the fourth of five children I still find myself looking to my older sisters with special regard and admiration. Pat was at the bridge table and I heard her say, "Mother was more brilliant than Daddy." I expressed my surprise. "But mother always said that he was the brighter," I countered. Then Jean joined Pat, "Mother was creative and enterprising; she developed so many skills like music, design, and creative writing."

My sister Kit then pointed out how well they complemented each other and recalled the time when mother's inventiveness saved our father's life and perhaps the life of an expectant mother. In a bitter snow storm my father was on his way to Jessenland to deliver a baby. While he was driving on the lower river road, the winds were not as menacing, but mother, realizing that as soon as he reached the top of Flynn Hill the drifts would be a formidable block, called the Gerarty's who lived near the top of the steep hill. "Bill," she said, "Trax is on his way to the Fineran's. Will you hitch up your team and meet him at your mailbox?" Then mother called the other farms along the route that our father would follow and she asked each one to swing a lantern in the night so that Bill Gerarty and our dad would have beacons to follow. Years later, Bill told us about that night and how the swinging lanterns kept them on the road to the bedside of the expectant mother.

Whatever the balance in the gifts of my parents, we adored them both and still see in them what should be the symbol of church, the voice of reason and wisdom, of tenderness, justice and love. "Holy" rules must never again be allowed to divide families, divide children from parents. There is no authoritative scriptural admonition that can be quoted to outweigh the Fourth Commandment. Sheer common sense directs us.

Ministry

Ministry is the second general area in my life that has been affected by renewal. I loved teaching, loved the students and, in effect, I have never really left it. For 17 years I was in the formal classroom, but since 1965, my school has been a larger one. In 1964, the civil rights movement was gathering momentum. The Catholic Interracial Councils were growing and these were coordinated by the National Catholic Conference of Interracial Justice (NCCIJ), whose offices at that time were in Chicago. Matthew Ahmann, head of NCCIJ, had convened the first National Conference of Religion and Race, which showed, in effect, that there was a relationship between religion and prejudice, a reality that seems clear now, but at the time was not always acknowledged. The late Rabbi Abraham Josuah Heschel, one of the speakers, said, "The main responsibility for people of faith must be to transmute prejudice into justice; and justice is another name for God."

One of the departments of NCCIJ was education. I was appointed to this office in February, 1965. I was initiated into the work with direct action that began the very next month in Selma, Alabama. When blacks were beaten with billy clubs in Selma, and national TV carried the pictures, we began to organize defensive action from the NCCIJ offices. The Catholic Interracial Councils, which were largely lay organizations, sent many delegations to Selma. Among the delegations were nuns recruited by our offices. The Maryknoll Sisters responded early, as did the Sisters of the Blessed Virgin (BVM's), Sisters of Loretto and the Benedictines. One mother superior said, "I will have to ask the bishop." Naturally, none of her sisters arrived.

We flew to Montgomery and drove the 60 miles to Selma. it was a cold, wintry day and the winds were harsh. The first place we went was to the black Baptist church, where people were singing and praying. When the ushers saw us in our habits, they took us to the very front benches. After about 10 minutes, the preacher came down and asked me to go to his pulpit to speak. "Tell us why you're here. Tell us what you think," he said. At first I was startled but I went to the pulpit and felt that the congregation would understand. They helped me along by answering back, as is the custom in black churches. "You tell 'em"; "Amen to that"; "Praise the Lord," etc. I soon got into the rhythm and together we prayed and preached our homily on race, religion and righteousness.

Before going to Selma, I had called my own provincial, Sister Bernardia Gores, in Minnesota. I had spoken of the Selma crisis and told her that I wanted to go. As usual (this was her gift), she listened. She gave me one admonition, "Stay in back, don't get hurt!" I thought of this when, after the homily, 10 of us sisters were ushered out into the street where rows of state troopers stood with their billy clubs in front of them. We formed a line, the sisters in front all the way across the street. People began to sing freedom songs and lined up behind us. The troopers stared at us, their necks red in the sharp March winds. I think of our singing now for there was a touch of prophecy, "No man's gonna turn us 'round."

This was my introduction to a new ministry and one which truly adhered to the apostolic dreams of my founder, Teresa Gerhardinger of Bavaria. In the years that followed I was able to carry out some fruitful education programs. For example, in one we placed several hundred college teachers, mostly sisters with doctoral degrees, in 112 predominantly black colleges. The teachers we placed relinquished their salary and took the places of black teachers, who needed several years off to complete advanced degrees. In the summertime, we found teachers for Upward Bound programs, in which young people received courses to help them prepare for college.

In this instance and in those to follow, I use the word "we" because in all the programs, even up to the present, others have helped me in significant ways. For example, in the college placement service, teachers did the work. In the Traveling Workshops of which I will speak presently, sisters traveled the country on behalf of improving race relations. The planning and coordination were my job, but others performed heroic services. Thus, "we" is essential in my judgment as I tell of our projects over the past 20 years. It represents a long line of marvelous women who helped make it all possible.

Another program NCCIJ founded and then replicated established summer schools in federally subsidized housing. These classes were highly successful in keeping youngsters well occupied for the summer months as well as preparing them for the coming school year. In all there were about 30 of these. Funding was facilitated by the War on Poverty, whose head, Sargent Shriver, served on the board of NCCIJ. I do not say that Mr. Shriver used his influence for us in a special way, but his name did not make our funding any harder!

In still another educational endeavor, we oriented inner-city teachers for the "new culture" of blacks and Hispanics. This urban education was affiliated with Mundelein College and was carried out for about five years. During this time we were consulted often regarding keeping the inner-city Catholic schools open. That many of them did remain open, we feel, even today, serves as eloquent witness of the church in these areas.

Perhaps one of the most far-reaching of the NCCIJ education programs was Traveling Workshops for Inter-group Relations. Each Traveling Workshop had five teachers and in a given year we had two and sometimes three teams operating at the same time. In all, there were 110 such workshops concerned with white racism and the practical ways in which to overcome it on an institutional and individual level. The teachers addressed the subject through the disciplines of sociology, economics, religion and psychology.

In a recent *National Catholic Reporter* an editor discussing race relations lamented that the church had not been present to civil rights. I shook my head at this naivete.

In the last three years of my service at NCCIJ (by that time I was executive director) we deposited our archives at Marquette University. Six tons of papers and manuscripts covering Project Equality, education, housing, medical care, employment, and investments told the story of lay Catholic commitment to social justice in race relations.

Now, almost 20 years later, such work seems rather traditional, but at the time it was considered by many as controversial. I recall a sister asking, "But are the black people Catholic?" When I answered that only two percent were, she replied, "Well then, how do you justify giving all your time to this work?" Another asked, "When are you coming back to our province to work?" As late as last year, my novice director looked at me and said, "I'll always regret that you left the classroom."

In Selma, I saw another classroom. I met another need and I have never doubted that our founders would have approved the choices that were made. It seems clear to me now, why Dr. Margaret Thompson called the years 1917-1962 aberrant years for nuns. Selma and beyond began years which for me represent the "tide of returning."

One wave in this tide occurred when I was a member of our general chapter in 1968 and 1970. Part of the 1968 sessions took us to Munich, Germany, the cradle of our order. One morning we were asked if we'd like to spend the day in the Bavarian Alps. Not realizing that this was a rhetorical question, I raised my hand and suggested an alternative. "I'd like to visit the Dachau concentration camp," I said. Silence ensued. There was a hurried huddle in the front of the refectory. They decided to be American in making the choice. "We'll vote," said the German provincial. The vote was unanimous. All American delegates, 40 in all, wished to visit Dachau.

Dachau is 20 minutes and a million light years from Munich. I was stunned as I viewed the ovens, the pond where human ashes were thrown, and the museum of photographs. The sign over it, "Never again," haunted me. I did not know how it would affect my life, but I knew six million Jews were killed by baptized Christians. That fact would be anguish in my heart until I could somehow witness to the meaning of this revelation. Four years later, when I was completing my work at NCCIJ, Rabbi Marc Tanenbaum read a news article in which I was quoted about Soviet Jews. I had said, "Here are the Jewish people in Russia, victims of centuries of pogroms and now again in our day, being persecuted and denied exit visas." It was a simple statement of outrage that prompted a practical idea from Rabbi Tanenbaum.

He wanted interfaith witness to the rights of Soviet Jews. I knew at once that this was an idea that was workable: to stand up to Pharaoh, to speak out to the USSR about our brothers and sisters in Soviet Jewry. We began that very day to plan a national consultation that took place in April, 1972. The office resulting from that conference exists today, and is staffed by Sister Ann Gillen. The official title is the National Interreligious Task Force on Soviet Jewry, and it has been a factor in the emigration of 263,622 Soviet Jews from the USSR for the country of their choice.

At the international meeting of Jews known as Brussels II, I was deeply moved to be among those who received a medal from the hands of Golda Meir for my part in this effort. Walter Hubbard, president of the NCCIJ board, also received a medal. As president, he helped us organize the events that led up to the founding of the Interreligious Task Force on Soviet Jewry. As Mr. Hubbard said, "We blacks know full well the meaning of discrimination and wherever it is found, we'll fight it." Our medals read, "Let my people go."

There is simply nothing I would not do, no effort I would refuse, to educate Christians about the history and implications of the Jewish heritage. As Sargent Shriver, head of our task force, said, "We can do nothing to change the past; but we must do all we can in the present in order to change the future."

In 1974 I went to the Middle and Far East to hear from women their perception of women's status in society. Their pain and frustration was no surprise even though men of those nations claim that "their women" have roles of preferment and comfort. In Syria, Lebanon, Iran and India I heard directly from women of all classes about their third- and fourth-class citizenship. Muslim women especially confided that they were often not even considered human beings. An Iranian woman told me, "A cow in my husband's stable is more valuable to him than a woman." They dreaded bringing daughters into the world, knowing that girls merely expand the slave class in their societies.

As a consultant on women's affairs for the World Council of Churches, I had many opportunities to hear women of all nations speak of their problems, but I was especially concerned about Muslim women, who belong to the fastest-growing religion in the world. I determined to spend the rest of my life in the struggle for recognition of women's equality, so I began plans to found the Institute of Women Today (IWT).

Composed of Catholic, Protestant and Jewish women, the institute's purpose is "to search for the religious and historical roots of women's liberation." In 1975, the first year of the Decade of Women, we held over 50 workshops for women discussing the status of women. The faculty of the institute is drawn from the disciplines of law, psychology, theology and history. Among the sponsors are Church Women United, the National Federation of Temple Sisterhoods, the American Jewish Committee on Women, the National Coalition of American Nuns, women of the AFL-CIO, National Assembly of Religious Women, the United Presbyterian and United Methodist women.

One of the contributions to women's studies initiated by IWT is the book, *Beyond Domination, New Perspectives on Women and Philosophy,*. Edited by Dr. Carol Gould, this book grew out of our Annette Walters Conference on the Philosophy of Women's Liberation, the first such conference to my knowledge on the philosophy of liberation.

The main work of IWT is on behalf of women in several jails and 10 prisons. We have about 50 teachers and volunteers who carry out programs for incarcerated women and their families. Three leading programs might be mentioned. We have initiated non-traditional building skills courses into three prisons. The skills are electrical wiring, plumbing, drafting, and carpentry. A second main service helps women in prison establish cottage industries in which they may make money. Teachers assist the residents in making quilts, comforters, handbags, etc. These are then sold through our Chicago office. At the moment we have a large contract for 5,000 handbags, which will bring the maker $3.00 apiece. This money goes into an account which the prisoner is free to use for her own needs and for her children.

A third major program has brought the Ira Progoff Intensive Journal writing workshops into United States prisons and jails. Sister Maureen McCormick and Sister Jeannette Normandan, certified by the New York sponsors, Dialogue House, conduct these highly therapeutic workshops for incarcerated women.

Sisterhouse, a 35-room home on Chicago's westside, for women coming out of prison is also a project of the institute. Sometimes, upon release, women have no one to take them in and help them re-enter the mainstream. This is what Sisterhouse does. Sister Anne Mayer and Sister Gladys Schmitz provide to each person whatever is needed for safe and secure re-entry. Residents may stay up to four months and as Sister Anne says, "Four months is just a time span to help the women aim for the future. No woman in crisis is turned away."

In 1965, when I began work in another province of my community and worked at an independent agency, our community directory showed that I was only one of several Notre Dame Sisters working thus. Now, 20 years later, our community directory shows hundreds of our sisters working apart from the formal institutions of convent and church.

Self-concept is a very important measure of self-esteem. When the avalanche of sisters leaving peaked in the late 1960s, our wise president, Sister Georgianne Segner, reported some insights about the letters of the sisters who sought dispensation. "One thing that occurred in almost every letter," she said, "was a recognition by the sisters of their poor self-image, their damaged self-concept." I cannot forget this as I reflect on the re-introduction of the word "Superior" at the behest of Rome into the new rules of sisters. There is but one antonym to superior and that word, "inferior," is destructive.

In dialogues with men of the Congregation for Religious, American sisters found these men are willing to "write off" this generation of nuns. However, we of this generation want the next and future generations of sisters, in whatever form they may serve, to know that we will not allow such conditions to exist in the years to come. The control, the demeaning of personhood, the oppression of sisters by many pastors, the counter-productive lifestyles, the destruction and control of conscience by superiors, confessors, retreat masters, male counselors who seek control over our leaders represent to us a sinful dominance and denial of basic human rights. This must not be allowed to happen to another generation.

The persecution of women like the Glenmary Sisters of Cincinnati by the late Archbishop Karl Alter, the persecution of the Immaculate Heart Sisters of Los Angeles by the late Archbishop James McIntyre, the oppression of Sister Agnes Mansour by Archbishop Edmund Szoka, and Archbishop James Hickey's maltreatment of New Ways Ministry are all cases showing young people that entering religious life is a dangerous and hazardous way for anyone who thinks independently and freely listens to the Holy Spirit for guidance.

For 17 years I taught young men. I loved them, and if I learned anything at all about them, I learned about their intense thirst for justice. They will agree to just about anything as long as it is fair. I cannot imagine a healthy young man today following a vocation to a priesthood that is denied to half the church's membership. This, it seems to me, would be intolerable for a sensitive, socially-conscious young man today.

Prayer

If renewal has improved my relations with family and ministry, there can never be adequate assessment of the helps I have received in prayer. Earlier retreats were usually in the heat of August during a period of fear and wonder about "transfers." Retreats were conducted by priests who were on a scale continuum from excellent to poor, from fine to ghastly. I recall one priest to whom we are forever indebted, who asked the provincial, "Why do you have an hour for spiritual reading in assembly?" When analyzed, they found that this was a custom from early days when some sisters could not read. Our retreats had too many general sessions when we were to meditate together, pray together or just sit together. There was little time for quiet reflection and private prayer. This "group-think" and "group-hear" all but destroyed our desire to "come aside and rest awhile," as Jesus invited.

Sister Margaret Brennan of the Immaculate Hearts Sisters of Monroe, Michigan, brought to this stalemate of sisters' retreats an innovation which now, almost 15 years later, has completely changed the old patterns. She made an individually-directed retreat and knew that this was a method of prayerful reflection for all her sisters. Not only did the IHMs benefit from this new method, but so did all U.S. nuns. The individually-directed retreat, a process of self-evaluation and prayer, has changed the prayer life of nuns, has brought a quiet revolution, and has made the older methods intolerable.

Individual spiritual direction of sisters by sisters has emerged. This also is a part of the prayer changes that have given new patterns to the spiritual lives of sisters. I made my first individually-directed retreat in 1972, and in all my 43 years of religious life, nothing has helped me as significantly as these exercises.

Worship is hard for a feminist in a church which discriminates against women and where men dominate all liturgical functions. Because women serve as excellent leaders in retreats and in spiritual direction, feminists do now have some access to the life of grace in the church.

Feminist prayer services, already common, also indicate a direction for future prayer. At the 1983 conference, "From Generation to Generation: Woman Church Speaks," there was profound evidence that feminist prayer services appeal to women. They have scriptural underpinnings, but also have dance, song, affirmations and testimonies. They are living liturgies. The critiques of 1300 participants at that meeting gave overwhelming affirmation that women wish to pray as women with women in a manner chosen by women.

Thus, renewal has called me to stand up like the bent-over woman in Luke 13:10-21. Through return to our founder's roots, renewal has called me from the infirmity of the aberrant years to the new healing and wholeness of prophecy and beginnings. Jesus said to the bent-over woman, "You are freed from your infirmity." He laid hands on her and immediately she was made straight and she praised God.

Bent over no more, I relish convent life. I relish ministry to a neglected and marginal church in jails and prisons. Bent over no more, I am again an active part of my own tender family and I hear with joy the God who calls us to the great tide of returning.

The Great Commandment

Fara Impastato

Sister Fara Impastato has been a Eucharistic Missionary of St. Dominic for 45 years. In her congregation she has been novice mistress, vice-president and finance officer. Since 1966 she has been on the religious studies faculty of Loyola University in New Orleans. She is active in adult Christian education and seves on the Faith and Order Commission of the Louisiana Council of Churches.

The story that I have to tell is in a way a strange one. It is more the story of a personal inner journey than of any great social changes, though of course they are part of it. Undoubtedly the permission for change, the actual changes, the atmosphere, the new philosophy asserting the appropriateness, the desirability, indeed the necessity of interpersonal relationships for religious who wanted to love God — these factors facilitated and perhaps precipitated certain stages of this inward adventure. Despite the fact that the inaugurating crisis for me was *not* Vatican II, the process of resolution was within the framework and shaped by the principles generated from the upheavals proper to this surprising council.

That is the first prenote: This is the story of what happened to me during the Vatican II period, not of what happened to my congregation, or in the world outside of me, except in so far as events impinged on my own development. Further, what happened is not single-tracked, just as God's great commandment is not. One part concerns him; the other part ourselves. It can, in fact, be thought of as two comandments. So, my journey ran along two tracks. Another image explains this better. My own consciousness does not perceive these two "tracks" as parallel roads bur rather as two tasks or two paintings, each of which, in turn, got attention and then had a cover thrown over it and stood untouched for weeks.

Indeed my story happens to tell itself in terms of these two commandments and to certain unconscious understandings I had about God unconsciously in relation to these dual laws.

I accepted, even before I entered the convent, that these great commandments were really the only commandment. Early, very early, I discarded attempts to practice this or that virtue and concentrated on "loving God alone" and translated "loving others like myself" into "serving others selflessly." How did I interpret this "selfless love"?

Love meant "effective willing of good to another." The trick, of course, was to discover what this good was. I had heard a beloved teacher say: "The best thing you can do for another is to teach that other the truth because the truth frees and makes persons able to be self-directing — like God." I wanted to "do the best thing." How was I "to teach the truth?"

I lacked two and a half months of being 19 years of age when I almost literally ran away from home to become a postulant with my beloved congregation. Very early I had read of some saint (later I discovered it was our father, St. Dominic) whose ambition was to "speak only to God or of God," and I promptly resolved to follow suit. In this way I would certainly be teaching the truth! Somehow I translated that to mean, "The only time you should spend with other people is time in which you can do them some good (i.e., talk to them about God), because you are a religious and a missionary and haven't any right to fritter away minutes in idle conversation."

I took these principles with absolute seriousness and daily made fresh resolutions to live according to them. I often broke away from a group if I thought the conversation was "idle" and severely scolded myself if I did not make every (translate "often ludicrous") effort to "elevate the conversation." For many years Aquinas' clear statement rang in my head: "Love is the effective willing of good to another." Along with that statement rang what I considered its logical corollary (it is not): "Feelings have nothing to do with it." True love is a matter of will, but Aquinas wisely explains the place imagination and emotion have in supporting and hastening love.

What did I do with my own private heresy of *apatheia*, my determination to disregard emotions? In the first place, and correctly as far as the intention goes, I struggled against *negative* feelings. And God in his gentleness either removed the object of my dislike or brought me to see the other with compassion (not altogether untinged with condescension) which, at any rate, freed me from the grip of hatred. Second, I considered any strong feelings I had for those whom I loved within the community an unfortunate distraction. Of course there were persons outside the convent to whom I felt drawn, both male and female.

The males I ruthlessly and carefully avoided — and I cannot say I am sorry I did. Given the strength of my passions and my utter naivete, that way of solving what could have become a dilemma was probably the most (unconsciously) prudent decision I could have made. As for the females, I listened to them, tried my best 'to speak to them about God, was nourished far more than I knew by their appreciation, and ascribed whatever pleasure I felt in their company to the glow of doing good. I would have considered myself deficient in proper detachment and failing against the first commandment if I had simply enjoyed their company or rather had admitted to such enjoyment. All this time of course I was convinced that I was indeed loving my neighbor as myself.

This attitude was further strengthened by my interpretation of celibacy: that you gave to God an undivided heart which found its rest in him alone. I had begun to understand at a very young age that created things were limited, and Augustine's cry aroused my conscience to all sorts of desperate resolutions: "You did create us for yourself, O Lord; and our hearts are restless till they rest in you." Furthermore, two other statements convinced me I was right: One, from Genesis, to this day stirs my heart with wonder and longing: "Abraham, I am your shield; your reward shall be great." Greedily, I dreamt of that reward. The second statement was from Aquinas on the object of prayer: "Ask from God nothing less than himself."

This combination of great truths, imperfectly digested, led me to generally avoid human love and plunged me into oceans of guilt over the absorbing affection that flared up in my consciousness.

The genesis of this affection would have been perfectly clear to any observer even superficially schooled in the ways of the human heart. During my 11 years as novice mistress, I regularly became intensely attached to the young women who came under my guidance. I loved them fiercely, protectively. Yet somehow, because I had a keen sense of the importance of my task and of the trust reposed in me, I loved them with a certain anguished clear-sightedness. Generously, I spent myself to the point, as it turned out, of dangerous exhaustion. I did not, of course, say to myself: "I love them." No, I was simply concerned for them as the future of our congregation. The desolation I felt after their first vows and their departure to the mission fields I put down to weariness, the disturbance of the familiar, and human weakness. And I drowned my grief, unacknowledged for what it was, in a frenzy of preparation for the postulants who were due to arrive within the next five weeks.

Remember that my definition of "willing good to" was to "teach truth to." Be assured I missed very few opportunities to teach our young sisters, to bring to them every ounce of art and music, of beauty and breadth I heard about or could dream how to get for them. My demands were high — for many, impossibly high. I was scrupulous about making sure each person was free to leave. They were really free, too; and knew it. I wanted only those to stay who wholeheartedly chose to; and when I felt that some intention other than God and his love was operative in a person, I worked hard to see that this young woman was helped homeward. I did not always succeed, but subsequent events proved that my intuition was accurate about the doubtfulness of the person's place in religious life, or at least in our congregation.

In the middle of my career as novice mistress, a somewhat older-than-most young woman came to the novitiate. She was very well educated, widely cultured, knowing far more about music and literature than I. She was endlessly creative, brilliant — and a superb teacher. She could be difficult, but I refused to see this or to admit it. I did not know it then — I did not merely love her, as I did so many others (not all, alas): I fell in love with her. Whatever physical feelings were involved in this experience were impatiently pushed aside with a certain angry embarrassment. I discovered Bartok; we read together *Four Quartets* and various abstruse studies on the Arthurian cycle; I felt again the wonderful excitement of graduate school. On her talent I built my plans for the future education of our young sisters. I saw her doing her stint on the missions; then returning to become my right hand, the years stretching before us, filled with absorbing work: teaching, planning, creating a small, elite academic Arcadia. Imperceptibly I'd drifted from my center. The voice from the cloud was silent. I had lost sight of the reward "exceeding great."

Three years after she left the novitiate, when she was due to renew her temporary vows, our five-member General council dismissed her with no prior warning to me. I do not know if they were right or wrong. I do know that all five of these women, my sisters, were good women. I know that they tried, with real effort and often painful searching, to do what they honestly felt was best for our congregation. I did not, however, want to see this at the time. They brought my dream to an end. I quite simply hated them and would gladly (I think) have destroyed them and the entire congregation if I could have. Concomitant with the dismissal of this women, on whom I had unconsciously built my own private world of intellectual pursuits and high culture, came something I had expected and, with a sense of relief, had been looking forward to: my replacement as novice mistress by another young religious, who also figured in my future. I had long wanted her assignment as my assistant and felt that her appointment augured well for the continuation of my carefully constructed program. But this "triumph" — the appointment of the person of my choice to succeed me — was almost literally ashes in my mouth when I was suddenly confronted with the loss forever as close companion and perennial co-worker of the other one on whom I had come to rest (though unwittingly) all my joy. I did not know I had done this until I breathed the thin and desolate air left in the void of her going.

The little Louisiana town to which I went was not, as I had imagined it would be before my friend's departure, a place of peace for me. It was instead the scene of raging interior battles. My congregation — my superiors and sisters — were astoundingly kind and gentle. My mother general (we still had Mothers general then) repeatedly went out of her way to try to help me, to get for me difficult-to-obtain appointments with excellent directors, but darkness had descended. "I will never forgive you," I had said to her, and I seemed determined to remain faithful to this terrible promise.

Into the eye of this storm wandered an innocent lay woman whom I had known for several years and who liked me immensely. Vatican II was over. The machinery of "renewal" had begun to hum: "Return to the basics," "respect for the person," "proper self-development," "nurturing one's gifts for God and others," and that wonderful shibboleth, "meaningful relationships" — all were bright slogans spinning in the air, promising to deliver religious life, released from the encumbrances of past generations, into the 20th century. The real sign of true emancipation was to have a friend outside the "confines" (the language is significant) of one's own community. I suddenly noticed the shy and diffident young woman who for a while had taught "my" novices and who now had an appointment at a nearby university. With barely conscious determination, I cultivated friendship with another human person for the first time in my religious life. To express as vividly as I could my "break" with my community the friendship was with a "secular": a neo-catholic, someone quite unconventional. Vatican II had only begun to be implemented, remember, so this friendship would need to be cultivated quietly, "in the shadows."

Now let us leave this canvas for a while and uncover the other one. I had progressed from vigorously declared "detachment" from human beings to deliberate "wasting" of time in languid drives around country places and long listening bouts devoted to electronic music of Koto or Curlew River. What had happend to my understanding of the first great commandment? Something weird and wonderful, despite all appearances to the contrary. I come now to what was to be for me the greatest gift of the renewal that followed Vatican II — freedom from (what I would never have called it until I began writing this account) superstition. Let me explain. I had a subtle but profound and pervasive sense that unless I "prayed," that is, spent some time in the motions of prayer or reading in the chapel which I carefully labeled "prayer," — *bad things would happen.* I was not driven to prayer at this time because I felt a profound need for God, nor because I saw or felt that without him I was less human, but rather because if I did not pray, I laid myself open to the traps and tricks of an unfriendly universe. This was not conscious, or course.

My notion of prayer, despite all that I knew intellectually and taught, with a great deal of success to others, was magical. One fine evening I went with several others to a lecture by a young Dominican who was soon to leave the priesthood. For me he was a tremendous source of light. He made clear that nature has its own virtualities; that these virtualities go their own way and are available to be used by the believer and unbeliever alike; that belief (according to him) had nothing to do with the success or failure of our human enterprises. Somehow, he said, "God's in his heaven — and let him stay there; all's well with the world." He insisted that we human beings are in charge down here, are meant to do things and run things, and that grace and the spernatural are *not* involved in all this. I understood him to say the exact oposite of what is implied in the teaching of Karl Rahner about the "supernatural existential." He seemed to be affirming *in a freeing way* the exaggerated distinction between the natural and supernatural that has plagued scholasticism's teaching on grace since the 16th century.

I would like you to understand the crooked thinking from which this young man delivered me. What he made clear was that God really respected my freedom, really left me free to love or not. Somehow for the first time I *felt* that I was being offered a gift — not having an unwelcome largesse thrust on me — and that I did not need to "love" God in order to avoid angering him and therefore calling down dreadful consequences on myself. Rather, I could love him as he loved me — "of free grace," "without charge." For the frst time in my life I felt I had a choice. Also involved in this was an urgent affirmation of the goodness of nature, of its validity for leading me to joy if honestly listened to and followed. For the first time in language which shook me to the roots he was introducing me to Rahner, who says:

> First, grace *is* experienced, but not as grace; it is indistinguishable from
> the stirrings of the transcendence of the human spirit. And, second, a

person's experience of the supernatural call and address of God is never
a perception or grasp of an object; grace appears rather as an unthematic
horizon of transcendence.

Strangely enough, I had reconciled myself to a supernatural and beatific
vision many years earlier, but I had never, never felt the enormous
gratitude, the flood of tenderness toward God which now arose in my
heart when I learned that I had been ordained from creation and in and
by my creation to God himself. I am not sure why exactly I responded
in this way. I know only that the realization of the nobility of human
nature, of its innate possibilities, of the "natural" gift of the spirit to each
of us filled me with fresh life, with tremendous happiness and with a
new openness to other human beings. I had a new respect for and acceptance of them. I do not mean I was converted overnight from all my
suspicions and arrogance. No. But I no longer felt I was the member of
a besieged and faintly weird but extremely privileged sect, a Roman
Catholic. No. I was simply a member of the human race, all equally loved
by God and intended by him for unbelievable joy.

I felt ashamed of the belligerence, the spirit of rebellion and revenge
with which I had cultivated the unsuspecting and affectionate young
woman who was my "friend." I understood that others were not mean,
were not objects — even of "charity" — but were mysterious and marvelous co-workers with me along the road to incredible fulfillment.

I say I "understood." I mean I began to see, to glimpse. I had miles to
go, many deserts to cross before I came to peaceful prayer and before I
came simply and gladly to love another human person. I went by fits
and starts. I continued to struggle with what I stubbornly asserted was
the *contradiction* between the commands of love of God and love of neighbor. I could not seem to accept our Lord's "The second is like the first."

Then in September 1983 I attended a workshop led by Jean Houston.
The theme was the search for the Grail. The aim was personal transformation. The framework and mystic background was the Parsifal story.
Two questions got to the heart of the matter. First, where is the Grail?
(The answer: within our heart, our human nature bears the Grail — the
sum of all that is, God.) The second question is: What ails you, uncle?
(an example of compassion, of the command to love). Do you see the
essential union between the questions and love, which is their answer?
I was in a group listening with open mind and open heart to another
woman whose Miraculous Medal was a huge silver amulet bearing the
image of the goddess Minerva. Never would this have occurred without
Vatican II. Vatican II had made it possible. I had grasped the possibility.

At the very end of this workshop I came not only to see but to experience
that to love God and neighbor are one. Let me describe for you the final
crucial hours of the workshop. Parsifal (after many misadventures) was
near the end of his search for the Grail. In Jean Houston's account of
the tale, he meets a lady on a mule. Then a storm arises, but beyond it,
in the darkness of the early dusk a light is evident. From the castle
beyond, in the midst of the woods, comes a glow. It is the Grail! Seeing
his determination to go on, the lady gives Parsifal the mule and a magic

ring. As he moves on toward a half-bridge made of crystal, he meets a knight who announces a tournament which cannot be reached except by crossing this very bridge.

What does Parsifal do? He rides to the end of the half-bridge. As he begins to step off into the depths, the bridge swings around, fastens itself on the opposite shore and bears him safely across. He arrives at the tournament, wins all the prizes and finds his beloved Blanche Fleur awaiting him in tent. He moves on, rides into the Grail Castle and asks the two questions. The lady who had given him the mule returns: She is the daughter of Merlin the archetype of wholeness, the invisible guardian of the grailseeker. All now is light, music, flowers, joy.

What of ourselves? What does the half-bridge mean? We need to go to the very end of our seen possibilities, past the end-of-the-usual. We need to be available to the depths, dare to step into them. At the moment of accepting the unfamiliar, the opposite-to-the-usual in our nature. We can move on; indeed that opposite is often the only way forward, to the Grail Castle. Only by daring the great turn-around, only by crossing the line of fire, can I come into the castle, find again my answers to the questions, and be united to the beloved of my soul.

The workshop ended with this exercise: Parsifal had asked the question: Where is the Grail? (He had accepted the challenge of finding the source, the inexhaustible treasure, God within). He had become compassionate, able to ask the second question: Uncle, what ails thee? And so had won permanent union with Blanche Fleur.

And ourselves? Each person received a lighted candle. Across the center of the room was stretched another line of candles. If one felt that she had indeed come to recognize the Grail, knew in her heart where the treasured beloved was, one could move slowly forward, cross the line of fire into the magic realm of union with the Beloved, sit quietly absorbing the flame until one gently blew it out. The external flame had gone within. One was surrounded by one's beloved. One had come home.

So I carried my candle, knowing God was drawing me when suddenly he made it clear that he was not alone. Only by embracing all those whom he held in his heart, all my human brothers and sisters, could I be absorbed in him. I could not exclude anyone, because to do so would be to not-be-with-him. And so the arms of my heart opened and to my human loves I said: "Come, let us be at home." And so we were.

What has renewal meant for me? The discovery of the unity of life, of love, of wholeness. God is indeed my dearest treasure, but he does not separate himself from all his creatures to whom he has willed nothing less than himself.

Open Windows, Open Doors

Carol Coston

Sister Carol Coston, a Dominican, is executive director and board member of Network, a Catholic social justice lobby. She currently chairs the Adrian Dominican Corporate Investment Board and has served on the boards of Common Cause, Bread for the World, New Directions, the National Center for Urban Ethnic Affairs, the Interreligious Task Force on U.S. Food Policy and the Religious Committee for ERA. She has a master's degree in speech and drama from the Catholic University and previously worked as an educator in Michigan, Puerto Rico and Florida.

In medias res — February, 1984 — how would I describe myself today 20 years after the renewal process began in women's congregations?

I am a feminist sister beginning my 30th year as an Adrian Dominican. I love and cherish my friends, delight in their company and need their support. I'm a social activist who needs quiet reflection times and I'm searching for a feminist spirituality that can nourish and inspire me. I have a huge reservoir of anger at injustice that is easily set off — particularly during this Reagan administration and the current papal intervention in the lives of women religious.

I just finished 11 years as a founder and first director of Network, a Catholic social justice lobby. Prior to that I taught all ages — from four-year-olds to senior citizens, from swimming to social encyclicals. I'm an active member of my congregation's investment committee and have chaired its portfolio advisory board for several years. Currently I'm engaged in a study of worker-owned cooperatives and organic farming as possibilities for my next work.

In reflecting on my personal response to the renewal within women's congregations, I find the freedom of choice to be the most significant change — choice of ministry, personal relationships, spirituality, lifestyle. Concomitant with choice is responsibility for the results.

> Fertility and choice:
> Every row dug in spring means weeks
> of labor. Plant too much and the seedlings
> choke in weeds as the warm rain soaks them.
> The goddess of abundance Habondia is also
> the spirit of labor and choice.[1]

I had experienced choice and responsibility prior to entering my community, but in the 10 years before renewal began, most choices were curtailed or were made for me by my superiors.

The whole painful and energizing renewal process which led us Adrian Dominicans to critique every part of our congregational life — rule, constitutions, original charism, customs, works, history, relationship with the hierarchical church — led me to reject much that was no longer valid or life-giving and to reaffirm or discover anew other aspects.

The women's movement, in which I participated enthusiastically, occurred simultaneously with renewal in 1960s and 1970s. Pope John XXIII used the image of opening windows in the church and letting in fresh air, but the women's movement opened doors. And as we walked through into new experiences of discovering ourselves and our shared stories, we began to develop a feminist perspective that recognized and critiqued domination wherever it operated — men over women, whites over blacks, U.S. over Third World countries, military over civilians, hierarchy over religious. At the same time women began to claim more responsibility for the shape of our world and became social change activists.

Other doors opened to the world of women artists, poets, singers, novelists, theorists and historians who began to peel away the myths and role expectations and negativity that had kept women's spirits heavy. From these women I began to experience myself as woman validated and affirmed, not belittled and negated as often happened in the institutional Catholic church. And as I discovered our lost, neglected or hidden stories I felt a pride in our foremothers in every field who dared to break with male dominance and tradition; I felt bonded with the many brave women religious who — against great odds — began new foundations or new institutes.

In my experience the women's movement was a significant shaper of renewal. Marge Piercy's poem "The Sabbath of Mutual Respect," quoted earlier, symbolizes positive aspects of both the women's movement and the renewal of religious life:

> Praise our choices, sisters, for each doorway
> open to us was taken by squads of fighting
> women who paid years of trouble and struggle,
> who paid their wombs, their sleep, their lives
> that we might walk through these gates upright.
> Doorways are sacred to women for we
> are the doorways of life and we must choose
> what comes in and what goes out. Freedom
> is our real abundance.[2]

To illustrate some of the doorways opened to me since renewal, I'd like to reflect on my activities in early 1984, the days around my 29th anniversary of entering the Adrian Dominicans. What choices and what responsibilities are represented by the following activities: writing a chapter on my friend, the late Clare Dunn, CSJ, Arizona state legislator, for a book on religious in politics; discussing financial difficulties with my living community — sisters from three other orders; eating dinner with

Maureen Kelleher, RSHM, longtime friend from beginning Network days in 1972, now finishing law school; discussing Network's participatory management with Nancy Sylvester, IHM, current coordinator, as we drove to North Carolina; visiting two black-managed, worker-owned businesses invested in by the Adrian Dominicans — Workers Owned Sewing Machine Company in Windsor, North Carolina, and Eastern Casket Company in Tillery; taking slides at both places for the Portfolio Advisory Board's slide show to educate the congregation on alternative investments; staying overnight with Helen Wright, SND, Network board member and director of an ecumenical emergency aid and referral center in Raleigh; swimming at the YMCA.

The events around that anniversary period captured most of the significant changes I've experienced and will provide a framework for the rest of this personal and historical reflection:

1. The freedom to choose a ministry or significant work;
2. The freedom to choose a living community, personal friendships and a life-style that supports the ministry;
3. The challenge to understand the connections among all forms of domination and the responsibility to try to transform them;
4. The need to develop a feminist spirituality that integrates all of the above.

Although I was taught history as a linear progression of events marching forward from war or from technical breakthrough to industrial revolution, I prefer to view my personal "herstory" as more of a spiral — with each pass of the spiral growing out of past experiences but adding new dimensions. I want to share the connections in my own life before, during and after renewal and relate these to the renewal spiral within my congregation.

My first significant ministerial choice was to become a sister and on February 2, 1955, at age 19, I joined the Adrian Dominicans — a choice I have never regretted and a real doorway that continues to open for me.

It was a totally new life-style. Having gone to a public high school in order to be on the swimming team and to join a sorority, and then to Florida State University, I had had no contact with sisters for years. Nor did I have experiences similar to most of my classmates, such as active involvement in a parish, attending ethnic churches, or even living where there were lots of Catholics. In West Palm Beach, Florida, there was only one Catholic church, almost all my friends were Protestant and my father professed no formal religion.

I had a full and extremely active high school life — almost daily swimming and diving practice, dancing lessons three times weekly, leadership roles in the sorority, lots of dating and overnight slumber parties with my girl friends.

I won two diving championships in my senior year — Florida State High School and Senior Women's Amateur Athletic Union (AAU). When I graduated I received the best girl athlete and the most valuable girl athlete awards.

My academic life was secondary and not as interesting as these other activities, but because of a solid foundation from St. Ann's Grade School, I achieved fairly good grades with minimal effort.

At Florida State University in 1953-54, I remained physically active but studied more and made the dean's list. I was also invited to join two well-respected sororities, was chosen cheerleader, did some diving for the Tarpon Club, performed two acts — acrobatics and the Spanish Web — in the Florida State Circus "Flying High," dated frequently and was unhappy most of the time!

Despite these achievements and affirmations I felt directionless and could not accept what I perceived to be the prevailing standards of the other young women — their lives seemed to revolve around their weekend date, or their "steady," or their plans to get married. Few seemed to have any ambitions for a career or challenging work.

During that year I became attracted to religious observances. I often went to early mass and thoroughly immersed myself in a class on St. Paul. I felt an incompleteness about my life and was finally able to identify this as not having a strong relationship with God. It became clear to me that what I really wanted to do was to learn to love God and because I felt I needed someone to show me how, the logical thing to do was to become a nun. That decision was clear and quick and because I was so grateful for some inner clarity after being quite miserable, I wanted to leave immediately and "join up."

After 19 years in Florida surrounded by the ocean and sunshine and spending a good bit of my life in a bathing suit or leotards, it was somewhat disorienting to enter the dark, imposing Dominican motherhouse in Michigan in February and put on black from top to toe. My father had once been featured in a plumbing magazine for his creative painting of a boiler room and its pipes in bright primary colors, so I was particularly distressed walking through dreary underground passages looking at rows of exposed pipe somewhat haphazardly covered with dull gray insulation.

Even though my physical surroundings were different, I did not find either the postulancy or the novitiate traumatizing or even disagreeable. Having had so much freedom and independence prior to entering, I was amenable to letting go and throwing myself into becoming a good Dominican sister. I liked living in community, being intellectually challenged and learning the order's traditions.

But what I did find traumatizing was teaching second grade in Grosse Pointe, Michigan, my first year out of novitiate. I had fantasized about being sent to Puerto Rico or the Dominican Republic, so I resented being in a rich Detroit suburb teaching generally well-to-do seven-year-olds. Nor was I prepared to deal with six subjects, several to be taught at three different levels, and over 60 pupils. No training was given as to how to design, duplicate and explain an interesting enough bit of seat work that could challenge the bright, be at least understood by the others, and last long enough for me to collect the following: milk money for the week, donations for the pastor's Christmas present, pledges for the Holy

Childhood pagan baby fund, grubby dollar bills and sticky change from the chocolate candy-bar drive, plus excuses for absentees. Nor was I warned that even during these omnibus tax collections second graders will choose to throw up — sometimes right on your desk!

During that dreadful year I had diarrhea every Monday morning and lost 17 pounds. I pleaded with God to release me from this burden (I had recurring nightmares of an endless series of second grade classrooms stretching painfully into my future). "I know I'm doing your will; I realize it is a privilege to teach these immortal souls; yes, I recall that you said, 'Let the little children come to me,' but did they throw up on you or have a nose bleed all over your white habit and newly starched veil?"

The only mutually rewarding relationship I established with a student that year was with Doug — a repeater. What he lacked in reading ability he more than compensated for in practical skills. I put him in charge of "throw-ups." At the first sound of a gag Doug shot out of his seat, sped to the janitor's closet, returned triumphantly with the bucket of green compound, broom and dust pan, and with an efficiency I can still admire, cleaned it up with a flourish. He was the only professional in the room.

Luckily, the next year I was sent to Guayama, Puerto Rico, where — without a B.A. yet — I taught freshman, junior and senior English, biology, general science and sophomore religion. I also ran the speech league, directed the Christmas pageant and was the only driver to doctors' offices and large grocery stores 40 miles away. To cap this outlandish schedule I had to squeeze in two university classes for my degree — Roman lyrical poetry and "Catholic" logic. Evidently, my existing logic credits from Florida State were somehow not acceptable. Recognizing the impossibility of doing any of this competently, I escaped into English translations of French writers such as Claudel, Mauriac, Peguy, Bernanos and the Maritains — reading being one of the few choices I had any control over.

Overall though, I loved my three years in Puerto Rico and one summer in the Dominican Republic. My spirituality was affected as was my polit-ical consciousness. The Puerto Ricans' and Dominicans' attitudes toward God seemed to be more open, trusting and natural; their religious cere-monies more lively and dramatic. Church was viewed as God's house and if God is really our father, why wouldn't you greet each other joyfully and talk to each other in "our father's house"?

My closest friends were native Dominican and Puerto Rican sisters and I began to resent the cultural imperialism being directed toward them and their traditions. Some sisters wanted to run Colegio San An-tonio like a U.S. military academy with undue emphasis on marching, straight lines, silence and order at all costs. The Puerto Ricans' natural vivacity and warmth was often squelched. And sometimes in the convent the native sisters' accents or speech mannerisms were mocked even though English was their second language and many of us spoke only one. I also observed an encroaching cultural invasion at its worst, in my opinion, as U.S. films, clothing styles, cold drinks and magazines poured into the island. Later I learned how U.S. businesses got all kinds of tax breaks and special treatment to bring business in and then pulled out when it was no longer to their advantage.

In 1958, following my first teaching year in Puerto Rico, I spent the summer in the Dominican Republic. This opened two more doorways in my life — living in a country ruled by a military dictator and learning the negative effects of U.S. foreign policy on Third World nations.

The first thing I noticed were the traffic control measures that greatly inhibited free movement by the civilians: road blocks, check points at all major highways, restrictions against headlights at night, and lots of raised mounds in the roads — sardonically labeled "dead soldiers." The second obvious curtailment was massive censorship not only of personal mail but also negative articles about Trujillo or his family in magazines. *Time* would arrive with holes cut out of the pages. I also noticed how guarded people were in talking about the political situation. As North Americans used to openly criticizing our government, we had to learn to be more cautious and to understand that indiscreet conversations could be dangerous to our friends.

Subsequent to that summer I twice returned to the Dominican Republic, read a lot about it and continued discussing the political situation with our sisters who lived and worked there. As a result of walking through this first doorway of political consciousness I learned two things about U.S. foreign policy which, unfortunately, continue to exist today: We will tolerate the most outrageous and violent dictators as long as they do not ally themselves with the Soviet Union or Cuba; and we have no qualms about interfering in the internal affairs of Third World nations, including their electoral process, if it is suits our "national interest."
I began to understand the deep anger and resentment toward U.S. policy by Latin Americans. We neither trusted nor allowed them to manage their own destiny, and by our intervention assaulted their national pride, self-determination and dignity. (And today our foreign policy makes the same mistake in not allowing Nicaragua to determine its own form of government, in interferring against a popular resistance in El Salvador, in supporting right-wing regimes such as in Guatemala which kill, torture and maim their own citizens.)

In the late 1960s, when I was teaching at Tampa Catholic High School, the first effects of religious renewal were felt. Although the initial community discussions about a new constitution were often painful, I personally became excited about the process. We really struggled to express ourselves openly, admit differences in perceptions or values, deal with hidden tensions which were blocking good communication, and be open to the risks of change. During those years we crisscrossed the state frequently in order to have cross-fertilization with other Adrians.

It seems to me that three aspects of the Dominican tradition fostered a personal freedom and creativity and thus provided a positive environment for change in our congregation:

1. The emphasis on study and the intellectual life;

2. The validity of dispensation from the rule for the sake of the mission;

3. The pattern of traveling to geographically dispersed missions that began with St. Dominic and continued in our own congregation.

Study was encouraged. It was assumed that you would get college degrees. Since we ran three of our own colleges many sisters obtained their Ph.D.'s and then were able to teach other Adrian Dominicans. For example, by 1983, of the 1,537 members in our congregation, 1526 had B.A.'s, 1144 M.A.'s and 94 Ph.D.'s. I believe that these intellectual opportunities helped us be more open to the new ideas of renewal.

Second, when St. Dominic started our order he wanted to insure maximum freedom to serve as the needs arose so he left a cloistered community and sought for a more flexible rule. Dominicans are taught that the rule is for the sake of the mission. For example, the earlier constitutions called for living in community, but if it was necessary for an individual to live alone because of the nature of the work, that person could be connected in name to a local community even though not living there.

And finally, the geographic dispersal of our sisters resulted in a group of over 2,000 women who had had diverse experiences. We had been sent across the U.S. from Washington, D.C., to California and from Michigan to Florida. We served in the Caribbean, the Philippines, the Bahamas, Africa and Peru. Many of those who had worked and lived in poor inner-city areas or Third World countries brought a particularly different perspective to prechapter discussions and to chapter decisions — more analytical, more challenging, and more critical of U.S. foreign and domestic policy. They had heard the "cries of the poor" and wanted congregational goals to reflect an option for the most oppressed.

With all this ferment taking place across the country, it is no wonder that our renewal chapter of 1968 was pretty bloody! The variety and intensity of perspective added to it — what to change and how fast to change. An important result of the deliberations was to support the principle of subsidiarity — that is, making as many decisions as possible at the local level — and to free the leadership to support and encourage the growth of the individual sister. Prior to this time the general councilors all had other full-time jobs and were thereby hindered in their ability to give advice and counsel, thus leaving an enormous amount of power and responsibility in one woman's hands — the mother general. (We have since dispensed with this title, to the relief of all of us with participatory or pacifist leanings.)

Because a congregation-wide study that would provide new data was in process, few enactments were made at this chapter. Nevertheless, an emphasis was placed on serving the poor, whether in inner-city areas o in the missions. The first strains of the strong social justice emphasis in subsequent chapters were beginning to be heard by 1969.

In 1970, my personal choice to leave a satisfying teaching experience at Tampa Catholic was influenced by hearing the cries of the civil rights struggle. I had grown up in segregated Florida surrounded by "Whites

Only" signs and "For Colored" drinking fountains, train waiting rooms, bathrooms and divided seating on buses. As a child I was vaguely uneasy about this. I loved the few weeks in second grade when the black students were bused over to prepare for first communion with us and then disappointed when we never saw them again afterward. In junior high I read copies of *Ebony* magazine brought to me by the black woman, Sally Williams, who had worked for my family since I was six weeks old. Sally and I would talk while she ironed and from her I began to learn the personal and structural effects of racism.

In 1963, I had been sent to Catholic University for my master's degree during the summers in speech and drama. In deciding on a theses topic I knew it had to be on something personally relevant and not just an academic requirement. I chose "Black Theatre in the 1960s" and compared the plays to the Kerner Comission's report on violence and civil disorders. I was then able to use these sources and insights in teaching religion, speech, English and forensics with the hope that my students would become more open and less prejudiced. In fact, a survey done by another teacher on racial attitudes in the student body showed a significant and positive difference in the students I had taught.

Even though I confronted racism through teaching and by encouraging all the black students to participate in the National Forensic League to better prepare them for leadership roles, I felt I needed to do more. I then organized a tutoring program for black grade schools, invited black leaders to dinner at the convent and to speak to the students, showed films on the voting struggles in the South and the viciousness of the Klan.

In 1964, my mother started an educational center in Boynton Beach. She had originally planned to work with about a dozen three-and four-year-old black children using some Montessori methods and other techniques to improve verbal and observational skills. Within a week she had 40 children and several volunteer mothers. When it was apparent that the church basement room was going to be too small, additional funds were procured to provide adequate space.

I went with her to Washington and made the rounds of several government agencies and children's advoacacy groups. Her educational approach preceded the Head Start program but eventually money for salaries was located through the Office of Economic Opportunity. Today the Child Care Center serves amost 90 children and plans are in progress for another building to expand the service. Some of the original volunteers are now salaried senior staff.

I spent time at the center during my home visits and began to learn more about the economic, employment and housing problems in black neighborhoods. But as I wanted to be more personally involved full-time, I asked my provincial for permission to work directly in the black community. She agreed to it if I could find a suitable job. In September of 1970 I began work as an administrator for the Department-of-Labor-funded Neighborhood Youth Corps, a program for high school dropouts. I tried to find high school equivalency and work training placements for black teenagers, the majority of whom were single young women with children.

In 1971 Kathleen Gannon, OP, and I moved into a newly built low-income housing project sponsored by the Kiwanis Club of Fort Lauderdale and the Methodists' urban ministry program. In exchange for reduced rent, we were asked to be available for social services after work and on weekends.

While these experiences opened new doorways and gave me some vicarious insights I realized that there is no way a white person can ever internalize the struggle to live as a black person in a racist society. And I made many mistakes in my attitudinal approach to the work — too much service-oriented and not enough empowerment; too much of "I'll fix it up for you" by badgering the welfare office or pulling strings through friendly contacts within the system, and not enough analysis of why these economic discrepancies continue to exist. We also questioned the validity of our using an available apartment in the housing project when we could have easily found other housing.

But through this Kathy and I did begin to learn the need for public policy changes and institutional reforms. We began testifying before the county commissioners on open housing ordinances, helped organize social justice forums in the diocese and worked in coalition with black and white religious and civic groups to open the voting registration process to make it more physically accessible to the black community and convenient for working people.

Then in December, 1971, Kathy was invited to a nuns' meeting in Washington, D.C., to talk about political involvement for sisters. It sounded so intriguing that I tagged along on her invitation and as a result became vulnerable to another life choice — Network.

The spiral image is especially apt for this next phase of my life because my experiences in Puerto Rico, the Dominican Republic, the black community and local politics prepared me to see the need for more just national policy; the open-placement concept in the congregation challenged me to choose where I might best serve; and the availability of the Adrian leadership encouraged me to take a risk.

The meeting at which Network was founded took place at Trinity College, December 17-19, 1971. At the final session, 47 sisters from 21 states voted by an overwhelming majority to form a network for political education and action — to be called simply, The Network. I volunteered to be on a steering committee that would lead us to the next steps. At the next meeting, I was asked to become the first staff member. I said that I had to call my prioress and provincial first and consult with them. Both immediately encouraged me to go ahead. Later a sister at the meeting commented on the rapidity of their decision: "If it had been my congregation I would have been told to write up a proposal and submit it to the ministerial needs committee who would meet in three months and then send it on to the subsidy committee which met two months later who would then send a recommendation to the general council which met once a month!"

The decision to start Network took place within the context of larger changes within the whole church. Sisters, inspired by the energy and new visions from chapters of renewal, were looking for extensions of their traditional ministries. They had seen the power of being organized. They had begun to get involved in local politics. Those who worked with poor people in the U.S. or Third World countries recognized the negative effects of public policy on the lives of the poor. They were ready to respond to the signs of the times found in their own experiences and to the challenges in the 1971 documents — the synod statement *Justice in the World* and Pope Paul VI's *Call to Action* both of which called for changes in political and economic structures.

The growth of Network from an idea to an organization is an example of cooperation and shared resources. Network has become a registered lobby in congress; decribes itself as a "Catholic social justice lobby"; has a membership of 7,000 — religious and lay, women and men; a paid staff of nine; an annual budget over $300,000; and is organized by congressional districts throughout the United States.

In its first years Network educated, organized and lobbied on issues such as: cutting off funds for the Vietnam war; reducing foreign aid to countries violating human rights; reducing the defense budget and increasing funds for social service; supporting the Equal Rights Amendment; establishing an independent public corporation to provide legal services for the poor; raising the federal minimum wage.

We viewed all of these actions as consonant with the Hebrew prophets' cries for justice and release from oppressive bonds and with Jesus' words in Matthew's gospel about feeding the hungry and sheltering the homeless. We also recognized similar challenges in the church's social encyclicals. We saw our work as a political ministry that tried to change unjust structures.

Network has never had the kind of political clout achieved by large sums of money at campaign time or by tens of thousands of members ready to spring to action. We have been able to make some inroads because of our unique constituency and the nature of our political agenda. We are not perceived as working for our own "special interests" but rather for the interests of those most marginalized and underrepresented.

The following newspaper headlines capture some of the media's perception of Network:

"Sister Uses Gospel Values in Washington, DC Post," Judy Ball, *Catholic Telegraph*, Cinncinati, Nov. 30, 1973

"Unorthodox Lobbyists Make Politics Ministry," Patricia Anstett, Dubuque, Dec. 30, 1976

"Nuns' Group Heeds the Calling to Congress' Not-So-Holy Halls," Barbara O'Reilley, *The Morning News,* Wilmington, July 19, 1978

"Catholic Lobby Organization Fighting for Social Change," Richard Starnes, *Pittsburgh Press,* August 2, 1978

"Priests, Nuns, Brothers Contribute to Leftist Lobby," Paul A. Fisher, *The Wanderer,* St. Paul, Sept. 11, 1980

At the same time Network was establishing itself as a credible lobby on Capitol Hill religious congregations were establishing justice goals in their general chapters. In the Adrian Dominican congregation this took place in 1974. A movement had been growing throughout the community that we needed sharper challenges in the general area of justice and specifically in the area of investments. I could sense that the time was ripe for both of these when about 20 Adrian Dominicans who were attending the June 1974 Network seminar met to discuss and to strategize for the upcoming chapter. Their enthusiasm for these objectives was a harbinger of the final chapter enactments in August, 1974:

GOAL 1:   The involvement of each Adrian Dominican sister in an educative process in social justice as an essential element of her gospel commitment for the purpose of working toward a more just society.

GOAL 2:   The evaluation of our ministries and the institutions in which they are exercised in the light of the gospel imperative of justice.

GOAL 4:   The evaluation of our congregational investments in relation to the gospel social principles and the identification of means to effect change toward justice in the policies and operations of corporations in which we hold investments.

As a result of these enactments an all-out effort in justice education began, but it was not greeted with universal enthusiasm. There were pockets of resistance. In retrospect I can see that some of the "justice advocates" contributed to this resistance as they bulldozed their way into people's consciousnesses and demanded that everyone be as upset at they over the dismal shape of the world!

In response to Goal 4 the Portfolio Advisory Board was established in 1975. I was asked to serve on it and in that capacity began to attend meetings of the Interfaith Center on Corporate Responsibility in New York and the annual shareholder meetings of corporations in which we held stock.

To speak out at annual meetings as I did at General Electric, Emerson Electric, and Gulf & Western is to experience being a minority voice with an unpopular message. The only leverage we seem to have is that the corporations dislike interruptions at their carefully orchestrated annual accountings and they don't like negative publicity, especially from religious groups.

In 1978, I was elected delegate to the chapter and served on the finance committee. Here we discussed the dilemma we faced as a congregation having a criterion of justice and at the same time gaining a significant portion of our income from large corporations whose policies and practices are often unjust. And like most other congregations we had an aging population with more members going into retirement than entering. The responsibility to provide for their basic needs plus infirmary costs weighed heavily on the delegates. This financial situation was exacerbated because of years of minimal — and often unjust — salaries received from schools and parishes, coupled with almost non-existent pension plans.

The delegates recongized that if more sisters could earn non-subsidy salaries then this income could offset some of the need for high interest on investment income and would thus free more funds for alternative investments in credit unions, housing projects or worker-owned businesses at a lower interest rate. While the final directives from the chapter reflected both these approaches, they also affirmed the Portfolio Advisory Board's continuing work in monitoring the existing portfolio according to criteria for socially responsible investments.

During the four years between the 1978 and 1982 chapters the Portfolio Advisory Board continued to attend dialogues with corporate managers and to make presentations at shareholder meetings. I went on a research trip to the Dominican Republic to learn about the effect of Gulf & Western on the economy. Our group met with economists, politicians, sugar plantations owners, reporters, a bishop, Gulf & Western officials and sugar cane workers. I saw some really appalling living conditions, especially for the Haitian workers. In a camp we walked through mud and garbage, saw one shower for dozens of workers, stood in rooms about six feet by ten feet that housed six grown men, and witnessed them doing their cooking in a little alley between buildings while trying to stay out of the rain. Then we attend Gulf & Western's annual meeting at the Breaker's Hotel in Palm Beach, where all the well-dressed and well-fed shareholders could sit comfortably in nice chairs on a parquet floor and look out a beautiful picture window at the ocean and the sea gulls. The contrast was sobering.

The questions Nancy Sylvester, IHM, and I raised about wages and the observations we made about the living conditions were not well received by either management or the assembled shareholders.

Other Portfolio Advisory Board members had similar experiences, and as we reflected together on what we wanted to say to the 1982 chapter, we all agreed that we were unable to effect real change in corporate structure and policy. We felt that we should continue to speak the truth as we discerned it, but without any illusions that corporations would change unless it was profitable for them to do so.

We had had good experiences in investing the $100,000 allotted to us for alternative investments and recommended increased efforts in this area. We further advised that energies and research be directed toward the creation of just and viable alternatives to the present economic system. These projects — housing, solar energy, worker owned co-ops, etc. — could provide employment for ourselves and others, as well as just investment opportunities for our monies.

The 1982 chapter endorsed all these suggestions along with a directive to divest ourselves of any stock we had in the top 100 Department of Defense contractors.

Since the chapter the PAB has continued to invest in alternatives such as:

Federation of Appalachian Housing Enterprises, Berea, Ky.
Visitation Community Credit Union, St. Louis, Mo.
Family Homes Cooperative, Beckley, W. V.

Industrial Cooperative Association, Somerville, Mass.
Workers' Owned Sewing Company, Windsor, N.C.
Church of Messiah Housing Coalition, Detroit, Mich.
Cincinnati Land Cooperative, Cincinnati, Ohio.
Southern Mutual Help Association, Jeanerette, La.
Eastern Casket Company, Tillery, N.C. and
Dungannon Sewing Cooperative, Dungannon, Va.

My two major ministries now are Network and the Portfolio Advisory Board. Both continue to be supported and encouraged by the general chapter enactments and both continue to open doors to exciting but often disconcerting and painful experiences.

As my life spiraled through the 1960s I became aware of the negative effects of racism and in the 1970s I began to see the classism inherent in the economic discrimination being practiced by both multinationals and U.S. foreign policy. But what I'm most aware of, all the time, is sexism, which cuts across all other forms of domination. I find it in church structures, economic systems, political parties, educational institutions, every profession and in any culture that now exists. Women are perceived as less than men in each of these areas and suffer accordingly.

In attending the International Women's Year Conference in Houston in 1977 and the Mid-Decade Conference in Copenhagen in 1980, I realized how many other women also recognize what an Indian woman described as the "anatomy of subordination" — a kind of skeletal structure that can be covered with different forms of domination while the pattern of control and exploitation is the same.

All my reading, writing and speaking about women's experiences, coupled with working on the Equal Rights Amendment and women's roles within the Catholic church, has not only provided exciting and energizing insights into our past achievements and future potentials, but has also developed a painfully heightened consciousness of the lies we've been told and the opportunities denied. I struggle not to let the resulting anger control me but it's always there — like a low-grade fever from the "dis-ease" of social justice. I'm reminded of a song by Margie Adam: "I've got a fury deep inside my very soul and it's going to eat me up or let me go."[3]

And in an effort not to get eaten up, I, and many of my friends, continue to search for ways to develop a feminist spirituality that reverences and recalls women's experiences, celebrates our life passages, nurtures our spirits and fuels our courage. One such effort was the initiation of staff reflection days, which helped us touch the religious and spiritual motivations important to us personally and allowed us to share these in an accepting environment. We also developed rituals around Epiphany, contract-signings and staff departures. Later, at the legislative seminars we tried to incorporate feminist readings and music into eucharistic and other celebrations.

Sisters Against Sexism, a group whose name was suggested by Elisabeth Schussler Fiorenza, meets in Washington. It provides another experience of feminist ritual. Each woman brings something for the shared meal — her gift to the group. The hostesses plan the ritual, which has taken many unique and creative forms. In this way leadership is shared and rotated. We usually end in a circle symbolizing horizontal relationships rather than hierarchical ones — Sarah's circle rather than Jacob's ladder.

I want to conclude this spiraling narrative by returning to Network because it epitomizes my response to both the women's movement and renewal.

I am often asked: "Has Network been successful?" A glance at its current legislative agenda — human rights here and abroad, reduced defense budget, non-intervention in Central America, a just immigration policy — shows that we generally lose on legislation more often than we win — at least in today's political climate. But I do believe Network has made a significant contribution in educating thousands of people, especially women religious, in the whole political process and the relationship of public policy to the needs of the poorest in our society. And the staff and board have created an organizational style that is a form of participatory management from a feminist perspective.

My reflections on what Network has meant to me personally since 1971 focus more on the women I have met over these years — the staff and board, my living communities, participants in the annual legislative seminars, and the local activists I've met in the 32 states in which I gave talks or workshops.

As I recall these women I'm struck by their richness and diversity, their common anger at injustice, and their sensitivity and humor in the midst of continuous struggle. I'm reminded of a section in Marilyn French's novel *The Women's Room,* which portrays the personal renewal of several contemporary women:

> I hear Martha's voice often as I walk along the beach. And others' too — Lily, Val, Kyla. I sometimes think I've swallowed every other woman I ever knew. My head is full of voices. They blend with the wind and the sea as I walk the beach, as if they were disembodied forces of nature, a tornado whirling around me. I feel as if I were a medium and a whole host of departed spirits has descended on me clamoring to be let out.[4]

Attending that first meeting in December, 1971, opened up a roomful of voices for me. I had never experienced so many strong, energetic and assertive women in the same place at one time. As we introduced ourselves the range of involvements and experiences was impressive. (This ritual of sharing recent experiences has become the opening of every Network board meeting and I'm always moved by the diversity, creativity and just plain doggedness represented in our common desire to take responsibility for our planet and its inhabitants.)

The friendship, inspiration and support I've received from all these *compañeras* — these "squads of fighting women" — is the most cherished outcome of my original choice to start Network. And I hope always to feel encircled by them and others who share similar values and vision, because to continue to open these doors is a risk. To keep feeling responsible for the public policy decisions in our country is a burden. To have the "dis-ease" of a social justice conscience is to carry inside a constantly nagging feeling that all is *not* right with the world.

The feminist singer Carole Etzler begins one song with "Sometimes I wish my eyes hadn't been opened."[5] But our eyes have been opened and there's no turning back. *Adelante!* Through the doors *and* the windows!

Notes

1. Marge Piercy, *The Moon is Always Female,* (New York: Alfred A. Knopf, 1980), pp. 104-107.

2. Ibid.

3. Margie Adam, *Margie Adam, Songwriter,* Berkeley: Pleiades Records, 1976.

4. Marilyn French, *The Women's Room*, New York: Simon and Schuster, 1977.

5. Carole Etzler, *Sometimes I Wish*, Atlanta: Sisters Unlimited, 1976.

Finding a Founder

Dorothy Vidulich

Dorothy Vidulich is a Sister of St. Joseph of Peace and a co-member of the Sisters of Loretto. She works as an agent for change in church and social structures. For the past 10 years she has been coordinating justice and peace ministry for the Sisters of Peace. She is currently Communication Coordinator of NETWORK, a Catholic social justice lobby.

In 1952 I entered a group of women religious then known as the Sisters of St. Joseph of Newark at their Englewood Cliffs, New Jersey, novitiate. This decision was preceded by years of searching for meaning in life and trying to integrate the traditional Catholic values I had been taught at home and in school into an experience of God that would somehow spill over into the lives of others. Seven years of social work in New York City combined with evening college classes had plunged me into the realities of the psychological and economic suffering of many people. I also experienced first hand the premium placed on higher education as I struggled to accomplish a B.S. degree from courses at Fordham and Seton Hall universities.

Throughout these years, I was searching for a grasp of the mystical, the unknown mystery associated with God. Long hours of travel by rail from the Jersey suburbs to New York each day allowed much time for introspective analysis of how to make the most of a given lifetime. I avidly read volumes on the spiritual life, ranging from Teresa of Avila to our contemporary mystic, Thomas Merton.

His *Seven Storey Mountain* was subway reading and in many ways guided my vocational decision. My Jesus-and-me spirituality thrived on daily mass (sometimes two a day!), rosary, novenas, visits to the Blessed Sacrament. The transition to religious life was not difficult, because novitiate training reflcted the basic attitude I had acquired about the Catholic church as a rock of immutable truth. I readily followed the rules as a result of my conditioning that the hierarchial institutional church flawlessly pointed the way to eternal union with God.

The early 1960s saw two dramatic shifts that were to upset my tidy mentality. John XXIII changed the image of pope from a reigning monarch to a listening leader; John F. Kennedy overturned the assumption that Catholics were an outmoded minority in the United States as he became the first American Catholic president. In a unique way, this combination of two charismatic leaders created a climate of open discussion and communication among U.S. Catholics. At this deeply historical moment, my convent blinders gradually let in another new vision. As the United States becomes increasingly aware of its global responsibility to the poor, the hungry and the oppressed in Third World countries, the Second Vatican Council documents spelled out the theological underpinnings for this responsibility.

I was then the principal of a suburban Catholic high school and superior of a large community. Responsibilities within convent walls and my religious congregation had been all-important to me. But word was out among students, parishioners and sisters that dialogue and a share in decision-making were toppling over autonomous structures hitherto controlled primarily by the pastor and, to a lesser degree, by the principal-superior. Lectures gave way to small group discussions; parish councils were formed; car keys and bank books — power symbols of the local superior — became communal property as part of the initial plunge into shared responsibility. God's will as the superior's will was blowing into oblivion!

A growing sense of personalism was emerging among the sisters, and within our convent group, several became skeptical of their commitment to religious life. The unmasking of a woman who had hidden behind a habit, an assumed name (often a masculine one), and a regimented life-style often revealed a woman with a newly realized sense of maturity who felt called to make a different life coice. The pain such women felt as they left the community was often offset by their joy of self-discovery and growth in deep relationships.

The summer of 1964 marked my exodus from secondary school work and I became assistant to our new provincial, Jeanne Celeste Keaveny. When I left the novitiate, she had been my first — and only — superior. Together we had worked in challenging situations in a struggling-for-survival south Jersey school and a creative new high school in California. Jeanne was held in loving esteem by sisters who had worked and lived with her. In the worst of pre-Vatican days, she knew how to slip legalisms under the carpet and make life more human and livable for us.

Our first year together in province leadership seemed unreal and smothering. We both found ourselves doing things we didn't believe in: voting on admitting postulants we knew only superficially; working on lists that moved a sister from one work to another without any dialogue with her; listening to the complaints of pastors and bishops who wanted sisters to fill slots in school faculties to keep costs down. It became obvious the precious lives of members were mere things that had to give away to church-organized structures. And so in 1965, we abandoned the traditional model of uprooting sisters from their work and sent out a list of staff openings, inviting them to apply for new assignments.

What seemed a big step then seems insignificant now, but the shift from dependence on orders from above to emphasis on self-responsibility in making decisions was to usher in a continuum of changes all aimed at making the institution secondary to the person. Then, in October of 1965, Paul VI proclaimed *The Decree on the Adaptation and Renewal of Religious Life*. The systemic weaknesses we had already recognized were now being addressed officially. Religious institutions were mandated to re-edit constitutions, directories, custom books, so as to suppress obsolete laws. The Congregation for Religious was offering a freedom ride but it would cost dearly in pain and frustration before sisters were ready to travel in new directions.

Throughout this time, the person-controlling aspects of religious life were continually under scrutiny: baptismal names were being reclaimed; scheduled prayer gave way to more intimate forms of faith-sharing; wearing religious habits that had defined us as sacred vessels in a secular world became optional. The question of garb was always a sensitive issue and giving it up took away from some women a special identity that seemed essential to their vocation. I decided in 1968 to wear ordinary clothes. It did not seem to me that "transition garb" addressed with clarity the identity-discovery that was emerging within me.

How to form community also became a key concern. Some sincere women were painfully polarized when they saw change as the destruction of cherished symbols that had set them apart as a group in the church. The matriarchal role of superior continued to be the most divisive element. As long as the superior was equated with authority and control, sisters who sought to take initiative in developing communal life-style were at an impasse.

Rethinking the role of superior was targeted as the first major step in the renewal process. Accordingly in the summer of 1966, some 30 local superiors in the province were called together for an intensive education on how to implement the Vatican Council renewal decree. We had resource people with great vision to help us in the journey but the burden of finding the way depended on personal insights exchanged in discussions and evening kitchen-table dialogue. Together we began to see our pyramid style of leadership was a freedom-repressing structure that reflected the values of a male-dominated Catholic system designed for efficiency and control.

Somewhere in the early part of our sessions we wrestled with a section of the renewal decree stating that "the spirit and aims of each founder should be clearly recognized and faithfully preserved." Our own history as a congregation floated in murky waters. In 1888, Margaret Anna Cusack, our founder, had been pressured by Rome into abandoning her Sisters of St. Joseph of Peace community. Eventually she left the Roman Catholic Church. She was indeed the skeleton in our congregational closet, and the church of Rome had succeeded by a direct command to have both her name and her memory effaced from our history.

As fragments of Margaret Cusack's story began to unfold and books she had written were gradually resurrected, a strong sense of reclaiming her emerged among many in the group. Some responded with rage at the church system that had repressed her memory. They felt this same system fostered the legalisms that still stifled personal growth in religious life in the mid-1960s. Before the sessions ended, the lid was off, and convent routine would never again be neatly laid out by superiors.

For at least a dozen of the women gathered together, this experience was the beginning of a realization that the restrictions of a vowed commitment bolstered by the mythology of being especially chosen to be a superior, were frustrating their life fulfillment. Within two years, they were to make new choices that were to prove freeing and enriching.

For myself, I was excited about the ferment of change that began to take place in such a short space of time. I also experienced a compelling drive to fnd out more about Margaret Anna Cusack. What was in her writing, her lectures, hr political astuteness, her vision in founding our Sisters of Peace community that was such a threat to the official church in her day? The decree to return to the spirit of our original founder seemed to hold a clue to identifying ouselves anew as a congregation. In the months that followed, I was to study her intellectual and spiritual conversion. I followed the steps she traveled in being a convert to Catholicism during the Oxford Movement, to intering the Poor Clares in Kenmare, Ireland, to founding our group of women in 1884. The shadow of her inescapable presence could not but help to shape the direction of our renewal process.

Indeed, we continued to remember, to renew and to risk. There were no blueprints to follow, only the constant need to research models for experimental chapters, for presenting proposals, for voting out obsolete materials in our constitution, for developing an interim "way of life." Our province was gifted with key resource people who became life-long friends: Mary Luke Tobin, Jane Marie Richardson, Helen Sanders of the Sisters of Loretto; Anita Caspary of the Immaculate Heart Community, Los Angeles; Mary Daniel Turner, Sisters of Notre Dame de Namur; Marie Augusta Neal who directed the *Sisters' Survey*. Basic to all experimentation was the involvement of our own sisters in presenting position papers, evaluating their ministry, paticipating in workshops, introducing change in leadership models, becoming formulators of new prayer styles and initiating liturgical groups.

At the same time, the Vietnam was was launching a growing political awareness, and some sisters were motivated to march, to fast, to demonstrate for peace. For the first time, a novice would knock at the provincial door to ask if it were all right to risk arrest; or a group would come to seek support in forming a new style of small community. Often, as personalism was appreciated, individuals made painful decisions to choose new commitments. The seeds of renewal planted in the rich soil of human relationships were often flooded with bitter tears of misunderstanding.

Despite the alienation and criticism that often accompanied initiatives for change, I was convinced that in peeling away old legalisms and patterns of dependency, a new sense of freedom and maturity would appear throughout the province. When Jeanne and I left provincial leadership in 1969, we knew that experimentation was leading not to superficial changes but to a transformation of lives. The movement could not be turned around. It would only gain momentum. New energies had been released, and world concerns now challenged our concept of ministry.

The transition from seeking to create models of renewal to actually implementing them in our lives now presented itself. Rather than be recycled into traditional works, both Jeanne and I wanted to determine our choice of work and living style. As in pre-convent days, I found myself searching classified ads and trying to formulate a resume of experience. Administrative tasks, which were scarcely describable in professional terms, left gaps in my job profile. Continued education seemed a cop-out for me as I felt I needed to be independent of community financial support. Besides, I had been saturated with the evolving theologies of the 1960s in workshops, lectures, resource contacts, reading. Finally, Jeanne and I decided to accept the post of religious education coordinators in a forward-looking post-Vatican II parish.

The four years that followed could probably be labeled bleak and blah, although I can still appreciate some good things that happened. Both symbolicaly and realistically we went "down under." Parish coordinators somehow always worked in the basement, and when the task involved catechesis with public school students in a Catholic school parish, subordination of our work was keenly experienced. One good that emerged was the close links we' established with the laity — volunteer teachers and parents — who had keen insights about the need for renewal in the church and were active in assuming ladership in the parish. A special bonus was a pastor who shared feminist values in his commitment to social justice. We sensed some accomplishment in our teaching by integrating justice issues as essential to Christian living.

My involvement in the renewal process of the province was now at ebb tide. Some of this was due to personal burnout but also to a belief that the process initiated among the sisters would best move forward on their own initiative. The *Sisters' Survey* of 1967 had indicated that although we were small in membership, we were among the leading congregations in responding to renewal. However, our philosophic understanding had not yet been translated into ministerial action. I wrestled with my impatience that the pace of change was too slow and I wondered why it took so long to get rid of what seemed the obstructive paraphernalia of religious life. life.

While I valued the contributions many of our women had made in education, nursing, work with the poor and the blind, I knew that viable institutions must be always open to change. As long as we continued to let our lives be influenced by canonical legalisms that had become anachronisms, we were stifling new calls to creative response. I had to keep moving on in vision and plans for the future or become schizoid.

Our general chapter of 1970, in Nottingham, England, reinstated Margaret Anna Cusack as our founder and changed the name of our congregation from Sisters of St. Joseph of Newark to our original title, Sisters of St. Joseph of Peace. A developing constitution, "Response in the Spirit," drafted in 1969, was introduced for in-depth study. The section on goals and spirit stated: "As Mother Clare (Margaret Anna Cusack) responded willingly, responsibly and courageously to the challenges of her times, so too we must courageously face reality even if it hurts, be critical of the conditions that must be criticized, and strive not only to bandage wounds but attempt to be innovative in building a better world."

Under the leadership of newly elected president, Louise Dempsey, the next four years were to give impetus to our commitment to work for justice locally and globally. Sensitive to the need to divest ourselves of excess property, we sold our motherhouse with its acres of land and moved our administrative offices to Washington D.C. In a mysterious way, the Cusack charism continued to pervade our efforts to move beyond a mediocre Christianity in speaking the gospel of Jesus Christ to our modern world.

This founder of ours, as we continued to study her works, emerged as a woman creating the feminist frontier more than 100 years ago. Her book, *Woman's Work in Modern Society,* published in 1875, developed her concern over the oppression of women. She appealed to women to "look stern facts in the face . . . for the future of the world will be what women make of it." She spoke against the doctrine of papal infallibility promulgated by Vatican Council I, evaluating it as a patriarchal threat that gave divine power to an individual. She openly criticized members of the hierarchy who used the power of their authority to obstruct and often destroy her efforts to provide education and housing for women victimized by poverty and inequality.

Her bold stance on women's rights was to influence deeply my own awakening to feminism. I like to believe that throughout the many years of religious life, at least I was aware of our dependence on a "to-God-through-father" mentality: priests provided spiritual direction, gave retreats, heard confessions, officiated at daily liturgy. Most intolerable of all was the pastor's dominant role in having the last word in school decisions that were clearly within the domain of the principal and her faculty.

In the early 1960s, the arbitrary firing of a dedicated teacher by the pastor taught me how deeply "nun-women" were oppressed and relegated to second class roles in the church despite professional degrees and job status. Such clericalism was to become a target of resistance as nuns refused to cooperate with pastors' mandates regarding religious garb, life-style, and restrictions on implementing Vatican II theology.

Throughout the 1970s, I was influenced by feminist theologians Rosemary Radfod Ruether, Nadine Foley, Elizabeth Carroll, Margaret Farley, Elizabeth Schussler Fiorenza and other women who spoke out against sexism. The Detroit Ordination Conference in 1975 was to interpret women's ordination in the wider spectrum of women's leadership in the church and world. I continue to grow in understanding that women have a responsible role in overturning dominant structures of oppression as they replace power with mutuality and share decision-making. This is essential as we work to overcome not only sexism but racism, nationalism and militarism.

As I reflect on the personal implications of this whole renewal process over the past 15 years, I keep rejoicing that the Spirit is at work in the church and that she enabled it all to happen. My social justice consciousness grew by leaps and bounds. Our 1974 statement of direction, "Mission: Peace Through Justice," committed us as a group of women not only to challenge all oppressive situations but to be involved individually and as a community in actions to create just structures. All of us were encouraged to reconsider our ministry choice in the light of this direction and we were urged to submit proposals for its corporate implementation. Renewal took on exciting meaning fo me again as experimentation went beyond the narrow concerns of religious identity dependent on garb, prayer schedule, titled authority. A group of the sisters in the province met and proposed a shared dream: the formation of a Sisters of St. Joseph of Peace Center for Peace and Justice.

By December, 1974, Jeanne and I were coordinating the center in a junior college building erected to educate sisters in formation but by the mid-1960s a place of empty classrooms and staggering debts. We had no precedent for developing a peace and justice center. It would evolve day by day in response to the growing awareness of social problems which gnaw away at human dignity. The peacemaker's path we learned, is traveled in solidarity with like-minded groups: the Intercommunity Center for Justice and Peace in New York City; Fellowship of Reconciliation; Mobilization for Survival; Church Women United, NETWORK and many others. Together we worked on issues of world hunger, disarmament, women's equality, human rights violations in Northern Ireland and Third World countries, criminal justice, peace education, ministry for the poor, and investment of province funds to seek reform of injustices in large corporations.

In 1975 the "Call to Action" in Detroit gave us great hope as it broke down barriers between laity and religious and revealed great leadership in women and men who wanted a voice in Church decisions. We hoped that our bonding together in common pursuits would lead to new concepts of community and we shared in general disappointment when the good initiatives from that conference fell by the wayside. Nevertheless, it was a bonding experience with many wonderful people.

Our center had meanwhile moved from the college building to an old coach house, originally purchased in 1885 by Margaret Anna Cusack where the atmosphere was very much in keeping with simplicity and the struggle for peace. On Sundays, it now became a place of worship as well as a catechetical center for children. The liturgy encouraged planning and faith-sharing among the families and emphasized the social justice imperatives in the scriptural readings. These were actualized in works for the poor and hungry. The liturgy group was an important step in broadening our Sisters of Peace charism to accomplish Cusack's goal of working for peace in families. It also pointed the way to a more inclusive understanding of membership and strengthened my conviction that the continuity of religious life is dependent on extending co-membership in religious congregations beyond a celibate community to women and men who identify with their goals and will work to implement them.

In 1979, I decided to move the work of the center to our Washington D.C. administrative office, and soon I found myself in the hub of political activism. The move to Washington also led me to experiment with living alone in an apartment on the outskirts of the city. This decision has allowed me to live out my belief that the design for expanded vision of religious life means bonding with others. I also found a support group of friends and activists at he Quixote Center. Our weekly liturgical celebrations continue to link me with prophetic people.

I had not been in Washington more than a week when a mailing from Jonah House invited me to take part in Holy Week anti-nuclear actions at the Pentagon. This was the radical incentive I needed to get into th heart of understanding the non-violent resistance/persistence of "peace people". Jonah House always plans fo peace actions within a reflection, and I will not forget those days together at St. Stephen and the Incarnation Episcopal Church. Liz McAlister gently shared her journey in the anti-war movement and encouraged us to tell our stories. Phil Berrigan was low-keyed but persuasive as he explored scriptural texts on peacemaking with us.

On Holy Thursday I participated in the first of many actions: a tour through the White House and civil disobedience in which our group threw blood on the White House pillars. This action was a protest against the blood that is spilled by U.S. weapons sold to countries at war; it was a protest against the madness of nuclear stockpiles. Since no pressure is put on participants to do civil disobedience, I chose to accompany the group on tour and after the action to distribute flyers of explanation to people on Pennsylvania Avenue. That evening we planned Good Friday actions at the Pentagon. I sat with Dan Berrigan, who advised me again that it was not necessary to get arrested in order to witness for peace. In deep reflective prayer, I struggled with my decision, and the next day, after our silent prayer vigil in front of the House of Death, we entered the Pentagon concourse. Dan Berrigan, wearing a white alb, carried a cross an we encircled him and prayed. At twelve noon, someone threw symbolic blood and ashes. The scream of sirens and police alarms sounded throughout the building. We were alerted that if we continued to kneel in prayer, we were subject to arrest. Despite shaking knees, I knew what I had to do and a strong sense of owning personal responsibility for our nations's power of nuclear destruction seized me. Risking for peace is what Christ's message is all about.

It would be hard to recall, since that event in 1979, how many marches, vigils, demonstrations I have taken part in. They have addressed many forms of injustice: solidarity for women's equality in promoting the Equal Rights Amendment and the Women' Ordination Conference; protesting the MX missile, cruise missiles, Trident and all nuclear weapons; witnessing against U.S. intervention in El Salvador, Nicaragua, Guatemala. It must be understood that these years have not just been a whirlwind of what might appear to be egocentric demonstrations. Actually, each is linked very closely to hours upon hours of social analysis and theological reflection.

Opportunities to visit countries where people are victims of oppressive systems have provided me with invaluable experiences. In 1979, I visited several peace groups in Belfast. Their dedication to peace and their efforts to heal the wounds of terrorism in the lives of children and ordinary people brought the reality of the Northern Ireland conflict into an awesome perspective. Likewise, in Nicaragua the ordinary people are suffering the horrors of militarization. I visited that country two years after the revolution and the defeat of Somoza. I found a genuine spirit of joy and hope among women, men and children who were busy trying to rebuild a life of peace. Meetings with Sandinista leadership groups convinced me the new government was making every effort to provide health care, education, land reform, religious freedom and cultural development for the people of Nicaragua. But a foreboding sense of fear that the United States would continue to oppose the country's efforts at self-determination by increasing the military strength of neighboring Honduras and by supporting the contra-revolutionaries undermined the fragile hopes of the people. These fears have unfortunately been proved well-founded, as U.S. policy in Central America continues to operate from the Reagan administration's stance of excessive nationalism and militarization toward Third World countries.

As I develop more political astuteness and analytical understanding of social problems, there has been an obvious shift in my approach to prayer and my understanding of spirituality. The pre-Vatican privatism of Jesus-and-me prayer and the elite timetable that religious followed have given way as personal liberation and a consequent Christian responsibility have emerged. In the 1960's, I had been greatly influenced by Teilhard de Chardin as he broke beyond the concept of privatized spirituality to show that we participate in the destiny of the universe. This spiritual outreach was extended as I began to read Gutierrez, Sobrino, Miranda and Solle.

I discovered that the Jesus Christ I had previously identified with somehow reflected the values of traditional middle-class culture. Re-reading scripture helps me understand that the God of justice and righteousness originally created a world of just order, and sent Jesus to us to help re-create that sense of just order in the contemporary world. The Jesus I now have faith in is indeed identified with the struggles of the poor and the oppressed. My personal experiences with people in Central America and so many refugees here attest to their "hope beyond hope" expressed in a faith that transcends overwhelming suffering as they seek justice and righteousness. Theirs is not the passivity of the pre-Vatican theology of patience with the promise of a reward in the life hereafter; it is the revolutionary patience that fights for justice. It is indeed the passioin of Christ.

The oppression of sexist language and symbols that still remain so obvious in church observances thwart my attempts to translate the mystery of God into a genuine experience. The propaganda of patriarchy is hammered out in the he-language of God the Father, the dominating rule of the Lord the Almighty, the rich embroidered vestments and golden vessels of the wealthy. A eucharist as genuine communion in love becomes aborted when sexual discrimination determines who will be the sacramental minister. My faith expands when I join women to celebrate joy, pain, oppression and freedom in prayer and ritual. Our being together in moments of transcendence brings me in touch with the Spirit of life.

Attempting to pick up the scattered pieces of these past 20 years has compelled me to come to grips with the relevance of religious life today. So many props of the past have been stripped away and I am left facing the naked truth that the core of my commitment is the pursuit of the gospel values of love and justice. This pursuit is to be shared with others as I seek not to withdraw from the oppressive situations of our world but to work to transform them. The 1983 SCRIS *"Essential Elements of Religious Life"* is a feeble recall to a lukewarm monastic style completely divorced from Vatican II theology. Its critique by so many U.S. women and men religious is a healthy and encouraging sign that our lived experience is basic to the emerging new theology of religious life. Several recent experiences have confirmed my hope for the future.

I am encouraged in my belief the 1980's is a critical decade for the church to appreciate a convergence of religious communities with faithful secular people with whom they work and share ministry. It is shaping a new model for religious life. Co-membership with established religious congregations, the growth of secular institutes, informally structured base communities of secular/lay groups, and an ongoing questioning of the value of canonical status confirm that we are moving in a new, vibrant direction. Among religious congregations there is evidence of our bonding together on issues of common concern that demand the strength of our solidarity. I arrived personally at this understanding in 1979 when I became a co-member in the Sisters of Loretto. For many years I had admired the risk-taking initiatives of the Lorettos and had identified their goals with much of the same founding spirit and objectives of the Sisters of St. Joseph of Peace. My application to Loretto represented the first request of a sister in full membership in her own community to join in active participation with another committed group. My dual membership the past five years has sharpened my appreciation of how much we are unified in our struggle to create a better future based on gospel values. I have keener insight into the dignity of the individual as each of us, independent of a congregational identity, assumes responsibility in her Christian witness through prayer and ministry.

The suppression of Agnes Mary Mansour is another rallying moment in our recent history that testifies to the togetherness of women and men as they oppose injustice within the Catholic church. Great hope born of pain surfaced when a group of us met in Washington, D.C., and we all identified ourselves as "sisters of mercy". Our concern over Agnes Mary's victimization moved to deeper levels of empathy when we heard the stories of other women present who had sufered condemnation from Church legalisms.

Women's ability to define themselves reached new heights in November, 1983, at the Woman Church Speaks conference in Chicago. Here the concerns of the 1975 and 1978 Women's ordination conferenees expanded to the wider vision of over 1,300 women from many life-styles who came to claim themselves as part of the sacred. They strategized to overthrow elements of oppression in the institutional church while at the same time celebrating their feminist religious identity and heritage.

Finally, my confidence in women to assume their leadership role in the church and the world was further affirmed in a recent visit to Holland. The Dutch church had been light years ahead of us in implementing change, and women in the Netherlands were already preparing for full ministry and ordination in the mid-1960s. In November, 1983, prior to the installation of U.S. Pershing II and Cruise missiles in Europe, I was invited to Holland as part of a Leadership Conference of Women Religious peace pilgrimage. I could quickly resonate not only with the Dutch commitment to seeking peace through oppositiion to U.S. natioinalism but even more strongly with the struggle of women claiming their equality within church structures. Rome's attempt to suppress renewal in the church in the Netherlands took the form of appointing conservative bishops and silencing forward-thinking theologians. But in our meeting many secular women and vowed members of religious communities voiced their determination to commit themselves to full ministry with the people of God. As I left for the airport at Schiphol, a sister promised me: "You sisters in America are now facing the same Vatican repressions we have endured. Just know we will come to stand with you in solidarity whenever you ask us to cross the ocean".

I conclude on an optimistic note. I express a need to rid our church vocabulary of words like "renewal" and "experimentation' which justified time limits on what are actually the natural demands of institutional growth or decline. Religious *life* must be just that: It must always give signs of growth, change, and response to the stimulation of an evolving world society. The adjective *religious* will demand more radical interpretation to include all persons in a faith community of gospel love and justice. Concern over lack of "vocations" will fade as elitist structures of the past erode to allow a new creation of expanded membership.

I rejoice in a special way that this year, 1984, marks the centenary of Margaret Anna Cusack's founding of the Sisters of St. Joseph of Peace congregation. Her bold vision back in 1878 of the "Coming Woman" will be realized as the majority of our vowed and co-members travelled together to England to proclaim that we have indeed *come* as Woman Church to speak and act for justice and peace. I respond with enthusiasm rooted in hope to our jubilee year call to move forward in risk, creativity and mutuality...to journey with others who loyally rebel against all oppressive structures that threaten God's justice in the world and its consequent claims to human dignity and self-fulfillment.

Diary of Change

Patricia Lucas

Patricia Lucas is the pre-release coordinator and caseworker at Cook County Department of Corrections in Chicago. Prior to that she taught elementary school in her native Harlem, New York, and both elementary and secondary school in Chicago.

Friday, September 9, 1955

Dear Diary,

Can you believe that I actually spent 28 hours and 15 minutes in the convent already? We go to bed with the chickens, get up before the roosters start crowing and keep silent from night prayers until lunch. Today the menu was tuna casserole à la institution style. I wish the novice mistress would let me call home for two mintues, so that I can tell mom that I miss her and her delicious meals.

Monday, September 12, 1955

Sister Miriam Cecilia just gave us our "permission card" and told us if we wanted our cards signed each week don't break any of the general permissions. If she doesn't sign it we will have to ask for every iota and that is not my style. Little Book, you shall be the recipient of all the things I am permitted to do. Imagine having to ask permission to:

1. accept candy

2. turn on the lights when it is absolutely necessary

3. borrow needle, threads and pins

4. exchange holy cards

5. go to my cell only when it is time for my bath and

6. take a glass of water.

Saturday, October 8, 1955

Rejoice! I've made it through one month. I was reading about St. Peter last night, and how he talked about leaving everything to follow Jesus. I thought of myself then and how I was bragging a couple days ago that I had left a really supportive family and the possibility of having a husband and children of my own. Sister Miriam Cecilia reminded me that perhaps two of the things I should have left behind were my terrible temper and my strong will. I was so embarrassed and humiliated. I am finding out fast that if I really want to be a saint and a good religious, I just have to give up more than I originally bargained for.

Sunday, December 25, 1955

What a fantastically beautiful Christmas it's been. Last night we woke up to Christmas carols instead of the usual cow bell. After midnight mass, we had breakfast and then rushed to the community room to get all of our mail and the presents under the tree. It was very hard doing without mail during advent but Sister Miriam Cecilia said that it was necessary in order to help us prepare properly for the coming of the Christ Child. I am glad he came.

Saturday, March 10, 1956

In a few weeks, I shall be received into the Congregation of the Franciscan Handmaids of Mary and I shall be one big step closer to being a professed sister. If I had to pick out the one thing that was the most difficult these past six months, it would be the rule of silence. I've broken it so often and so many times for no reason at all except that I love to talk. One of my greatest joys is having Sister Miriam Cecilia for a postulant/novice mistress. She is so innovative.

Wednesday, April 25, 1956

It's been a month since my reception and I've made it to morning prayers everyday on time. I am still finding it difficult to wash up in ice cold water but I know I shall be a better religious for it — at least I think I'll be. Of course, my biggest problem is still my temper and my lack of self-control.

Was I steaming this afternoon when one of the novices walked on my newly waxed floor. How inconsiderate! I am glad I remembered the comment Sister Miriam Cecilia made this morning after I read my meditation. She said to offer up everything that hurt for the success of the general chapter. Well, if the chapter is not successful it won't be because I have not suffered enough for it.

Friday, June 29, 1956

Today, is the saddest day of my religious life. Sister Miriam Cecilia was elected first counselor and she'll have to leave us to be the assistant to her aunt, Reverend Mother Eugenia. I know she does not want to leave but she feels this is God's will.

Sunday, January 20, 1958

Deep down inside I know that everything that has happened during the past 18 months has been the will of God but I still cannot help feeling bitter and scarred. I am keenly aware of the lack of competent people in the world, still more in a community the size of ours, but I still feel cheated of a good formation program. I wish I could remember where I read that it is not the extent of the pain that counts but rather the extent of the sensitiveness to the pain, because the author dwelled on the various ways of coping and I need to learn to cope.

I have grown and I now understand that this life is not and never will be Utopia. It is Good Friday with the promise of Easter Sunday. Tomorrow my third novice mistress in 28 months will arrive and I'll also find out if I'll be admitted to first vows on March 25th or if I'll have to wait until August.

Tuesday, March 25, 1958

In less than three hours, I shall finally be a bride of Christ. I vow stability now and forever, which means that I shall with God's help remain a religious for the rest of my life. I am determined to put behind me all negative feelings and to keep the following quotation engraved in the depth of my soul so that in times of immense trial I shall be able to reflect upon it and re-enkindle the commitment I am making today:

"O Thou Soul, most beautiful of Creatures, You who long to know where Your Beloved is
You, Yourself are the very vessel in which He dwells."

Wednesday, June 18, 1958

My mother died last night and Sister Consuella took me home for what probably will be my last visit to the old apartment. I felt a little foolish sitting in the living room with my hands tucked modestly under my scapular, while sister rambled through mom's closet picking out the dress she felt most suitable for the wake. In less than an hour we were back in the motherhouse and I overheard Sister Maureen asking reverend mother to allow her to accompany me to the wake. Oh, how I hope she will get permission. I do so want to be with my brothers. We need each other.

Saturday, June 21, 1958

Mom was buried today and already I miss her very much. Surely her life was a living example of love and dedication to the will of God. I used to associate sainthood with religious life, but mom was a married saint, who died as she lived — giving of herself to others.

Sunday, May 31, 1959

Larry's first mass was exquisite! Everyone and everything was great except that my parents were not physically present. Mom always said that she would not live to see Larry ordained and dad died before he even started school. I guess the good really die young.

It's amazing how mom, in her own quiet way, implanted in us a respect and reverence for God and our father. Without fanfare she would generally start each reprimand with either one of her two favorite quotations, "What does it profit a man or woman if he/she should gain the whole world and suffer the loss of his/her soul," and, "Remember you are a Lucas." I only hope and pray that we will always remember and observe those quotations.

Sunday, June 24, 1962

I cannot help but think that the relative peace and serenity I've experienced the past three years are merely the summer warmth that comes before the winter storm.

The 1960s are a great time to be young and alive. In the church we talk about "aggiornamento" and in the world it is Camelot.

Thank God, Mother Miriam Cecilia was elected mother general. We need someone to help us move ahead with the times and she is the most innovative person we have.

Sunday, December 22, 1963

Just a year ago it seemed like nothing could go wrong either in the church or in the world. Today, two great leaders are dead — John XXIII and John Kennedy.

Four short months ago, I made my final vows. I know that I should be ecstatic but my spirit is desolate. So far, I have not voted for any of the minor changes we've made in our habit. I love it and would like it to stay the same. O God, why do I feel so depressed!

Sunday, March 15, 1964

Give Mother Miriam Cecilia another "A." Her major theme this year is to go back to the gospels. She brought in two renowned scholars to prod us into reading and understanding sacred scripture — Father Barnabas Ahern and Mother Katherine Sullivan.

I love the talk that Mother Sullivan gave us on the Acts of the Apostles. She said that if you are conservative you will like the first five chapters because in it the motto of the Jerusalem church was, "If we have done it before let us always do it in the same way." On the contrary, the church in Antioch motto was, "If we did it before let us never do it again."

Seems like a good way to reflect on Vatican II and the changes that we've seen and probably will continue to see for the next 10 or 15 years. We are a perfect community moving neither too fast nor too slow.

Saturday, September 6, 1964

What a fantastic summer I had — one of the best! I really and truly love Greenwich and the Sisters of the Sacred Heart. The best part of the whole summer occurred when some of us celebrated the death of God. That God, the Untouchable One in the heavens, that Recorder of all our misdeeds, the Great Chess Player that moves us like pawns, had to die so that the "Ground of My Being," as Tillich calls him, could truly live in me.

The freedom to be and to love is mine. The God that dwells within the being of my sisters, my students and all people is not to be feared and held at a distance. It is only after finding God in the depth of my being that I shall be capable of sharing him totally with others.

Saturday, March 25, 1967

Our customs are really changing. Today I received several gifts instead of the traditional holy cards to celebrate my feast day. Only Mother Miriam Cecilia remembered that the feast of the Annunciation is my triple-decker special day.

Twenty-five years ago, I received the body and blood of Jesus for the first time. I was six years old and very much aware of the great privilege that was mine. Sister Olive Mary, my first grade teacher, told us stories of Blessed Imelda and St. Tarcisius. Without realizing it, I believe it was then that the eucharist became the apex and foundation of my life and perhaps the beacon light that drew me to religious life.

Nine years ago when I pronounced my first vows I did not know that in less than three months my mother would be dead and in some metamorphic way my perception of the vows would alter.

The vows are merely the tools, the instruments I need to chisel away at the desire to hoard or possess money, objects, or even my time which I am beginning to value far more than I should. To be chaste is to be faithful to the Beloved.

Monday, May 29, 1967

The Sisters of the Sacred Heart are really a great community! Mother Miriam Cecilia is forever teasing me and telling me that I am going to join them. I think she really believes that I am going to transfer to another community. I do enjoy the intellectual stimulus the sisters afford me but I don't want to join them nor any other community. Like all the other young sisters, I too am looking forward to many meaningful changes in our upcoming chapter. Mother's first five years were great but some of the sisters feel that the plentiful harvest will give way to a period of immense drought. I do hope that they are wrong but it is scary seeing so many of my friends making preparations to leave even before the chapter begins.

Tuesday, June 25, 1968

It's hard to believe this is really happening to us. Every meaningful change that would attract young black women or even whites, now that they are running in herds to the inner city, is being either deleted or tabled. It almost seems like someone learned a new word and is trying to use it in every sentence. Delete this . . . I move that we delete . . .

At lunch break when most of us were crying or just simply disgusted Sister Elaine suggested we pray and sing "We shall Overcome." We did not overcome anything. The afternoon session was another disaster. Perhaps tomorrow will be better.

Friday, November 29, 1968

Ten years in the motherhouse and I can't stand it any longer. I need space to think and reflect. The community is stagnant, refusing to move ahead.

11:20 p.m.

A fashion show was held tonight next door in the juniorate. Mother Miriam Cecilia would have died if she had seen some of her former novices modeling the clothes they were going to wear when they leave in a few weeks. The fashion show is over and the exodus is in full swing.

Saturday, June 14, 1969

It is 1:20 a.m. and the "Flame," as we nicknamed her, just left my room. After she told me that she was in love with a priest, I told her that Jesus didn't want us to live like this. She wouldn't even let me explain what I meant, she simply got up and said, "When I feel like that, Emmanuel, I am going to leave." (Emmanuel was my religious name.)

What I wanted to share with her was that it was the Emperor Constantine, not Jesus, who deemed it necessary for religious men and women to follow a distinct set of rules, thereby setting up an elite group of lay people, namely, sisters.

Friday, June 5, 1970

I just saw the *Man for All Seasons* and the one sentence that is still haunting me is, "When you go to heaven for following your conscience and I go to hell for not following mine, will you join me?" My conscience tells me to go back to the gospels and live community life in the manner that I feel Jesus intended it to be lived — literally being in the world but not getting caught up in the entrapments the secular world offers.

I don't need a habit if what I am speaks louder than what I wear. Please God, help me to explain myself to Mother Miriam Cecilia. I still like her very much. It probably was not her fault entirely that the community stopped growing. We probably expected too much from her with very little support or encouragement. We should have remembered the 13th beatitude, "Blessed are they who expect nothing, for they shall not be disappointed."

Friday, March 26, 1971

I think this is going to be a very informative weekend. I am glad Drew talked me into coming with her to meet and learn more about the Sisters For Christian Community. The foundress, Lillanna Kopp, is certainly to be commended. It takes a lot of foresight and downright courage to establish a religious community for the 21st century. It is a community in which individual members are responsible for themselves while striving to build Christian community wherever they live in whatever field the Lord calls them to work. I love the motto of the Sisters, "That all may be One." One in the Body of Christ. What a beautiful concept!

Drew has decided to make her commitment when Larry and Jo come for a visit next month. I shall be a supporter for I feel herein lies the future of religious life.

Tuesday, June 29, 1976

It's a great feeling being back in my old room at the motherhouse even if it's only for a few days. I am glad I went to my trunk and found you, little book. It's been four years since my last entry and my experiences are too many to enumerate.

Imagine me teaching high school on the westside of Chicago and living in an apartment. I am sure some of the sisters feel that I not only lost my mind, but also am about to lose my vocation. Perhaps that is the reason Mother Loretta Theresa (she was elected mother general at the last chapter) wants me to make retreat with the community this year. She said it is going to be a charismatic retreat.

Wednesday, December 8, 1976

For weeks I have thought and prayed about the response I must make to Mother Loretta Theresa's question, "What is God's will for me?"

In general, God's will for me is to live out the promises made for me at baptism and to realize fully the mandate I assumed at confirmation. In baptism, I was taught to have a "child-like" faith in God and to trust him explicitly, especially when his demands seem contrary to right reason. The sacrament of confirmation enabled me to make mature, free and conscious decisions in fulfilling whatever I felt God was calling me to do at a given time.

In particular, I feel that God's will for me is to continue my present life-style and to re-enkindle within my sisters the knowledge that we, as Franciscan Handmaids of the Most Pure Heart of Mary, are called to be prophetic witnesses to an entire new life-style based on the message of the Acts of the Apostles rather than that of Constantine.

God, when Mother Loretta Theresa reads this she is going to think I flipped, but somehow I have to make her realize that we must be women of vision, not clinging to the old, beautiful ways of the past but rather seeking the precarious new and frightening paths that will lead us into the 21st century.

Sunday, February 11, 1979

It's no use hanging on any longer. I know now that I cannot and shall not return to the Franciscan Handmaids of Mary. No significant changes will take place. I feel like I am watching one of my best friends die slowly of terminal illness.

Tuesday, August 22, 1979

My indult of secularization just arrived and although I feel a little disappointed, I am not unhappy. The indult severs my legal ties with the Franciscan Handmaids of Mary. The mere stroke of a pen cannot, however, abolish nor alter a commitment I made to God and one that I desire to keep for the rest of my life.

The Handmaids will always be a part of my life for I know that they contributed to my spiritual growth and it was the commands of my superiors that led me to this particular junction in my life. Fiat.

Saturday, August 23, 1980

During the past year I have gone to several meetings with the Chicago Hub of the Sisters For Christian Community. Something is missing — although I fully support them I cannot embody their spirit totally. Sometimes I feel that I am merely drifting with the tide but on days like today I know that God is here and he is merely telling me to be patient. Truly, I have come this far, as the song goes, by faith and I must trust and believe that in time I shall know precisely what it is God wants of me. I must learn to be patient and courageous despite the fact that Good Friday is lasting much longer than I feel it should

Sunday, September 26, 1982

The last thing in the world I wanted to do today was to go on a Day of Recollection. I enjoyed myself immensely and learned a lot about and from my three companions. Tomorrow, I shall call the contact sister in another community. I think my searching period has ended and now the waiting begins. Waiting to know if it is truly what God wants — I want it and I only hope He does too.

The term "mother church" has finally made sense to me. The people of God, the "anawim," the institutional church and all the faithful striving to become church is truly mother. As mother the church nourishes and gives life to souls entrusted to her at baptism, constantly giving grace to the faithful until the cry of birth is sounded and the soul begins its own journey in faith. I feel, no, I am impregnated with desire and I only hope the birthing cries will be loud and joyous.

Sunday, July 3, 1983

History was made today — the first Lucas family reunion. Not only was it delightful but also extremely informative. One of the highlights of the day was when Uncle Cyril, our patriarch, told all gathered from first to fourth generation, how he came to America as a young man, finished law school, served as a criminal lawyer for many years and then entered the ministry. Today, he is a retired Lutheran pastor, extolling the blessings and sacredness of a good marriage. He and Aunt Janet have been married for 64 years. Tomorrow is Aunt Janet's birthday and she will be 86 years young. God bless the both of them!

Like a true West Indian, Uncle Selywn couldn't let his older brother outshine him. He said, "Well if the wife dies, marry another" and he and Aunt Mabel got a round of applause. Forty-five years is not exactly a new bride but that fact did not deter our enthusiasm.

Special greetings came from our cousin, Bishop Telis-foro Isaac, in Santo Domingo. He is the first bishop in the family. I certainly hope he is not the last.

Our forefathers and mothers left us a rich heritage and I can never thank God enough for it.

Saturday, May 19, 1984

Today is one of the happiest days of my life! I almost feel like shouting "I am accepted" from the roof top. Barring some unforeseeable accident, I shall start a growth in the spirituality and spirit of my new community in September.

Funny, this is the last page of my little journal and I've come full circle. I am ending as I began 29 years ago with a new beginning — a new birth in the spirit. I can only hope that this one is as bountiful as the last.

Doors to the World

Mary Luke Tobin

Mary Luke Tobin, a Sister of Loretto for 57 years, coordinates the Thomas Merton Center for Creative Exchange in Denver, Colorado. Formerly president of her community and of the Leadership Conference of Women Religious, and a former national staff person for Church Women United, she devotes much of her time to lectures, workshops and retreats on peace, women's issues, Thomas Merton, and the integration of faith and action. For many years, she has been actively involved in movements for peace and justice.

Sister Tobin tells her story in an interview conducted by Cecily Jones.

Q. If you were to specify just one incident to symbolize the way the renewal has affected your life — at any time since the renewal began, say, in the late 1960s and into the 1970s and beyond — what would it be?

A. That's hard to answer, of course! So many experiences in the last 15-20 years might qualify. Perhaps, though, I'd choose a peace pilgrimage to Europe in which I was involved, along with five other United States religious leaders, early in 1973.

What were you doing? And who were the others?

It was just after the massive U.S. bombing raids on Hanoi at Christmas in 1972. Since the religious community in this country had not been able to exert enough pressure on our government to stop those terrible raids, Harvey Cox organized a hurried trip during which we visited several European church leaders to ask them to intercede with President Nixon in a kind of international voice of conscience. Besides Harvey Cox and myself, Rabbi Leonard Beerman, United Methodist Bishop James Armstrong, Episcopal Bishop Robert DeWitt, and Robert McAfee Brown were in the group.

Why that particular event?

As I said, there could be others. But I think this one illustrated the connections among several aspects of renewal as I have experienced it.

What were they?

I guess I'd name three chief ones — involvement in peace and justice issues; an increasing ecumenical awareness and action; and a new sense of maturity, individual choice, and community decision in carrying out our work.

That 1973 trip wasn't your first experience in working for peace, was it?

No, that's true. And today I suppose one might think about sisters' involvement in such efforts as rather ordinary, that is, rather to be *expected* of them. But then, in the late 1960s and early 1970s, to be involved in protest against government policies constituted a different posture for nuns. For me — and I feel that many other sisters would respond in the same way — renewal meant that I began to see the gospel in a new way, as a call to respond to the problems of the world and the world's people. That has shaped so much of my outlook and my actions in the last 15 years or so. The peace trip was an example of that aspect of renewal.

As we talk more, I'll certainly want to come back to your work for peace. But what about the ecumenical aspect of that particular trip?

To me it was an example of the way in which the religious community — I'm using that term widely — began to act more and more in areas of justice and peace. This, I feel certain, would not have happened before the renewal. I think the Second Vatican Council opened the way to greater ecumenical awareness for many. Certainly this was true for me, for it was at the council that I came to know persons such as Robert McAfee Brown, who was a Presbyterian observer, Albert Outler, a Methodist, and some Jewish leaders such as Rabbi Marc Tanenbaum and Rabbi Abraham Heschel. Of course, when I met them in Rome in the mid-1960s, I didn't realize how the paths of some of us would cross again, especially in the peace movement.

On that peace trip to Europe, there we were — men of several Protestant denominations, a Jewish rabbi, and I, the only Catholic as well as the only woman. We shared common hopes for peace, and were engaged together in a project which we thought might bring peace faster. I must say that I felt very much at one with my companions and respected their commitment to our common religious values and to peace. And that trip was one of the ways I learned that there is no substitute for involvement and action.

Each of your answers leads me to another question! Just now you mentioned the Second Vatican Council; so that's another area to return to. And there must be much more to say about the whole ecumenical dimension of your experience of renewal. But before we discuss these, could you expand a bit on your third point — maturity and individual choice?

Here we're talking about an area of renewal which has had great significance for me and, I think, for our community and for U.S. sisters generally. Concretely, I'd say that being on that European peace mission, my increasing involvement in various other peace activities, and my taking a job that very month (it was January, 1973) on the national staff of Church Women United — none of that would have happened without the emphasis on personal choice and personal responsibility that was so important in renewal.

How did that come about?

I look back to the early 1960s to answer that.

You were the president of the Loretto community then?

Yes. The early 1960s began for us in our community — and I'm sure in many others — a period of deeper insight into the dignity and worth of each person. You know, it was a time of so many changes in all the fields of human learning — scripture, theology and psychology were especially important for us. And we were listening to those changes. The listening and the study helped us to adopt principles that stressed the truth of the priority of persons over institutions. This understanding, of course, then led to the policies we adopted — an emphasis on personal decision-making and the responsiblities connected with it.

Wouldn't that personal decision-making strike some observers as being quite individualistic?

Only if they saw the picture incompletely and inaccurately. I think we were moving into a time of recognizing in a new way the true importance of each person. This was a recognition affirmed by faith. If we believed in the value of each person, *really* believed it, then each person should have a say in her own decisions, choices of work, living situation and so on. But we also learned, of course, the importance of listening to one another in making these choices.

So you'd point to an element of communal help in this?

Yes. I mean that these big choices were not made without communal reflection and without seeking the opinions and advice of others. You know the questions: What would this new job . . . or change in living situation . . . or move . . . or big trip . . . or study for a new career . etc. . . . mean for me and for others? What are the advantages, the disadvantages? Is this what the gospel is calling me to do? Am I suited for it? Is this the best use of my talents? Eventually, of course, the decision would be a carrying out of personal responsibility, a mature exercise of choice. But, of course, that also demanded confidence on the part of others. And I think we have learned the importance of trusting one another in the decisions that each one makes.

And in the case of the European peace mission?

Well, I think that's a good illustration. I decided to take part in it because of a whole background of realizing my presence might help, that it was a response to a gospel call, that perhaps it could mean one step closer to ending the Vietnam war, that the community steadily encouraged my work in peace activities.

You mentioned the Second Vatican Council. Do you date renewal in religious life from that event?

Yes and no. I don't think the council was the only channel to renewal for religious women. Even before the council, as I pointed out, there were threads of so many new developments in theology, bible study, psychology, and so on. I remember that I tried to learn as much as I could by questioning and listening to some of our sisters who had gone to study at good theology schools in Europe and in this country. We paid attention to those new theological voices and psychological insights. Some of the repeated themes in all that, I think, were the importance of the person, the development of interpersonal relationships, and the call to work against injustice. So I think the impetus for renewal really pre-dated the council.

But I'd also say that Vatican II gave affirmation to those new insights and understandings. You might say it provided an acceptable base from which to draw plans for the future. And I think many religious communities took advantage of that, releasing enormously creative ideas which are still unfolding.

So would you say that Vatican II sped up renewal in religious life?

I'm sure it played a vital role. One could see (and can still see) the principal themes of the council being listened to, reflected on, and integrated into the life of religious communities. The council was dealing with questions such as: Who is the church? Who are the other churches? How does the church face the world? Should there be a change in that stance? Is the church faithful to the gospel of Jesus? Those were some of the dynamic issues dealt with by the bishops of the world. I think the parallels in the renewal of religious life are obvious.

You've referred to religious communities in connection with Vatican II. What about the council's effect on you personally?

Of course, it affected me deeply. And I think the opportunities given me because of my participation as an auditor helped to promote the renewal of religious life in this country. Even though there were many limitations on an auditor's role, nevertheless the experience itself and the chance to see, hear, and even take part in a minor way were greatly enabling for me, and, through me, I think, for others.

Were you surprised at being asked to be an auditor?

I suppose that all of us hoped that women would be represented at the council, for we were certainly aware that a new era was beginning for the church as a whole and for us. And Cardinal Suenens from Belgium — who just a bit earlier had written a breakthrough book, *The Nun in the World* — had urged the bishops at the council to invite women observers. At the end of the 1963 session he questioned how the bishops could deliberate about "the church" when half the church was unrepresented.

And you were invited then?

No. My invitation actually came in late September of 1964 when I was on shipboard on my way to Rome. That August I had been elected president of the Conference of Major Superiors of Women (the CMSW), and the executive committee felt that I should proceed to Rome during the forthcoming third session of the council to see what I could learn even if I were just on the edges of the council. Cardinal Suenens had urged religious women to be present at whatever other meetings would be held in addition to the formal council sessions in order to exercise some influence by their presence and their evidence of interest. I was elated by the prospect of being there, even on the periphery, so I was eagerly on my way.

So you were actually en route to the Vatican when your invitation came?

Yes. One evening during the ocean trip I received a phone call from a *New York Times* reporter asking, "How do you feel about your invitation to attend the Vatican Council as one of the 15 women who have just been invited?" This was news to me! Of course, 15 women among 2500 bishops would hardly be a challenge to them, but it *was* a beginning.

Would you say some more about the council's impact on you?

At the council I heard many clear statements about justice as a mandate of the gospel. I felt that one of the tasks to which the council called all Christians was that of helping to create a freer and more human world. So I was eager myself, inspired really, to join that task, and I hoped that participation in work for justice would become an essential part of all religious life. For me the council focused greatly on that part of renewal: taking responsiblity for the world in which we live.

In addition, my auditor's role and my presidency of the Conference of Major Superiors of Women gave me many opportunities to talk with other groups after the council about what I had learned and what I hoped for. I was launched into activities which, a few years earlier, I would not have dreamed of. It is hard for me now to separate the council experience, the already developing renewal, and my own involvement with both.

At the council itself, did you have any voice at all?

We 15 women auditors occupied a tribune, a sort of "loge," one of the four facing the high altar in St. Peter's; and across from us were the "Protestant observers." They observed; we audited; none of us spoke! However, I would add that we did have some voice finally. Through the efforts of Bernard Haring, who felt that we should have more than a listener's role, three of us were invited to attend the commissions drawing up the documents on which the bishops would vote. We — Rosemary Goldie, from Australia, Mere Guillemin, the superior general of the Daughters of Charity, and I — were involved in the commissions dealing with the church in the modern world and with the laity. And we did have a chance to speak out in these meetings. I recall feeling that this opportunity to speak was important for women, at least in setting a precedent for the future.

Of course, the Vatican atmosphere was not terribly conducive for women to take a leading role, was it? I wonder if there were at least some signs of a breakthrough.

You're right about the atmosphere. And as I said, 15 women among the 2500 bishops was really token representation. Of course, Mary Daly was in Rome then, too. I recall her urging us sisters to recognize our veils as signs of submission to men!

During the council, Cardinal Suenens continued to evince an interest in our ideas. I remember his frequent meetings with religious women during the sessions and his invitations to groups of us women to meet with him in Rome to share our thoughts. He was genuinely eager to hear from us and to learn our concerns.

You said that you hoped that work for justice would become an essential part of religious life. Has that hope been realized, or partly realized?

I feel that more and more the whole Christian community has responded to what the gospel calls us to — speaking out clearly and without hesitation in situations perceived as unjust and oppressive. You might remember that one of the stirring sentences in the statement from the 1971 bishops' synod was: "Action on behalf of justice is a constitutive element of the gospel." One effect of the renewal has certainly been for me that I cannot *not* be involved in the peace movement and in many struggles for justice. That is where I feel I find my identity as a Christian and as a religious woman.

You've taken part in so many kinds of work for justice and peace through these years of renewal. Earlier you talked about the 1973 peace mission to Europe. What other involvements were significant for you?

A question like that could lead to hours of remembering! I suppose that in the area of peace, one of the most significant events took place in the summer of 1970. I was invited to join a fact-finding mission to South Vietnam, sponsored by the Fellowship of Reconciliation, to look at the situation there from the viewpoint of those within Vietnam who were seeking peace. I was the only Catholic in the group of 11, which, though not exclusively a religious group, did include an Episcopal bishop from New York, an executive of the National Council of Churches, and a Jewish rabbi. It was also a biracial group with two black participants, one of whom was the only other woman on the trip.

That must have been a very special experience.

Yes! We met with lawyers, professors, wives and mothers, farmers, students, social workers, Buddhist monks, publishers, Catholic priests. And we learned that while there were many peace efforts, these often resulted in imprisonment and torture. For a long time afterward, I could vividly remember students who still bore scars from being tortured for their dissent. And visits with women whose husbands or sons had been imprisoned or lost were poignant experiences. On our last day there, when we participated in a peaceful march to the U.S. embassy, we ourselves were tear-gassed!

Did the timing of that trip — just at the end of your term as president of the community — have some added significance?

Yes, certainly for me, and I think for the Loretto community. First of all, for several years before that, our community in its assemblies (or chapters as they were called then) had begun to deal with what would certainly have been called one of the "signs of the times" — the growing discontent with the Vietnam war. I remember very well that at our 1967 assembly we strongly supported a resolution then being introduced into congress. It was called Negotiation Now and urged our government to begin negotiations to end the war. I think that was a striking example of our deepening awareness that we were responsible citizens in a country involved in a wrong and very harmful war. In a way, that action set a tone for us, because we took a step we could never turn back from. And each of our assemblies ever since has included strong stands on important issues of justice and peace.

You were very strong in your conviction about the importance of speaking out, weren't you?

Well, I was so convinced that the gospel calls us to a world view and to actions rising from that view. So, it seemed natural that when I was invited to join that fact-finding trip to Saigon, I would say yes at once. In a way, that trip symbolized a transition point between the rather circumscribed life and tasks connected with a somewhat institutionalized role and the more demanding, much wider vision of what it means to be a citizen of a world where injustice and war demand that the Christian take some action. After such experiences, I could never return to the narrower view!

I know that in addition to your work for peace, you were also a part of many efforts for social justice. Could you talk about one of them that you recall as especially important?

Sometimes, when there's an occasion to assess the "successes" of our work for justice and peace, I like to recall that it was the people who finally brought the Vietnam War to an end. And in the same way, I remember the long struggles for justice on the part of the United Farm Workers — struggles in which so many church people shared. In the late 1960s, we invited some farm workers to address our assembly, and then as a body we took a resolution in favor of the United Farm Worker boycotts. That was the start of a great deal of work in solidarity with the farm workers in which many of our sisters were very active. I myself didn't realize that in just a few years from the time I listened to the farm workers at our assembly I would have a more direct experience of their situation.

Say some more about that.

I learned firsthand something of their struggle when I responded to a call to join the farm workers' protest in the Coachella Valley in California. It was another experience for me of how involvement is so much better as a learning process than reading, talks, etc. To be in the line, confronted by the police and the Teamsters across the road, in the midst of 114-degree heat — all this opened my eyes to the needs of these workers. It also showed me the effectiveness of protest, even though it may take a long time.

You referred to the 1970 Vietnam trip as a kind of transition point. Were there other transition points in your experience of the renewal?

I think one aspect of renewal which has affected me deeply over the years is the ecumenical dimension. At the time of the Second Vatican Council especially, I think we began to realize the importance of valuing the best in each faith tradition rather than of emphasizing the weaknesses of other religions and denominations in contrast to the strength of ours. My life has been so greatly enriched by my contacts with persons of different faith traditions!

Could you elaborate on some of these?

Of course, there were already the beginnings of ecumenical activities in the late 1950s and early 1960s. In Kentucky, for example, where I lived at the time at our motherhouse, Thomas Merton was inviting groups of students from the various Protestant seminaries in the state to spend retreat days at Gethsemani. But it was the council which really strengthened the whole inter-religious connection. Nothing was as important for me as the actual meetings with real persons who embodied their faith. When I met Robert McAfee Brown at the council, for example, his insights were pushing the gospel imperatives of justice along the lines I was also beginning to see. With him and with so many others in the Protestant and Jewish communities (as well as in some understandably fewer contacts with Buddhists and Muslims), I discovered such common aspirations for justice and peace.

Actually you worked in an ecumenical situation for some years, didn't you?

Yes, my job as citizen action director on the national staff of Church Women United put me into constant contact with persons of other denominations. And I always found very warm relationships with other staff and with the constituency.

That was somewhat unusual for a nun to have such a job, wasn't it? How did that come about?

I suppose one could say that it followed from the renewal as I experienced it. In my case, it was a matter of personal choice of that kind of work, which combined ecumenical contacts with raising concern and planning action about justice issues. I had become acquainted with Church Women United when I was invited to talk to their national meeting in New York just after Vatican II. So, the eventual job offer was another direct result of the council.

Does that ecumenical dimension still affect your life?

Oh, yes, very much so! It would be hard for me to imagine my life in an exclusively Catholic ambience. Today about one-half of the workshops, seminars, and retreats which I lead are for Protestant groups. In the last several years, I've been involved in conducting pastors' schools, leading clergy retreats, and teaching Methodist summer schools of religion. It's interesting work for me and satisfying. When I teach or give talks, I am speaking from my own roots, steeped, I hope, in the gospel and tradition, and I think I speak to the hearts of my Protestant brothers and sisters.

You've done some teaching at a Protestant seminary, too, haven't you?

Yes. For several summers I've taught courses, chiefly on the thought of Thomas Merton, at a Protestant seminary and at one of its summer extensions. That experience and also my involvement with an ecumenical campus ministry group have brought a whole different dimension into my life, a dimension that would be missing had it not been for the renewal.

What was the campus ministry connection?

Well, for a number of years I served on the board of the National Institute of Campus Ministry, which introduced me to wonderful Protestant and Jewish scholars. I think the campus ministry institute was unique in that it included Jews, which made it quite different from many other campus ministry groups. It was a difference that I valued very much. Rabbi Arnold Wolf and Richard Levy are two of the friends whom I came to know and value through this connection.

Would you say more about your contacts with the Jewish community?

First, I would point out that my life has certainly been enriched and my own faith has been deepened by the witness of some Jews of such profound faith commitment. In my years with the National Institute of Campus Ministry, I valued so much the scripture reflections presented by the Jewish scholars in the group. Their profound learning about the ancient texts has helped to illuminate my own understanding of the scriptures. I've already mentioned Rabbi Tanenbaum and Rabbi Heschel, who had such an impact at Vatican II. Rabbi Tanenbaum has even come to Loretto, Kentucky, to talk with the motherhouse community. He can point out in a powerful and convincing way instances of anti-Semitism, which unfortunately still prevails.

And Rabbi Heschel?

I will never forget a marvelous occasion of meeting him at a Vietnam War protest held in the rotunda of the capitol in Washington. I remember how he led our large group of protesters in prayer and reflection. What a gentle person! His long beard and prayerful gestures recalled the Old Testament prophets of whom he wrote so well. Many of us were arrested that day (for continuing to pray in the rotunda after closing time).

What about your experience of being arrested? How did that affect you?

We spent a night in a Washington jail. Many other war protesters went through much more than I did, in my few encounters with the law. But even that brief time of imprisonment provided an important object lesson, for I understood in a small but real way some of the dehumanizing experiences which all jailed individuals undergo. Being treated as a number or a thing — being thumb-printed, photographed, given a number, being marched around by wardens — all that is depersonalizing. We spent the night, three of us sharing a metal slab as a bed, in a crowded concrete cell under a glaring light. I'm sure that my sympathy for all those imprisoned was deepened by this slight but demeaning experience of incarceration.

I'd like to explore a somewhat different topic, Many persons both in and

*out of religious life recall your efforts in the late 1960s to further renewal
among religious women. How did that role affect you?*

Of course, now, these 15 or 20 years into the process, as I said, much
of my activity in those early renewal years merges together in my mind!
I would say that I felt a great responsibility to communicate to my own
community and to others many of the insights I had gained at the council
and in our study of the new theology.

Such as?

Mostly, I'd say, a new look at the church as the people of God and at
the gospel call to work for justice. The document on religious life, *Ecclesiae
Sanctae,* drawn up in Rome in 1966, cheered me on and reinforced many
of my ideas. That document stressed that only the religious communities
themselves were to determine the path of their own renewal. It also
authorized any experimentation (including canon law!) provided it did
not change "the nature and purpose of the institute." We all know how
that paved the way for much that was then to happen.

It was clear sailing then?

Oh, no! I suppose that as with all new developments, especially with
changes in traditional patterns, resistance is inevitable. And, of course,
I found that true both in my own community and in others.

How did you work with it?

It seemed crucial to me that if we truly believed what we said about
personal responsibility for decision-making and about self-determination
rather than legislating from outside, then we had to be ready to accept
the consequences. We had developed new insights on the value of the
person, on the demanding call to work for justice, on adult responsibility
for our choices. And as these insights were carried out into practice, there
were both positive and negative consequences.

And these consequences affected you in a heightened way, right?

They really affected all of us. On the positive side, for many sisters
the times and the new directions were liberating and challenging and
refreshing. New growth was in progress. But the negative result was
that for others everything was going too fast; some sisters were leaving
religious life; others were very reluctant to go along with the renewal.
Yet I felt that we could not really "pace" what was happening. World
events and the current developments in theology and psychology were
moving us onward. We had to continue on the path to renewal. So I
suppose that in my role as council auditor and as one who then promoted
the renewal I was the target of some criticism. But I felt I had to keep
urging on and moving ahead, even though there were many difficulties.

*Did you ever feel that maybe the struggle wasn't worth it — that it
would be easier not to keep pushing ahead?*

No, I don't think I ever did. You know, I'm essentially a rather hopeful
person. And, as I said, our growing insights into shared responsibility,
personal decision-making, and the gospel demand to work to eradicate

injustice — all these were so convincing to me. So I really believe it was worth it, even though at times in the early years I had some discouraging moments, especially cases of misunderstanding on the part of some in the community who did not agree with the changes.

But, remember, I was certainly not alone. In our community, everyone had the opportunity to take part in discussions and to serve on various commissions set up to renew our way of life, our government structure, and so on. And I also had working with me in leadership positions in our own community as well as in the Major Superiors' Conference women of great insight and courage. We did much searching and reflecting and talking and discussing together as we moved farther into renewal. And even though I sometimes worried that time constraints made it difficult for everyone in the community to assimilate the new insights, I also knew that there was urgency in making the shift from outside regulation to self-determination. We had to keep moving. Yes, it was worth it!

What about outside the community? You had many dealings with church authorities. How did that part of the renewal process affect you?

Well, religious women have been struggling for a long, long time to have our participation as full members of the church recognized. That, of course, is not true of sisters only, but of all women — that's another whole area that needs discussion. In my own case, I'd say that in the late 1960s the struggles for renewal were in many respects uphill all the way, especially as far as our dealing with the institutional church was concerned.

What were some of your experiences?

I remember the summer of 1965, which was the summer between the two sessions of the council that I attended. We — the religious women of the U.S. — were asking for a voice in church decisions that affected our lives. You know, canon law, and so on. I had asked the Conference of Major Superiors of Women for the approval of such a request if I made it to the U.S. bishops, and there was almost unanimous agreement. So I felt that we should make every effort to ask the bishops to implement our request. I remember taking the major superiors' formal statement to some members of the administrative board of the U.S. bishops, among whom were Cardinals Sheahan and Ritter. I can still recall the great politeness of each of them when I paid my visits. But I could tell that for them to take our request any farther would have required enormous courage on their part. And the hour was not ripe for that. So that was a painful disappointment. I expected more.

Did you find church officials at the Vatican more receptive?

No. I recall feeling that there was some sort of discrepancy between the new notions of flexibility and openness called for by the bishops at the council, and provided for in the 1966 document on religious life, and the stance of Vatican officials in the Congregation for Religious. Somehow, we were eager to get on with "the renewal and adaptation of religious life" that had been called for, and they were not. Now I realize that the

central curia never really wanted the changes in religious life that the
council had evoked.

Even during the council, when I was invited to speak to various groups
around Rome and at press conferences, I was conscious that a subtle
censorship was being exercised. Once I was asked by the Congregation
for Religious to submit to a bishop, their representative, a copy of a talk
I was going to give. Another time, a bishop was sent to caution me about
speaking in front of the press. However, I did give the talk and the interview. The Congregation for Religious seemed obviously worried about
the influence of a U.S. nun both during and immediately after the council!

You mean that you had to be "kept in line"?

I think there was an element of that. I recall being in tears after a
scolding given to me by a U.S. official at the Vatican. I felt he was under
pressure from somebody to get me in line. What was so difficult was
being misunderstood and being unable to do anything about it. That
certainly convinced me of my status as a second-class citizen in the church.

I suppose that in a way I may have been considered a threat, a person
to be kept track of! Once, Cardinal Ritter told me, with some amusement,
that during one council session, when he was seated just behind Cardinal
Antoniutti, who then headed the Congregation for Religious. He noticed
that Cardinal Antoniutti was busily reading a European newspaper con-
taining an article about me, including my photograph. Cardinal Ritter
recounted this in a gently amused way.

Do you think that the officials were perhaps also motivated by fear?

Yes, I think that was part of it. I often felt, for example, that the stance
of Cardinal Antoniutti came from a fear that maybe the innovations
would get out of hand. We were just poles apart in our views. He seemed
to believe that things should remain as they were; I believed that changes
were in order and that flexibility and experimentation must happen so
the renewal could go forward. I remember coming from meetings with
the cardinal with tears in my eyes and keen disappointment in my heart.

Actually, I suppose we both felt our goals were the same, for I recall
my last meeting with him, after the council, and not long before he died.
He said, "I want you to know, sister, that what I did in regard to the
innovations in religious life, I believe I have done for the good of the
church." And I remember answering, "I, too, Your Eminence. What I
have done to encourage these new developments in religious life, I believe
I have done for the good of the church."

That whole experience must have been hard.

Yes, but there were some marvelously supportive persons, too. I found
such understanding and encouragement from Mère Guillemin. What a
strong and courageous woman! To my sorrow, she did not live long after
the council. I know she would have had the ability to carry renewal into
many parts of the world. We understood each other as friends.

What about the broader question of the role of women in the church?

*Would you say that the renewal has brought a kind of feminist conscious-
ness into the religious community?*

Oh, yes, very much so. There's an ever greater awareness of the second-
class position of women in the world, and, of course, in the church.

*How does that affect you in terms of the overall renewal? Will there be
some change?*

Some of my thoughts on this go back as far as the council. I've often
recalled an incident when Rosemary Goldie, the Australian auditor, said
forthrightly to some commission members who had tried to write something fine about women, "You can leave out all the flowers and pedestals
and incense in speaking of women's contributions. Just say that what
women want of the church is to be recognized as the full human persons
they really are, and treated accordingly." The simple directness of that
statement seems to me sufficient to set the stage for correcting the gross
injustices to women in the church.

If we really believe that full human persons have equal rights and
responsibilities in the church, we must certainly promote full ministry
for women. I was delighted that the Women's Ordination Conference in
the 1970s made great strides in supplying a forum for women who felt
themselves called to the priesthood.

Were you — are you — one of these?

No. I can't say that I feel called to the priesthood. But I do feel the
official church must straighten itself out and *repent* of its treatment of
women so that those who do seek ordination may participate in that
ministry. I suppose the reason I have not considered it seriously is that
I believe such profound changes must occur first within the church, especially with regard to women, that we must push forward in that area. I
do love the church because of its mission in promoting the gospel and
because of its rich tradition in which we all share. But mixed up, sadly,
with that tradition is the patriarchal history and practice which must
be changed if the church is to be true to itself in promoting the gospel.

*Would you say that your role, the role of women in the church, has
improved?*

Yes, of course, it has *somewhat* because there's renewed consciousness
of the injustice toward women, due primarily to the hard work of women
committed to the struggle. It's true that women (and many sisters among
them) have been invited into some new roles in the church since the
Second Vatican Council. But the advances have just inched forward. And
as real countervailing trend depends on a much greater awareness of
the whole problem of injustice by both women and men. No amount of
admitting women to certain roles in the church will substitute for the
correction of the refusal to admit women to full ministry.

But you think it will happen?

Yes, I think the injustice will finally be corrected because the power of
truth eventually overcomes. But it's sad it's so slow. Because of their

unjust treatment, many gifted women have left and will leave the institutional church. And, of course, the church will be all the poorer because of their dropping out. But, as I said, we've been in the struggle, both as women and as sisters, for a long time!

In that struggle you've been associated with many other women. Are there some you'd single out as having had a special influence on your life in these years of renewal?

Of course, many women in the Loretto community have had special roles, particularly Helen Sanders and Jane Marie Richardson. The latter wrote our beautiful guidelines. The strength, intelligence, and support of both of them have been very important to me. And in the Conference of Major Superiors of Women (and its later development, the Leadership Conference of Women Religious), I would name those with whom I worked, especially Betty Carroll, Mary Daniel Turner, and Francis Rothluebber, whose vision and courage are still an influence on religious women.

What about women theologians?

I've been inspired by some women theologians, especially Rosemary Ruether, because of her clear thinking in regard to feminist theology, and Dorothee Solle, a woman whose work to end the nuclear arms race is so motivated by her deep faith and challenging theological insights.

Several stalwart leaders of Church Women United have touched my life. Margaret Shannon and Margaret Sonnenday were in leadership roles when I was invited to work on the national staff. Through that work, I met so many other courageous women — To Thi Anh, a Vietnamese nun whose beautiful spirit blended the thought of the East and the West; Oo Chung Lee, a Korean woman who worked bravely for human rights in her country; the Irish women peace workers; and so many other international women whom I met through Dorothy Wagner of Church Women United.

In the work for nuclear disarmament, I have been moved by women such as Randall Forsberg and Pam Solo, by the women of Greenham Common, and by so many others strongly committed to peace.

You said that involvement in peace and justice work was one of the chief aspects of your experience of renewal. I've been aware that some persons worry that "all this work for justice detracts from the life of prayer." What do you say to this?

I'd say that the faith life proclaimed in the gospel has no meaning without concern for others and especially for "the least ones" that Jesus singled out. I think that that love which sees God's purpose as the improvement of the human situation wherever suffering exists is in full accord with the admonition to "love one another as I have loved you." It seems to me that the more deeply one lives the life of faith, the more one is impelled to try to identify with the life, words, and actions of Jesus who set his life aside for the truth he lived by: Persons are above all human institutions and laws.

So in your own life, you do not see any kind of dichotomy, as they say, between action and contemplation?

No. I think that prayer and action in a faith context are very integral. I believe that *every* person has been graced with God's own self-communication. Making the realization of such a profound truth our own, I think, leads to such deep respect for the dignity of every other person that we resist any form of dehumanization. I've always appreciated Thomas Merton's statement that 'There is no contradiction between action and contemplation when both are raised to the level of love." I feel that *learning* to love in the reality of struggle in our lives and especially in our efforts to build a more just world flows normally from prayer. I know my own prayer has become an increasing effort to be aware of the hurts and injustices in the world as well as to be more sensitive to the needs of the persons in my immediate life.

I know that in the last six or seven years especially you've done a lot of work on Merton. In the area of renewal, would you talk about your connections with Merton when you knew him?

Because he was our neighbor in Kentucky and because of our acquaintance, he was very interested in the renewal of the Sisters of Loretto. During the last 10 or so years of life, when I knew him, I found him very interested in ecumenical developments, in the need for greater institutional honesty in the church, and in Christian responsibility for the world.

And your own work on Merton? How have you carried it out?

He shared so much in the areas I just mentioned as well as on the topics of prayer and the contemplative life. Many people today seem especially concerned about the integration of faith and action, and Merton was a profound guide here. I think the continued interest in him points to his role as a greatly important contemporary religious figure. So I've tried, through the Thomas Merton Center for Creative Exchange, to share some of his insights and to disseminate some of his manuscripts and tapes which I have.

I've heard you say that Merton was ahead of his time. In what ways?

I think that his insights into justice issues, especially racism, and into the threat of nuclear holocaust are just being appreciated today. Especially in the nuclear area, it's incredible that as early as 1962 he was writing about such topics as counterforce, deterrence, a preemptive first strike, the neutron bomb — warning us of this country's precipitous course down the path to nuclear ruin. The world has continued along that road. It's surely the most critical problem of our times.

Could you talk a little about your own work for nuclear disarmament?

I think the most important demand on Christians and on all others today is to end the nuclear arms race. Many, many sisters are working in this effort. As I said earlier about the peace movement, I could simply not *not* be involved, because I feel that in our almost desperate times today we need to follow every possible course to halt the weapons buildup. We've worked from so many approaches — contacting our congresspersons, collecting freeze signatures, promoting study of the bishops' peace pastoral, taking part in rallies and demonstrations. The list of ways of

resistance could go on and on. In my own work of giving talks and workshops, I make the connections between the urgency of working for peace
and the faith orientation of Christians. In the past couple of years, I've
had the opportunity to travel to Europe twice to learn more about the
connections between the peace movement here and over there.

*Were those trips with religious groups similar to some of your efforts
during the Vietnam War?*

Yes, they were religious in orientation. In 1981, I was one of several
observers at the World Council of Churches conference on disarmament,
held in Amsterdam. We not only listened to theologians, scientists, and
others from various countries discuss the need for stopping the arms race,
but we also had good meetings with the Dutch peace movement, itself a
development from church groups, as well as with peace groups in Germany and England.

In 1983, I was invited by the Religious Task Force of the Mobilization
for Survival to take part in demonstrations in London at the time of the
huge international protests against the deployment of U.S. weapons in
Europe. There, too, I met with many peace workers, church-based and
others, and with a number of religious groups. I think all those linkings
— with persons of other religions and with people of many countries —
are crucial as we work together for peace — really for the survival of
humanity. Certainly these are all involvements that would have been
impossible in the days before renewal.

Are you hopeful that nuclear disarmament is possible?

Yes, we must never give up hope. I think I feel most encouraged when
I see the hundreds of ways in which persons are working for peace, when
I see the burgeoning of peace groups, and when I see the hundreds of
thousands of persons from all walks of life, all ages, all faiths, joining
together to say no. In some ways I think I'm always trying to answer a
woman who sat next to me once on a plane when I was going to Albuquer-
que to give a talk about stopping the arms race. She asked me what I
was writing, and when I told her, she replied, "Why waste your time on
that? We can't do anything about it. It's out of our hands." I think her
attitude somewhat typifies the fatalism of many today, but I believe that
people *can* make a difference. I think that I cannot be silent.

*It seems that working for disarmament — for the nuclear weapons
freeze, for example — and for other justice issues actually means some
political involvement. What about that?*

Of course it does. It's crucial that we affect policy at the government
level. That's why we carry our concerns to Washington or to state capitols
or city council chambers. I feel that I could not be truly a Christian
without this kind of involvement because it is one of the critical ways of
working for justice and peace. To me it's simply a fact of life — a fact of
how I live out my faith.

*Have you ever considered taking a public office — that kind of political
action?*

No. But I know that that's a role which numerous sisters have filled admirably at various levels of government. I myself have been very active in NETWORK, the social justice lobby which was begun by sisters about 14 years ago, and which has consistently tried to keep congresspersons aware of the justice issues that must be addressed. My experience with NETWORK, with Carol Coston, its founder, and with its board has been one of the most encouraging results of the renewal for me. Besides the important work the NETWORK lobby does to promote "people" issues, I think the way it has educated so many sisters and others across the coutry has been invaluable. Also, the NETWORK board carries out the feminist principles of process and concern — real collegiality and consensus — that have been important aspects of our renewal.

I'd like to ask you two final questions. One concerns some specific kinds of work which sisters in the Loretto community are now engaged in which they perhaps would not have undertaken prior to the renewal. As you look out — as the former president and as one who promoted renewal — what do you see?

I could give numerous examples. Not long ago I visited two of our sisters in Appalachia who are working intensely with a group organized against strip-mining. They are really opposing systemic injustices. I also visited three of our sisters in a part of southern Colorado which is actually the poorest county in the state. These sisters chose to build their community where the needs of poor Hispanics are so great. Very often the choice of work dictates the kind of living situation which sisters decide on. Flexibility in this, of course, has been possible because of the way in which the principles of renewal have opened up our lives.

The sisters in southern Colorado work for the needy aging, in basic education for adults, and in the local educational system where bilingual teaching is a necessity. There are also some in our community working in the disarmament movement and the nuclear freeze movement on a national level. One of our sisters, just now completing law school, has been doing her internship in legal aid services to the poor. Well, the list could go on and on!

My other final question deals with what's ahead. How do you think the years of renewal have prepared the way for the future, for next steps for sisters?

As I reflect on my responses to you, with so many of them related to the call to build a more human world, the word *world* stands out. We used to shun "the world." (Of course, I understand why. We didn't see ourselves as part of that world.) But now I believe we find ourselves in the stream of those trying to enable and empower the people of the world to overcome the inhumanities and injustices that exist. Continuing this movement seems to me one of the healthiest aspects of renewal; and I'm happy that the future beckons us in this direction.

For me, renewal has opened the doors to the world. In this sense, the world is people — a broader cut of people, a whole suffering world with all the political, social, and economic factors that keep it from being the

truly human and just world that God intends. If I might connect this
back to the Vatican Council, I think that the deliberations of the Commission on the Church in the Modern World indicated a whole new direction
for church thinking. In the same way, the renewal has done that for us,
and we've been following that direction now for several years. I think
that we religious women are more free, more experienced, more acquainted with risk and disappointment, and especially more committed
to share in the attempt to create that more just world which the gospel
promotes. I think that world is where our future lies.

Dying and Rising

Rea McDonnell

Rea McDonnell, a School Sister of Notre Dame, is director of continuing education and assistant professor of scripture at the Washington Theological Union in Silver Spring, Maryland. She also conducts workshops and retreats on scripture.

I never "entered the convent." I always spoke of "joining the sisters." By the grace of God to this 17-year-old, I viewed religious life as an opportunity for relationship. Yet, reflecting on the most significant changes since my joining the School Sisters of Notre Dame (SSND) in 1959, I find that they are transformations of structure. In the past decades Roman Catholics have, through the leadership of our bishops, been encouraged to broaden our understanding of sin and grace. We experience not only personal sin and grace unique to each of us, but whole families, communities, societies can be caught in structures of grace.

Paul the Apostle, ambassador of reconciliation, was furious with his community at Galatia who entertained those who would divide, classify, categorize the young Christians. "In Christ," Paul insists, "there is no Jew nor Greek, slave nor free person, male nor female" (Galatians 3.28). My earliest experience of religious life, however, was one of chauvinism that divided women religious from lay women, from men lay or clerical, even from women of other congregations. Barriers were erected and the "perfect ones" were enclosed, not primarily for the sake of solitude, which is truly a value, but to keep us uncontaminated.

When I reflect on structural sin in the world today I am amazed at Paul's inspiration. It seems every structural sin can be traced back to classism (slave/free person), racism/nationalism/sectarianism (Jew/Greek) or sexism (male/female).

What renewal of religious life has meant for me personally, then, is a weakening, even a dissolving of some of these structures of sin as they impinged on the life of vowed Catholic women. I credit the Spirit at work not only at the Vatican Council but in our own prophetic leadership, the leadership of women religious. I am grateful, too, for the work of the Spirit in the followers!

Women religious, most of whom joined their congregations seeking a higher, more perfect way of life, a surer path to God, were rudely faced with their own elitism when they were told by the Vatican Council fathers that religious life was no "higher" or "holier" state of life. God calls all Christians to holiness and some choose to live out that call in marriage, others in religious community *(Lumen Gentium, V)*. Women religious in a slow, often excruciatingly painful process gave up their sense of privilege, their classism, and began to think of themselves as laity. At this time (1984), they are consciously uniting with their lay sisters. Thus we name ourselves "women religious," because lay women are also "religious women." Within the community, we have worked at being sisters to one another, eschewing both privileges and titles which bespoke classism: mother, superior, general. "In Christ, there is no . . . slave nor freeperson."

Vatican II was an ecumenical council and women religious responded with an ecumenism of their own. Many began to dialogue and work with ministers of other denominations, especially among the disadvantaged. A significant number of sisters studied theology in ecumenical environments, sometimes because certain theological degrees were unavailable for women in Catholic schools. International congregations grew proud to be sisters transnationally. Various congregations of women began to speak with one another, to organize together, to work with one another, to live intercongregationally. "In Christ, there is no Jew nor Greek. . . ."

Perhaps the most crucial structural sin to weigh upon women religious at this point in history is sexism. Sexism is even dividing sisters themselves at the moment. The structures that kept us from knowing, living and working with men have been breached. The pain for some sisters is to have watched their friends move out of the congregations into marriage. The pain for others is to have the spotlight turned full force on the way we women have allowed men in church and society to use us, patronize us. Some sisters are disgusted by community members who insist on changing the sexist language in common prayer; some are deeply hurt that their own sisters cannot see or feel the male oppression that they experience in the church. "In Christ, there is no . . . male nor female."

In my own life I have experienced the Spirit's freeing me from these structures. "Where sin abounds, grace more abounds." Freedom is born of pain, however, and so I choose to cast my story in images of dying and rising, "growing ever more in the pattern of the dying of Jesus so that the life of Jesus may be revealed in our body of flesh" (II Corinthians 4.10).

Much of my "dying took place in 1968, a crucial year for the whole United States. My heroes, Martin Luther King and Robert Kennedy were killed. My first close friend left the community. Most devastating was my "loss of faith." I was studying for a master's degree in theology in summer school. A teacher announced to us: "God is not a person." He went on to explain that God is more than a person, but that we humans can only speak of God by way of analogy. I could not hear his explanation. I heard only that my whole theological system was shattering. It continued to fall in ruins around me as I taught high school religion, fearful that I might infect my students with my lack of faith. What was happening, I realized later, was that I was beginning to reconstruct a "theology from below," a never-ending task that I am still about. I began to search for God in my own lived experience of community, teaching, politics, prayer. I began to let God reveal himself to me.

An important moment in 1968 was a discussion with Marcia, a member of my community who was a dear friend. We attended a lecture on vocations, in which a priest explained the Vatican II statement that the only vocation is to holiness, given to all. How we are to become holy and to help others grow in holiness is our own choice, based on who we are by nature and by grace and on what we want. The lecture pointed out that God doesn't "call" us to marriage or to the School Sisters of Notre Dame or to medicine or to street cleaning. We choose. Right, I said. But Marcia's image of God and God's will was distorted. She had joined the community because she thought God demanded sacrifice from her. This lecture freed her to voice her desire, her choice of marriage. She left our community. I was sad, but I was where I *wanted* to be. So much for the mystery of it all! I was in charge of my own life.

Five years later I fell in love, I who always insisted that I was not gifted to be wife and mother. Now I was free to look at both styles of life for the first time. In this freedom, paradoxically, I did not choose, but instead felt chosen. I cannot explain that. I can only claim mystery. Paul's experience seems to elucidate my own: "I stretch forward to grasp Christ who has already grasped hold of me" (Philippians 3.12). Just as my married friends feel grasped by Christ and held in their commitment to him, to their spouses and to their children, even when the grass at times looks greener, so I can only believe I stay in religious life because God is deepening my commitment, confirming my original choice. It has become more God's choice, God's mission and I only respond to this initiative.

Community and mission, chief experiences in my life, were shaped and reshaped for me in perhaps the most excruciating incident of my life. In 1970 I was fired. I had been teaching religion in a School Sisters of Notre Dame high school when my provincial leader broke the news. I marched out of her office and stomped down the corridor, hell bent on walking the mile or so to my family home. A friend was teaching and heard the heavy, angry steps as I passed her classroom. She stepped into the corridor, held me by the shoulders as I sputtered out my story and where I was headed. "Rea, you can't leave. *We* need you!"

I didn't leave. I carried my case to our chapter looking for justice, and as the chapter refused to overturn the principal's decision, one sister smiled at me and in sugary tones promised me, "Out of every death a resurrection will come." I was furious. Yet that moment was grace. I began at that point in my history to see the movements of my life as sharing in Jesus' dying and rising. I was asked by my provincial to find my own job since she could not place me in a School Sisters of Notre Dame setting. I thus became the pioneer in "open placement" in my province. It was not by choice that the structures of mission and ministry began to open for me. But *"we* need you," carried me through, kept me still deeply attached to the community.

The "we" were a group of friends and companions in my province who were beginning to move out of institutional convents into smaller groups, into homier situations. I was part of a group of six who moved to an abandoned convent in the inner city of Chicago. We ranged in age from me, the youngest at 28, to Philemon, aged 75. We commuted to work and bonded closely with other sisters in similar "experimental communities." "We" were forging new experiences of community.

Three months after I was fired, our community of six was given two weeks notice by the new pastor to leave the abandoned convent that we had scoured and renovated — another experience of the "dying of Jesus." This was for me a brief but profound experience of solidarity with the poor who are homeless or subject to eviction. The "resurrection" came quickly however. The six of us found an intercongregational community welcoming us. Being "shoved out of the nest" again opened new structures for our province.

Within those few months, both at home and at work, I was beginning to understand that indeed, out of every death a resurrection does come. This first intercongregational living situation brought a new and important dimension to our province where now a significant number of our sisters are in community with other groups of sisters. School was my delight. Freed from institutional commitments (at great cost, however) I could ask myself: What have I always wanted to do? I had always wanted to teach the poorest and the slowest. There was such a high school in Chicago, operated by the Institute of the Blessed Virgin Mary Sisters (IBVM), which took those girls who did not score high enough on their entrance tests to be accepted by other Catholic schools. These students were usually from poverty-stricken families. The IBVMs were my constant inspiration. Most of what I know about mission and ministry was forged in my work with them, work for the outcast of society.

I taught English and reading as well as religion. So many of the girls were hungry for belief in themselves, for individual attention that our small school with its programs for slow learners could offer them. They blossomed, they learned, they became creative. I responded with joy when a sophomore wrote her first complete sentence ever; with gratitude when a 14-year-old moved from a second grade to an eighth-grade reading level in six months; with awe at the delicate poem crafted by a street-wise young woman. Fostering human development became as important to me as fostering spiritual development. Out of the death of being fired came new and abundant life for me.

To educate in the area of spiritual development, however, was where I felt I belonged. With regret I left Chicago's inner city. I wanted to study for a doctorate in scripture at Boston University, a Methodist school of theology with an ecumenical faculty and student body. "Doing theology" from below made me acutely aware of the power of scripture to illumine our contemporary search for God in history, in community, in politics. Even more important than four rich and nourishing years of study, however, was the nourishment that fed a hunger in me I never knew I had. I lived in a community with men.

We School Sisters of Notre Dame are missioned by our revised constitution "to make one." This group of men religious have reconciliation as their central mission. How opportune that I and another sister from our community, also a student, should happen upon their house of studies for seminarians. It was policy for this group of priests and brothers to invite women to form community with them so that the seminarians could experience formation in a more normal setting. It was formative for us as well.

As we were being interviewed to see whether we would fit in, we were interviewing them too. "Who does the laundry, cooking and sewing?" I asked somewhat defensively. Women's private rooms were on the top floor, but everything else we shared: cooking, cleaning, prayer, meals, celebration. If I taught a man how to sew a seam, he taught me to patch my own bicycle tire. The men cooked well, the women shoveled snow well, and we all discovered in our weekly community meetings that our values were held in common. At the end of my four years there, the topic of a community meeting was why this mixed community worked so well. My own response was a religious experience, one of being brother and sister to each other. In this community the opposite sex was de-mythologized. We were not sex objects, neither objects of fear nor objects of fascination. We were not objects to one another at all. We were a praying community with the dying-rising Lord as center. Jesus "dies to gather all the scattered children of God into one family" (John 11.52). With their charism of reconciling and ours of "making one," we had experienced being one family of God, brothers and sisters in life-giving relationship.

Now I live alone. The dying and rising is much more interior now. Community is more interior now. I have lived for 11 years outside the geographical boundaries of my Chicago province, but I belong profoundly to the Chicago School Sisters of Notre Dame. The "we" of "we need you" have, many of them, left the congregation. I am at work where I should be: administrator at a Roman Catholic graduate school of theology, the Washington Theological Union. I also teach scripture on some weekends at Emmanuel College in Boston; on week nights in the pastoral counseling program of Loyola College in Columbia, Maryland. In the summer I teach in Boston, Baltimore and Vermont. I preach and direct retreats, lead adult education sessions in parishes, publish cassette tapes, write articles and books on biblical spirituality. Offering spiritual direction is an important ministry for me, too.

Community continues to mean to me my definition of 1964: sharing goals on a deep level. However, instead of sharing goals with a group under one roof I find I am facilitating other adults' uncovering their deepest goals in life and thus am challenged to hone and deepen and share my own goals with them. I find community with my continuing education students, especially those men and women experienced in ministry who spend their sabbatical for renewal and theological stimulation at Washington Theological Union. I pray with them, play with them, often cook with and for them at our potluck parties. They are a source of refreshment for me.

Those to whom I minister in spiritual direction minister to me. They speak of their life with God as he reveals himself uniquely. Together we search for God's movement, God's direction in their relationship with him and with their peopled environment. I stand in awe and pray in gratitude often as they speak, often long after they have left my office. They are community for me as we share not only goals but God on a deep level.

My scripture students, adults preparing for ministry, are community for me because of my strong conviction, practice and experience: Scripture study is formative of community. My goal is to help them "make the word of God their home" (John 8.32) and in that common home we always seem to discover that we are brothers and sisters.

A number of sisters from my community in the Washington, D.C. are in ministry to and with adults and are thus challenged to share goals and lives on a deep level. Many of us live alone needing solitude after intense hours of sharing with our peers in ministry, or with clients to whom we listen with intense and emotional involvement. We need solitude, but are completing six years of experience of "community without walls." Every two weeks a small consistent interprovincial group of School Sisters of Notre Dame meets to pray and eat together and to share the major movements of our lives. Although not gathered under one roof, we have a quality of community which many sisters would envy.

We do not necessarily have intimacy. Community — sharing goals on a deep level — can be extremely satisfying. For myself, however, intimacy with friends both inside and outside the congregation is a necessity. I remember teaching I Corinthians 7, Paul's explanation of sexuality, to a class of college students, most of whom were Catholic. I gave a soft pitch on the value of celibacy for the sake of the kingdom. One young man shot up his hand to announce: "But there's no intimacy, so how can you celibates be fully human?" Sometimes when I teach, the Spirit says something I never knew before, and that day the Spirit was teaching me as well as my class. It suddenly dawned on me that intimacy is both a choice and a gift, within marriage and without. I asked him if he knew of marriages in which there was no intimacy. He and other students had to admit that they knew many marriages without intimacy, as I had to admit knowing many religious and priests who never had had an intimate friend. Both the married and the celibate can choose, and refuse or receive the gift of intimacy.

I know that I need, want and make decisions that lead to and foster intimacy. Not only sharing goals, work, prayer and play, but sharing my responses to life, my visions of life, my emotions, my history, my craziness, my friends and enemies, my sins and graces are some ways which I have learned to grow in intimacy. Perhaps the most important way in which I came to enjoy intimacy in my own life was to let others love me. The abyss of loneliness is filled for me because others mirror and even embody for me God's unconditional and faithful love. These are my intimate friends, my greatest blessings.

These friends encourage me to move more deeply into the interior of who I am. I have discovered that the process of living more deeply from within is really for the sake of mission. Obedience is not external conformity to law but internal openness for dialogue, not only with authorities but with community, friends, students — all those who mediate God's desire for me and my ministry. Poverty is not measured by possessions or lack of them. Instead, like the rich young man of Mark 10, I have learned to see Jesus looking at me tenderly. As I grow more and more convinced of his loving look, I keep my eyes fixed more and more on him and I discover myself gradually, gently, respectfully being weaned from the things that surround me.

For myself, chastity has been rather central. In our day, we made a vow of chastity. I define "celibacy" as the state of not marrying for the sake of the kingdom. Celibacy may well be a choice, a lifestyle, but chastity can only be a gift. Once there seemed to be scores of regulations in the rule to keep sisters chaste. Now chastity means for me an interior response to God's gift of unconditional, faithful loving-us-first. That response grows continually more free and more joyful. It is a life-long process, I believe, to become chaste, to receive fully the gift of God's total love. More and more religious, priests and laity to whom I listen are opening to that interior experience, for all of us are called to receive the gift of chastity according to our state in life.

These religious, priests and laity tell me that their goal in life is to love well. Once every Christian was told to "be perfect as your heavenly Father is perfect." Religious and priests were supposed to shoulder double responsibilities for perfection. That seemed to be our goal. The church had been reading the version of this saying, however, found only in Matthew's gospel: "Be perfect." Today we read and want to obey the evangelist Luke's version of the same saying: "Be compassionate as your heavenly Father is compassionate (Luke 6.36). Bearing one another's burdens is how we fulfill the law of Christ (Galatians 6.2).

Like Peter at the first council at Jerusalem I have come to believe that our external perfection in the law, in the system will not only not save, it will drastically harm the church and "provoke God" (Acts 15.6-11). Not by any work, not by any life-style, not by any vow, not by any perfection am I saved or made holy. "It is God's gift" (Ephesians 2.6-9).

It is by sharing in the dying of Jesus that the life of Jesus is continually revealed in our body of flesh — our body as person, our body as congregation, our body as women religious, our body as church. All of us, lay and religious, women and men, bear witness to the Risen Lord at work. What an adventure: to experience the Lord gathering into one family all the divided, broken, scattered children of God. What an adventure to share in Christ's mission and ministry of making all people one.

Don't Fence Me In

Lillanna Audrey Kopp

Lillanna Audrey Kopp, sociologist-anthropologist, has spent 45 years researching sisters and has written two books on the subject New Nuns: Collegial Christians *and* Sudden Spring: Sixth Stage Sisters. *She was a co-editor of* Trans-Sister, *and co-founder with Margaret Ellen Traxler of the National Coalition of American Nuns. She was the originator in 1970 of Sisters For Christian Community, the fastest-growing sisterhood in the world. She has lectured widely on religious life renewal — most recently to the sisters of Holland at the 1984 International Interdisciplinary Congress of Women at Groningen University, the Netherlands.*

Pope John Paul II and I were born a few months apart, not exactly on separate planets, but in such dissimilar social and religious climates that our horns are locked in respectful confrontation over what each of us perceives to be the essential elements in the renewal not only of religious life, but of Christian life as well. He supports patriarchy and pyramidal model of organization for the church, and sisterhoods within it, controlled by a monarchical, all-male bureaucracy in Rome. In contrast, I and other feminists and futurists subscribe to the theory, supported by an alternate scriptural interpretation, that Jesus Christ was an ideological revolutionary who came to challenge the sexist, patriarchal status quo by calling his followers to egalitarian, circular-model relationships, to authentic community and mutual ministry where "there is neither male nor female, free nor slave . . ." (Galatians 3:28)

Pope John Paul II's Eastern European socialization disposes him toward spurring his subordinates to help round up the strayed American sisters and return them to total institution-like corrals of the pre-Vatican II design. There he purports to supercede the group-made constitutions and the sisters' own leadership charisms by being the ultimate superior (trail boss) for sisters throughout the world. My over-arching vocational goal, in contrast, reflecting ideals of the American West and what I believe to be those of the primitive, pre-patriarchal church, is to remove from sisters the harnesses and halters of bureaucracy and total institution, to throw wide open the corral gates and turn sisters free into fields where their personal and communal charism, in oneness with Christ, will forward their spiritual maturation and that of the entire church as the people of God in community.

And herein, in my opinion, lies the essence of the renewal tensions for more than a half-million sisters and two billion other Catholics worldwide. We all stand watching together the deaththroes of the patriarchal, Constantinian era of church history; we are taut and bloodied by the birth-struggle of authentic Christian community.

My life's journey and involvement in the birthing struggle of church as community is uniquely my own. But because I am journeying in the company of hundreds, even thousands of sister and brother companions in the United States, Canada and beyond, the telling of my experiences in religious renewal is the telling of their stories, too. Like the other writers in this collection, I want to share in sketching out the answers to questions Catholics and others at home and abroad are asking: What makes American religious women a Roman problem today? What in the renewal of sisterhood as in parish, diocese, and total church renewal, must be wholly new?

A cattle ranch burgeoning in golden wheat and edged in purple peaks was my first setting and locus of contact with institutionalized Christianity. Its initial representative in my life was a candy-toting pastor of Holy Rosary Church, Bozeman, Montana, who back in the Roaring '20s often visited my family on Sunday afternoons.

On this western ranch, when I was four, my spiritual development took significant, long-lasting turns as the result of two events. One day, convulsed with horror, shuddering, crying, yet utterly mesmerized and magnetized to a barn-wall knothole, I watched the throat-slitting, skinning and evisceration of three steers as ranch hands slaughtered them for market and our table. That overwhelming revulsion left me with only a fragile and cautious trust in the genuine sensitivity of men, not because of any innate killer instinct in them, but because they are too often socialized to be tough, macho, dominating and uncaring in the presence of the pain, the personhood, or the emotional travail of others. I always regarded my gentle father and brothers as rare exceptions to this pattern, men who somehow escaped the twin brand marks of patriarchy and sexism.

My spirituality, suffered another blow the following Sunday at mass when my mother explained to me that my candy-bearing friend up at the altar was eating the body and drinking the blood of the Jesus whom I nightly asked to bless each family member and every pet. The impact was devastating! I confess that to this very day the mass evokes memories of the traumatic barn scene and never became the high point of my religious worship as I was later told it should be. So I am definitely not among the women who might relish celebrating the reenactment of the sacrifice of the Lamb of God. Ordination in the present Roman rite — with its borrowed accouterments from ancient Rome's mother goddess cults: priesthood, vestments, and a sacrificial meal — is not for me.

When my older siblings were at school, I played away the hours with our dogs out in the fields and pastures. There a contemplative bent was mushrooming within me. Multi-shaded mountains, wild-flower-flecked foothills, or winter-whitened ranchlands provided an ample chapel for my offbeat worship and friendship with a tag along, ever imaginative God who kept filling my world with astonishing forms and brilliant colors.

Soon came an era colored green and black. In late adolesence, after a year in a Catholic college, I said hesitant goodbyes to friends, parked my bike in the garage, left my graduation watch on my dresser, as though I might be right back, and exchanged a life of carefree ranging and informal spirituality for the ordered program and highly structured regimen of religious life at a novitiate in Oregon. The long waxed hallways, the silent lines of black-clad sisters, the bells punctuating each interval of a rule-determined horarium, tethered my spirit. The rain-lush, forevergreen environs of Oregon became a confining corral like none I had ever envisioned. Yet I found joy in praying, studying, and teaching children.

Finally, with a master's degree in psychology and counseling, I plunged enthusiastically into work with divorce orphans, emotionally disturbed girls and court-committed delinquents at a social agency, operated by my congregation and the state of Oregon. The agency stood at one end of a large campus; at the other, a grade school, high school, college, novitiate, juniorate, provincial house, retirement center, golf course, orchards and cemetery.

Although I was an efficient teacher, principal and counselor for the girls at this social agency, the provincial superior one day asked me if I would "sacrifice" my specialization in psychology and study for a doctorate in sociology and anthropology at St. Louis University. Neither the provincial adminstration nor I could have even faintly anticipated that the following years of study of social structures and their massive, sometimes devastating impact on persons would utterly revolutionize my own outlook on religious life.

Sociology, the scientific study of the structures and functions of human groups, from tiny friendship clusters to international cartels, enthralled me. Especially was I intrigued by applying what I learned to the Catholic church structure in general, and to sisterhoods in particular. I devoured every piece of available research in the study of formal organizations. I probed additonal data in anthropology, social psychology, historical and political analysis. All corroborated the mind-rocking conclusion that metamorphized my evaluation of religious life.

Across an ocean another young student, Karl Wojtyla, the future Pope John Paul II, was learning the same from his social anthropology classes and from experiencing the structures of fascism and communism firsthand. Later he would write a monograph, *The Acting Person,* and I two books on Catholic sisterhoods. Both pointed out that

> persons blocked by authoritarian structures from participation in decision-making on their own behalf or for the common good of groups to which they belong, become malformed, closed in personality, stunted in maturation, alienated and estranged from the persons or groups suppressing their initiative and dominating their lives. Even were they to initially concur in the suppressive system because of religious or political beliefs, the infantilization from perpetual submission to the will of others, almost inevitably occurs.

Years later I would attempt to remind Pope John Paul II, through the

January 13, 1984 issue of the *National Catholic Reporter,* of his earlier monograph and of these very words, now so applicable to his concern for the vocation crisis in sisterhoods. Only recently have sisters begun to struggle out from the grasp of authoritarian structures imposed by canon law and the Sacred Congregation for Religious and Secular Institutes (SCRIS).

Domination-submission patterns in totalitarian nations are broadly perceived as evil and dehumanizing. They are condemned as immoral because they throttle the freedom of persons to think and act independently or in concert with others. Authoritarianism is recognized as a manipulation of power over another, and an abuse of genuine authority because it causes those whom it controls to regress and strangles their right to self-actualization and growth to full personhood. Unfortunately, persons who readily disavow totalitarian governance on a national scale as in Russia, China and Cuba, seem oblivious to the same suppression patterns in micro-totalitarian organizations operating in backyard USA — in the Ku Klux Klan, a Jamestown cult, or even a Catholic sisterhood.

Sociologists categorize these micro-totalitarian units as total institutions because they swallow the total or near-total decision-making freedom of their inmates. Within total institutions administrators plan the hour-by-hour activities, determine who will do what, set up rigid rules and relentlessly supervise their enforcement. Among the many groups that social scientists define as total institution are these familiar forms: prisons, boarding schools, military barracks, navy ships, homes for the aging, asylums, convents, monasteries, concentration camps. Prior to Vatican II and subsequent renewal efforts sisters have been, in varying degrees:

— obliged to follow a rigid hour-by-hour horarium;
— required to eat, sleep, work and recreate together under supervision;
— issued institutional, group-identifying clothing;
— made to break with their pasts;
— limited, scrutinized, censored in letter writing;
— allowed to visit parental homes only at times of death;
— permitted infrequent visits from family and friends;
— urged to relinquish all personal property, including family pictures;
— required to ask permission for new tooth paste, shoe strings, etc.;
— given identifying numbers for ranking and roll call;
— stripped of surname, even baptismal name usage;
— assigned a new name, even masculine names by a bishop;
— deprived of decision-making, and hence of an adult self-concept;
— required to ask permission to leave a room;
— divested of autonomy to come and go at leisure;
— asked to expose personal lives for the records;
— assigned jobs without consultation or preparation;
— subjected constantly to the benevolent or despotic will of superiors.

These centuries-old patterns and the serious problems related to them, which I had observed or experienced during my first 20 years as a sister, I now know were not due to autocratic tendencies or personality imbalance in superiors or subjects. Scientific research showed many of the dysfunctions of religious life to be obsolete culture patterns, built-in consequences of unwholesome, person-deforming, community-destroying social structures, especially bureaucracy and total institutions. Yet total institution was the taken-for-granted, unexamined structure of religious life imposed by ecclesiastical authorities. Individual sisters had no input into the design of those structures, just as they have had no input into the 36-page document on *Essential Elements of Religious Life* published by SCRIS and approved by Pope John Paul II in May, 1983. It is probable that most sisters, clerics, and even popes lack the faintest suspicion that the authoritarian structures in religious life, like authoritarian structures in homes, schools, or workplaces, are malfunctional and actually destructive.

But how could a relatively young sister-sociologist fresh out of doctoral studies confront her superiors with such information? How voice her grave concern over the immorality of using total institution structures to those who not only affirmed them but promoted them as the will of God? Face saving, I knew, was a factor in religious life that had to be reckoned with. Even were the mother superior to allow me 20 or 30 minutes for a conference, how could I encapsulate all the research of the past 20 or more years that would lay bare the seriously dysfunctional aspects of even a modified Christian totalitarianism, with its emphasis on blind obedience and self-abnegation? How could I share with sister friends that our congregation, like sisterhoods throughout the world, was an oligarchic bureaucracy and definitely not a community, as we so naively and euphemistically called it? Who would listen, or if they listened, understand what three years of doctoral study had seared into my heart and mind?

I knew that it had taken decades for the science of psychology to gain respectability, and for official church personnel to finally shift "blame" for many problems from the realm of personal sinfulness to psychological causes. How many more decades would it take, I wondered, for this new sociological insight to gain acceptance?

Returning from doctoral studies to teach at a college of my congregation compounded my frustrations. Where were the administrators willing to consult sociology for insights relative to the renewal of religious life? I yearned to be allowed to utilize sociological insights and be among the planners, nationally, for the operations which I sensed would be necessary if religious life were to survive.

My opportunity was to arrive circuitously via the civil rights revolution. It exploded in the United States concurrently with the ferment from Vatican II, and the *moto proprio* from Rome for sisters to update and renew. In the mid-1960s, blacks were taking to the streets in protest both peaceful and violent over their centuries-long domination and suppression. Many inner-city Catholic schools began to close as blacks inundated the old neighborhoods. Second generation Catholics of immigrant parents were fleeing to the more affluent suburbs, followed by their pastors and teaching sisters. In the midst of this intense racial upheaval and population displacement, an urgent call ran forth from the National Catholic Conference for Interracial Justice (NCCIJ) in Chicago, asking religious congregations to volunteer qualified sisters for race relations workshops to be set up around the United States in areas of greatest racial strife.

Research was indicating that working-class Catholics were among the most strident racists. When Dr. Martin Luther King led a peaceful march into the Lithuanian Catholic neighborhood of Cicero, a Chicago suburb, *Newsweek* captured on camera for its front cover a white boy in a Jesuit letterman sweater throwing a brick at the head of a marching sister as he yelled, "And that's for you, *nun!*" It was vehemently resented in such Catholic ghettoes when a few priests or sisters marched for racial justice. For the most part, however, the official church was relatively silent and uninvolved in the great revolution. Lay people and sisters operated the NCCIJ. It was a decade after the black rights movement and the assassination of King that the American bishops' conference made a formal statement that racism is a moral evil.

I rejoiced to be among the 15 sisters loaned to NCCIJ for their Traveling Workshops in Race Relations, accredited by Loyola University, Chicago. We traveled thousands of miles by plane and station wagons during four racially hot summers and some school year weekends providing in-service training sessions for Catholic and public school teachers, police forces, federal employees, social workers and some diocesan conferences. For me, this was a tremendously enriching experience on two fronts. It allowed my energies to be unleashed in this great cause of social justice for blacks. It placed me face-to-face, mind-to-mind, and heart-to-heart with hundreds of deeply dedicated and courageously involved sisters from various ethnic origins, geographic areas, cultural backgrounds, and educational specializations. When race relation sessions ended each day, informal, unscheduled, spontaneous sister gatherings occurred in lobbies, school cafeterias, local convents, church basements. Into the night we shared pent-up dreams with one another over what we envisioned as necessary for a renewal and florescence of religious life. From city-to-city, state-to-state, and coast-to-coast our race relations team traveled with a double agenda. We prayed that we might somehow make a small gain toward bettering race relations. We'll really never know. But that our gatherings made an impact on American sister renewal, we have no doubt. During them, American sisters envisioned together wholly new religious life models for the 21st century, and they are working still to make them a reality. Our mutural concern for genuine change in sisterhoods was so intense, it lighted a prairie fire of determination, a grassroots revolution among sisters.

One lazy summer Sunday of 1967, as our race relations workship team rested between sessions at a convent in Little Puerto Rico, in Chicago, the faculty at Mundelein College invited us to liturgy, dinner, and renewal discussion with an assortment of sisters from summer sessions and local convents. We had now become used to the shuffled mixture of black, brown, blue, gray, and white habits in a room, and the confidential sharing of renewal issues rarely raised earlier outside one's own convent, or even within it. Trans-congregational meetings of sisters were occurring on the national level through the recently organized Conference of Major Superiors of Women. But these assemblies, in their early years, were more audience sessions, with learned male clerics addressing the sisters while the sisters of each congregation sat segregated with their own kind throughout talks and meals. Dialogue was minimal, the sharing of religious life problems was almost prohibitive. So we recognized fully the tradition-breaking significance of these unique gatherings of grassroot sisters, the "inferiors" in the superior-inferior dichotomy and class levels imposed by religious structures.

It was heartening to realize that so many women religious were not passively relinquishing to administrative elites and clerics the full initiative for change. Cracks were definitely appearing in total institutions this decade. The Sister Formation Movement, begun in the 1950s, was in large measure responsible for this grassroots assumption of personal responsibility in a small but growing number of U.S. sisters. This movement had urged that every teaching sister have at least a B.A. degree. Sisters operating high schools, colleges, nursing programs and hospitals needed more advanced degrees for their institutions' accreditation. So sisterhoods in the mid-1960s were at peak performance. Novitiates and juniorates were filled to near capacity or over. The United States sister population crested at the all-time high of roughly 182,000. Catholic schools were bulging with students.

No one could anticipate in 1967 that within 15 years 47 per cent of the U.S. sisters would have disappeared. A natural death rate and vocational decline could account for but a tiny fraction of the loss. The deadly D's (disaffection, disesteem, and disillusionment) were decimating sisterhoods. In many congregations, where Vatican II principles were resisted and renewal was a shallow facade, sisters left knowing, in conscience, that they could no longer support an outmoded, autocratic system by their presence. The story of the travail of the renewal in religious life would be an unauthentic, whitewashed account were it not recorded for historical purposes that much renewal enthusiasm and expertise was silenced and censored. Hundreds of sisters threatening to the status quo were invited to "put up, shut up, or get out."

One sunny Sunday of 1967 in Chicago, our workshop team was invited to join the faculty at Mundelein College for liturgy, dinner and discussion with an assortment of sisters. This day we shared confidently and intensely with one another as though we were all of one spiritual family. So intense was our experience of commonality and trans-congregational community, we agreed that this type of dialogue not be a one-time event. Our destiny as women religious was uniting us as never before, and we wanted to sustain our closeness by setting up ongoing communication channels. A cross-congregational nuns-to-nuns-only newsletter was proposed. Somewhere in the crowd a voice suggested the newsletter name, and *Trans-Sister* was born. Volunteer editors emerged when Margaret Ellen Traxler, Mary Ellen Muckenhern and I agreed to edit and publish the newsletter on the condition that all present be volunteer reporters.

Thus emerged the first newsletter uniting U.S. sisters in their renewal goals. *Trans-Sister* was enthusiastically welcomed; subscriptions soared. Even from far-off Rome a sister-librarian at the Vatican wrote the editors that she used its renewal news in bimonthly broadcasts from the Vatican for African sisters. *Trans-Sister* was published bimonthly until 1971, when newsletters of other sisters' organizations replaced it.

In the late 1960s sisters throughout the world began holding renewal chapters in preparation for rewriting their constitutions. Directives from Rome insisted that every sister be involved in committees and commissions for this renewal. Sisters were invited to prepare position papers on issues of concern, which were purportedly to be shared with all their sisters and chapter delegates. Many congregations went through the process with openness and integrity; others, like my own, limited renewal participation to a few chosen persons, made only selective renewal readings available, and filed position papers of members in unaccessible places. Select committees prepared the new constitution statements, and delegates attending constitutional assemblies often felt they were expected to simply rubberstamp these after minimal dialogue with constituents, and only superficial modifications from the floor.

With simplistic trust I had carefully prepared a position paper for my congregation's renewal chapter, a sociological analysis of the structural changes needed to free religious life from bureaucratic patterns and the sociological-theological nature of the replacement: collegial community. When Father Andrew Greeley and Sister Marie Augusta Neal solicited research papers for the National Catholic Sociological Association's conference that year, I sent them my position paper, — an analysis applicable to all sisterhoods. They scheduled it for the opening session and invited the major superiors of American congregations to attend.

The coming of many major superiors to our meeting in Florida and their enthusiasm for my sociological analysis altered my life enormously for the next three years. Invitations to renewal chapters or weekend conferences throughout the United States and Canada, precipitated me into a hectic, challenging lecture circuit on American sisterhood renewal. My two-day presentations were often attended by the local bishop, vicar for religious, or a canon lawyer. In highly polarized congregations, the change-resistant sector often insisted that a canon lawyer be present on the stage with me to critique my presentation or to field questions. Quite naturally, I had conferred hours with such professionals long before I dared venture out on a three-year lecture tour. I knew my data was sound both sociologically and theologically. An illustrated summary of my lectures had been published by Argus under the title *New Nuns: Collegial Christians*. Its front page bore an imprimatur. Argus supplied thousands of these to congregations, many of whom ordered a copy for each member.

I became inextricably caught up in writing and lecturing on the Vatican II-inspired structural renewal of sisterhoods, on their needed radical transformation from top-heavy, work-orientated, person-manipulating organizations into person-centered, Spirit-directed, collegial or consensual communities of co-equals — women penetrating the total American culture with Christian values rather than concentrating exclusively on traditional ministries, mainly teaching and providing hospital care.

After several years on this renewal circuit the collective impact from facing problems within sisterhoods pressed heavily. I often realized that no sister in the world, and certainly no cleric, was learning more about the internal erosion in sisterhoods than I. Congregation administrators often shared detailed accounts of internal disorders hoping to better equip me to address the issues when I talked with their sisters. I was particularly devastated when major superiors, almost in whispers, spoke of the loss of some of their finest women, women with mature convictions about their lifelong commmitment to Christ, but nevertheless convinced that their religious life must be expressed in alternate patterns in other places.

I too dreamed continuously of the possibility of a wholly new structure for the consecrated life, a fresh creation without rents and patches, a fresh start that would obviate the present polarization and pain of renewal. I became increasingly aware that in every congregation I visited, in every audience listening to renewal discussions and proposals, there were other sisters dreaming the same dreams. I kept wondering if it were too late to stem the exodus of more sisters and summon back to an experimental grouping many who had already left. The grouping would be a national experiment in truly collegial community. Because I considered it the leadership responsibility of the American bishops and Conference of Major Superiors, I raised the question of such an experiment whenever possible, especially if I spotted a bishop in the audience.

Finally the probing question triggered action. A bishop in Colorado flew the next week to confer with a bishop in Michigan, the latter being, at the time, the official intermediary between U.S. sisters and bishops. A few months later, when I was lecturing in Michigan, this bishop and a Canadian cardinal associated with the Congregation for Religious were present to hear me and share views concerning the proposed pan-congregational community. Both prelates agreed that the bishops and major superiors were too preoccupied with their own internal problems to address the larger issue of a national experimental community that would embody the principles of subsidiarity, collegiality and co-responsibility from its inception. Why, they asked frankly, do you not undertake this task yourself? American sisters know you and trust you. If such a style of sisterhood is viable and of the Holy Spirit, it will grow and by its fruit we will know it.

My initial anticipation that such an experiment be blessed, assisted, and given canonical approval by Rome, was the only aspect of the proposal that the prelates opposed. If it were to be canonically affirmed now, they reminded me, it would require a predetermined constitution that would cement a breath of the Spirit into concrete. If it was to be truly and freely open to the needs of each moment of history, the charisms of the members, and the continuing direction of the Holy Spirt, then the seeking of canonical recognition should be postponed indefinitely — under present circumstances, perhaps forever. My convictions about the need of this new, free-form sisterhood were so deep, I became determined to risk all and be a catalyst for its birth and growth. This would mean dissociation from my original congregation and distancing myself from the crush of renewal activities.

The distancing was beautifully facilitated by an offer from Chapman College, California, to teach anthropology for a year aboard their university of the seven seas, World Campus Afloat. With a faculty of 70 and a student body of over 700, I set forth on an exploratory adventure — a period of praying and planning.

Slowly, as we encircled the world, the profile of a wholly new-style, post-conciliar religious community took shape. It embodied the visions of Vatican II, my own sociological dreams, and the hopes shared by thousands of sisters at home. In addition, at every port around the world where our ship docked, I pursued with avid interest two preoccupying goals: to deepen and enrich my understanding of world cultures, and to use free hours away from students and scheduled tours to seek out convents and exchange renewal ideas to the extent we shared languages. By the end of this slow voyage around the world, I knew for certain that no other woman in the entire world had shared the renewal dreams about religious life as extensively and intensely as I. I was aware that the same Holy Spirit who was urging me toward collegial, consensual community-in-Christ was instilling similar hopes in sisters everywhere.

When our floating university cast anchor at Puntas Arenas, the southern-most city of the world, on the eve of a new year, rerouted from Oregon, dispensation papers from Rome were awaiting me. I kissed them in welcome for now I could begin a new year and a new life at the same time.

As 1970 dawned in the Straits of Magellan and antarctic glaciers glistened against a chill cobalt sky, in the presence of God, a priest-chaplain, and a sister who taught Spanish, I signed the dispensation papers freeing me from a bureaucratic congregation and, at the same time, renewed my Christ-commitment as a Sister For Christian Community, less a title than a goal for any bonding of women which would help the birthing of church as community.

My new vows of serving, loving, and listening were simply contemporary counterparts of the traditional ones of poverty, chastity, and obedience, cleansed of patriarchal interpretations and archaic cultural accretions. They were promises simply to respond to the evangelical counsels in Christ's Sermon on the Mount. I did not assume the title "sister" but identified myself by my legal name. In this new sisterhood, we share the ideal indicated in passages throughout the Vatican II documents, to penetrate the world incognito and be hidden yeast for Chrsitian community and/or human values wherever we live and work. This is, of course, a Vatican II challenge to all Christians. *Lumen Gentium* reminds us that we are all invited to observe the evangelical counsels, not just the commandments; that we are all consecrated to Christ and made a priestly people through baptism. Many of us envision a coming era of church history when the old separation of Christians into priests, religious, and laity will be laid away as part of our patriarchal past. In that day all of us will serve one another, will love and listen to one another, and sense our common vocation to be catalysts for Christian community.

Before we dropped anchor in New York harbor, *Trans-Sister* had already beamed forth the good news to waiting sisters that a new-style sisterhood was emerging. It would be open to any woman who relished the risk of helping to pioneer a consensual, free-form community. Response was immediate and continues to make Sisters For Christian Community (SFCC) the most rapidly expanding sisterhood in the church. At this moment when traditional congregations are welcoming the average of one or two sisters a year, our community is welcoming an average of five each month, an acceleration already reflecting, we believe, the enormous frustration of sisters who have labored in renewal efforts for 20 years and now see their insights negated and their work dead-ended.

Today, renewal in sisterhoods seems to have traveled full-circle from authoritarian, pyramidal congregations of 20 years ago, through a hopeful springtime of collegial community and flowering ministries, back to a mandated winter. Rome's non-acceptance of new constitutions until they provide for institutionally-issued uniforms and superiors as ultimate decision-makers, is a continuing patriarchal affront to the intelligence and integrity of women. If these mandates and the SCRIS document *Essential Elements of Religious Life* are put into effect, renewal efforts toward an authentic community structure will have been reduced for one portion of the world's sisters to futile rhetorical exercises. But the sector that has consistently resisted the freeing insights of Vatican II will savor a triumph.

Through *Lumen Gentium,* the bishops of the world at Vatican II challenged all Christians to recognize the world as their locus of life and ministry. Yet 20 years later, sisters are being asked to return to convents and cloisters, and abandon homes and apartments in the midst of Christian community. Reacting to religious women who act on their belief that leaven must be within dough and not segregated from it in a convent one subculture away, patriarchal prelates have reached into the mixing bowl to extricate sisters from worldly pursuits.

Within recent months one dedicated U.S. sister who was determined to be yeast on behalf of the poor by becoming director of the Michigan State Welfare Department, was wrenched from membership in her religious congregation when given an either-or-choice by Rome and two hours for making it.

Today, even as I write, international TV cables are putting forth the news of another sister, an esteemed attorney and longtime advocate for persons too poor for legal service. She is being mandated by her bishop to give up seeking a more powerful advocate role for the poor as attorney general for the state of Rhode Island, or sever connections with her religious congregation.

A watching world must view this dilemma of U.S. sisters as an anomalous tragedy where good persons negate the Christian ministry of good persons for unfathomable reasons. Christians who have read these accounts and also the documents of Vatican II must wonder what the Holy Spirit was really communicating through the bishops of the church at Vatican II when they wrote:

> This council exhorts Christians, as citizens of two cities, to strive to discharge their earthly duties conscientiously and in response to the Holy Spirit . . . . This split between the faith which many profess and their daily lives deserves to be counted among the more serious errors of our age . . . Therefore, let there be no false opposition between professional and social activities on the one part, and religious on the other . . Christians should rather rejoice that they can follow the example of Christ, who worked as an artisan. In the exercise of all their earthly activities, they can therefore gather their humane, domestic, professional, social and technical enterprises into one vital synthesis with religious values, under whose supreme direction all things are harmonized unto God's glory. (*Gaudium Et Spes, IV,* 43)

If sisters continue to be denied the "vital synthesis" of their professions and religious life commitment, *if* sisters' new constitutions continue to be rejected by well-meaning but uninspired clerics in Rome, *if* the enforced roundup of sisters back into archaic superior-dominated patterns of governance is actually accomplished, even against the collective best judgment of the sisters involved, *if* sisters and other Catholic women continue to be excluded from sharing genuine co-responsibility for the church as Christian community, then it seems inevitable that some sisters must bolt free from canonical corrals. They can certainly remain Christian community but in respectful confrontation with all persons, patterns, and policies of domination within church and society. Such bolting-free sisters are and will no doubt remain a powerful spiritual force to be reckoned with. They will march free as an integral part of the feminist revolution sweeping the world, determined to level its structures of oppression. They will be the midwives at the birthing of authentic Christian community, the ultimate renewal.

Looking Back, Looking Ahead

Kaye Ashe

Kaye Ashe, a Dominican, is author of Today's Woman, Tomorrow's Church. *She is dean of the Rosary Graduate School of Art in Florence, Italy. She earned her Ph.D. at the University of Fribourg, Switzerland, in modern European history. Women's lives, past and present, and women's voice and vision as expressed in the feminist movement are of vital interest to her.*

How difficult it is to express what has happened in U.S. religious communities of women since the 1960s! We have witnessed so much courage, eloquence, vision; so much conflict, hurt, bewilderment; so much questioning, discovery, growth. We have studied, argued, protested, met, strategized, prayed in new ways and old, discovered one another across congregational lines, and found our common bond with all women.

We have changed our "life-style," yes, but the surface changes reflect only superficially the transformation that has occurred in our concept of ourselves, sex and sex roles, work, prayer, life in community, ministry, church, authority, power — in short, in the central aspects of our being as women and as religious.

In the days when I "entered the convent," (today one "joins a community") young women were donning habits in droves. My personal motivation sprang from a vague feeling that the Dominican Order was where God wanted me to be coupled with the conviction that the charms of marriage, while alluring, would be short-lived. I wasn't sure in 1948 how one legitimately dealt, as a Catholic, with the prospect of an endless succession of children, and it didn't occur to me to ask. I had a strong suspicion that there *was* no legitimate way to curb what I feared would be my tendency to reproduce abundantly. More importantly, I deeply admired a number of the Sinsinawa Dominicans who had taught me from first grade to first year college. They were women who respected and sought truth, whose faith was reasoned, who knew the secrets of literature, who were ecologists before conservation became a national movement, whose interest in their students was sincere and unflagging, and who were warm, intelligent, and witty. The life that helped shape them, whatever its sacrifices, seemed a desirable one to me.

Religious sometimes dwell now on the senseless regulations, the repression of feeling, the loss of personal identity, and the power wielded arbitrarily by superiors, that they feel characterized sisters' formation in pre-Vatican II days. Who can deny that those elements were present?

But the novitiate and convent life, in general, also offered a pleasant rhythm of study, work, prayer and play. At Sinsinawa, Wisconsin initial formation took place in a setting of great natural beauty, where the seasons were experienced with an immediacy new to a young woman from Chicago.

What sort of training in pre-Vatican II days was designed to transform a crop of raw candidates, many fresh from high school, into "nuns" and teachers? We were acquainted with canon law regarding the vows and religious life, introduced to scholastic theology and philosophy, to Garrigou-Lagrange's *Three Ages of the Interior Life* and to various works by and about Dominican saints, provided with college-level courses designed to move those who did not have one toward a degree, and encouraged to adopt the demeanor proper to a religious: one did not run, make oneself conspicuous in any way, cross one's legs, use slang, or gaze about in public places. Our contribution to community life was to maintain peace and charity, do a generous share of the work, and be punctual at community prayers and meals. Our contribution to the work of the church was to maintain good schools, respecting the person of our students and furthering their intellectual and moral development. Our training for this task often took place largely on the job with the collaboration of first-rate teachers who had spent years refining their techniques. Congregational superiors decided the level on which we would teach, and the place where we would exercise our apostolate.

We were to spend our lives largely within the walls of convent, church and school. To leave these premises we were obliged to ask the permission of the superior, and we never left them except in the company of another sister. One sister was responsible for the financial transactions of the community; she generally bought everything from the sisters' food to their underthings. The others had little or no notion of what things cost.

Decision-making was in the hands of superiors who were appointed by the mother general. They, together with a certain number of elected representatives, elected the mother general at general chapters. These bodies, meant to inspire and to make policy for the congregation, were often reduced, before renewal, to reiterating small rules and regulations bearing on behavior. Convents of a certain size themselves constituted a "chapter," but the only chapters held were chapters of faults, in which sisters accused themselves of such matters as breaking silence, breaking dishes, neglecting spiritual reading or office, and at which they asked for permission for things they needed: soap, shoelaces, shoes, medicine, dental work, and the like.

Community relations were marked by consideration and courtesy, essential for those living in close and constant contact with one another, but seldom by any profound sharing of faith, personal goals, doubts, hopes, ideas, or ideals. We seldom analyzed or expressed emotions; indeed, we barely acknowledged them. Conversation bore most often on our pupils and school work. Most of us spent long hours in the classroom, and work, if not an obsession, was a driving-force in our lives. We felt guilty to be found leisurely persuing a newspaper or magazine, or listening to music or a baseball game. Even recreation was scheduled: a half hour in the evening when we might play cards, knit, chat and laugh together.

Our relations with the outside world were strictly limited. Contact with parishioners was virtually restricted to school conferences. Relations with priests were discouraged and somewhat suspect. The only approved one was that of spiritual direction, priests dispensing it and we receiving it. Superiors could read our mail, coming in or going out, if they chose to do so. Incoming mail was put, opened, into our mailboxes. Outgoing mail was left, open, to be posted by the superior.

Within the community, however, sisters found lasting and meaningful friendships. Many maintained correspondence and contact with former students, sharing the joys and crises of the various stages of their development.

Pre-Vatican II convent life was, then, not devoid of meaningful work, warm human relationships, or humor. But it made inroads into our sense of self. We gave up our names for those of saints (many of them male), and our birthdays for the feast of the saint whose name we bore. We wore habits that may have had a certain beauty, but which hid most of our body, limited our movement, deprived us of any personal expression in dress, set us apart from other laity, and encouraged the adoption of a role. We were, in some senses, kept in a state of childish dependence, shielded from financial realities, and relieved of the making of choices and decisions that characterize adult life. We found our place in a hierarchically arranged church somewhere between clergy and laity, and in a hierarchically arranged congregation where obedience left little room for discussion, dialogue, or participation in decisions which affected our lives. We adhered to a theology of religious life which emphasized personal holiness to be attained through faithful observance of the rule, and which fostered a large measure of suspicion of the "world".

All of this now seems long ago and far away. But the first steps toward modernization and renewal were modest ones. Invited by Pope Paul VI to examine our constitutions, eliminating from them outdated practices and restrictions and adapting them to the needs of changing times, we centered our attention at first on eliminating the obviously medieval references to strange penances, and to practices that had long ago fallen into disuse. Modernization of the habit consisted in its first round in a barely noticeable modification of the veil. Several factors, however, contributed to more profound changes at an ever-accelerated pace. Sisters in greater numbers avidly studied the new theology, and entered high degree programs in various disciplines: science, psychology and sociology. The philosophy of personalism touched us with particular acuity, and we sought ways to express and develop our personhood and to enter a wider range of human relationships. Our political awareness was raised by participation in anti-Vietnam protests, and the civil rights and feminist movements, both of which questioned time-sanctioned structures and emphasized individual rights.

All of this was bound to affect our life in community. Concern with the minutiae of the rule and constitutions gave way to larger questions of how to live gospel values authentically. We struggled with the meaning of poverty, chastity, and obedience, maintaining the essence of the vows but redefining them in ways consonant with the contemporary world and with the demands of personal freedom and growth. We placed them clearly in the context of apostolic community and mission. We challenged the kind of linear authority that had characterized religious congregations, and moved together toward interdependence, collegiality, and collaboration. We became impatient with repetitive prayer forms in impersonal settings, and sought new ways to pray and worship. We extended our participation in the church's ministry beyond school. Most of us adopted contemporary dress. We learned to relax more and to communicate better. We shared our doubts, our frustrations, our hopes for the future, and discussed passionately the changing realities of our life together as well as the political and social realities of the larger world. We asked for mutual trust in rapidly changing times.

It was exhilarating; it was also painful. Some felt that the changes devalued the former order of things, and rendered meaningless the lives they had so carefully constructed. Some, whose identity was closely associated with their role, suffered a loss of sense of self. But most felt that their "self" had been restored; that they could proceed in new ways as responsible adults on the journey of becoming human and becoming holy with the rest of the church.

The first wave of renewal centered principally on life in community: How would we dress? How would we pray? How would we relate to one another? How would we govern ourselves? We asked ourselves repeatedly who we *were* — as members of a local community, as members of newly-formed provinces, as members of the Sinsinawa Dominican congregation, as women, as women in the church, as women religious in the church. As we redefined ourselves through a scrutiny of the present and a rediscovery and rereading of the past, and as we worked to create communities built on trust, tolerance, and appreciation of one another, emphasis gradually shifted to a deepening and renewal of our sense of mission. We looked outward more and more, eager to respond to the cries of the poor, to enter the struggle for economic justice, for the end of discrimination against women and minorities, for peace, for conservation of the earth's natural resources. While education in general, and schools in particular, continue to play an important role in the congregation's mission, sisters in increasing numbers choose to minister as members of parish and diocesan teams, hopsital and university chaplains, and social justice advocates. They staff shelters for battered woman, give legal and medical assistance to the poor, work with migrant groups, and with native Americans.

If some have chosen, in the course of 20 years of experimentation and renewal, to leave religious congregations and to live out their Christian commitment in other forms, those who have chosen to stay have committed themselves more deeply to one another and to a way of life that is meant to provide a prophetic sign of hope to a wounded world.

Two issues stand out as particularly striking in the evolution of American women religious since the early 1960s: their construction of participative forms of governance and their increasingly feminist consciousness. These trends conform to the spirit and even to the explicit exhortations of the Second Vatican Council, but they run counter to strong currents through centuries of church practice. The misunderstandings caused by this tension sometimes place American women religious in confrontation with Rome. Further, they embarrass certain American bishops who maintain excellent rapport with the women religious of their diocese. The bishops find themselves between women who take a large measure of autonomy for granted and the pope who is urging them to exercise stricter control over religious orders.

Since these two issues are vitally important to American women religious, and to the church in general, they bear closer scrutiny. A "transvaluation of values" of such dimensions has taken place among U.S. congregations of sisters that there is little likelihood that we will march in reverse at this point. It is crucial, therefore, if a serious rift between the American church and Rome is to be avoided, that we attempt to keep the channels of communication open, while making clear our determination to move firmly and finally out of the position of second-class minors in the church.

Let us look first, then at the question of authority, leadership, and governance. The Catholic church did not escape the crisis of authority which touched all institutions in the 1960s. Indeed, since the Catholic church entered the 20th century with an exaggerated and stubborn form of the hierarchical and patriarchal organization characteristic of all social structures, the tension was greater here than elsewhere. The documents of Vatican II, while addressing the problem, vacillate between naming the people of God as primary bearers of the power of the Spirit and casting the hierarchy in that role.

Today, two concepts of authority, each with historical precedent, inspire different sectors of the church. The first one, which took shape in the Constantinian era and crystallized in the Middle Ages, presents the church as a pyramid in which power and status are clearly defined, and reside principally in the higher reaches of an all-male clergy. Ministry in this model of church is exercised by the ordained, and the ordained hold virtually all of the important posts on the parish, diocesan, and curial levels. Power relations are vertical and decision-making is centralized. Authority figures tend to assume the functions of protection, legislation, and control.

Since Vatican Council II, another concept of authority, and consequently of ministry, has gained ground. Its roots extend to New Testament times. Those who adhere to it envision the church as a community of equals. Relationships between members are characterized by mutuality and collegiality. Governance is participative; power is shared. The pyramid in this model gives way to interlocking circles. Leaders are chosen who can motivate, inspire, and provide living examples of the ideal of the community. Ministry becomes the responsibility of all of the members of the community; each is called upon to witness, to proclaim the word, to reconcile, to be a sign of unity and hope.

Congregations of American sisters were quick to adopt the second vision of leadership and authority, and to enunciate principles of mutuality, collaboration, and interdependence in their revised constitutions. Linear authority gave way to shared authority, patriarchal structures to participative ones. Members were to be co-responsible for establishing goals, framing policy, and making decisions, and this at every level of the congregation's structure.

American sisters gradually translated the principles enunciated in revised constitutions into their lives. They more readily accepted primary responsibility for their own spiritual and professional development. They accepted mutual responsibility for one another and for the work of their congregations. They entered into the decision-making process at all levels.

The experience of 20 years of participative government and of leadership which encourages independence has, of course, affected the expectations that U.S. sisters bring with them to their work in parishes and dioceses, and to their relations with Rome. They are increasingly unhappy and impatient with authoritarian styles of governance, or with any hint of an attitude that men were born to rule and women to obey. American women religious accept responsibility for their lives in community and they expect to collaborate as equals in the work of the church at all levels.

This, perhaps, explains the suspicion with which some sisters have viewed the establishment of a commission of bishops to serve American religious in various ways. In his letter to them the pope drew attention to the bishops' task, in union with himself, of authenticating the discernment of a religious community's proper ecclesial charism. But, since religious have worked within the church's teachings and their own traditions, the result of their study, discernment, and experience constitutes, in *itself,* an authentic discernment of the community's ecclesial charism.

Archbishop John Quinn, of San Francisco, as pontifical delegate heading the commission has, to be sure, included three sisters on a consultative committee, and one as consultant to the entire group. He will certainly be sensitive to their views and open to their suggestions. But true collaboration would have called for sisters to be part of the commission itself. With the present setup it is difficult not to feel like the object of an investigation rather than partners in an honest effort to review and evaluate the experience of the past 20 years. Given the nature of the commission's work, John Paul II might well have invited the major superiors of religious to form a commission which would include bishops, while exhorting bishops to seek to understand and support religious in their efforts to strengthen and renew their commitments.

The Agnes Mansour case is a sad illustration of the distance that separates Rome from American sisters in matters of governance. The pope through his emissary operated out of a monarchical framework of government in confrontation with sisters accustomed to democratic forms of due process. Agnes Mansour, respecting at once her own Catholic conscience and a U.S. Supreme Court decision in the matter of abortion, and working in the interests of the poor in an influential government post with the approval of her religious superiors, was forced to either resign her post or be faced with dismissal from the Sisters of Mercy. We know the struggle, the frustration, and the pain behind her choice to ask for a dispensation from her vows. There is not only a question of differing views of the exercise of authority here, one representing a morality of command and obedience and the other seeking a morality of justice, there is also behind this whole scenario a strong strain of anti-feminism that brings us to the second issue of importance in the post-Vatican church.

Feminist thought took root in American religious communities during the period of renewal. It was impossible not to see how the feminist critique applied to church institutions. From canon law to the practice of many local pastors, from the realm of liturgy and symbol to that of ministry, from theology to the organization of church structures, women religious found patriarchal assumptions solidly in place. The "good sisters" were expected to be self-abnegating servants, caring principally for children and the sick, with little voice even in matters that directly concerned them and no place, of course, among the ordained. We found ourselves, with all women, absent from the liturgy except as passive listeners. We were exhorted, having renounced physical motherhood, to embrace spiritual motherhood, since, presumably, we could not claim womanhood without *some* form of motherhood. We did our spiritual reading from books by men written from their point of view and experience. We made retreats directed by men whose understanding of our needs was often limited. But, like all women, we expected to find salvation in and through males. We doubled our own powers to theologize, to heal, to reconcile. We hardly suspected our own strength and wisdom.

This has begun to change, but the full realization of female autonomy within the church will be a critical issue in the continued process of renewal. Women theologians and ministers, social activists and educators, whether members of religious communities or not, must continue to deepen and to act out of a feminist consciousness. Apart from the question of our rights in church and society and of the more profound one of identity, are questions of survival of the human race and of the world about us. It is not simply, therefore, a question of minor concessions to women, or of appointing token women to a few positions of importance in church or state. The task before all of us, women and men, is the reconstruction of society's values and of a mind-set in which domination, violence, and abusive power characterize domestic, national, and international relations. In the world that feminists envision, dialogue, creativity, harmony, and nurturance replace repression, competition, war, and conquest. It is a world in which the marginalized and the exploited empower themselves and discover new ways of conceiving and exercising power.

The role of U.S. women religious in this struggle and this process will be an important one. While we work with women and men everywhere toward a world of peace and justice, we must continue to insist on our competence and rights within the church, and be willing to experiment in order to create new forms of leadership and new modes of worship and service. We must theologize from women's point of view, and help shape an ethics that takes women's experience into account. We must bond with all women in the effort to recognize and break through the economic and psychological obstacles which impede the full realization of our being.

The renewal and updating called for by John XXIII and by Paul VI will not be complete until women's voice and experience find full expression in the church's decision-making process, ministry, and sacramental system. Women religious are in a good position to further this process and to help create the church of the future, one in which new patterns of thought, relationship and governance will give witness that community is possible in a world which hungers for it.

From Good Sisters
to Prophetic Women

Jeannine Grammick

*Jeannine Gramick has been a School Sister of Notre Dame since 1960.
As co-founder and co-director of New Ways Ministry, she has conducted
a research study on the coming out process of lesbian women and edited*
Homosexuality and the Catholic Church.

I was an old-fashioned, pre-Vatican II Catholic. I grew up believing
that God spoke through the lips of my grade school nuns, except the
grouchy ones; I made excuses for them. In the extended family in which
I spent my first 10 years after my birth in 1942, parents, grandfather
and uncles thought I was a devout and obedient child. I remember daily
mass and holy communion and periodic fears for my family's eternal
salvation because they didn't always "do what sister said." As an only
child, I shouldered a grave responsibilsity for my family's spiritual welfare.

God was my best friend and I, in turn, knew that I was his best friend.
(In those days I thought of God as "he.") I loved God so much I thought
I would burst; I wanted to shout "God" to everyone. At the same time, I
was astute enough to realize that I couldn't bring people closer to God
if others considered me an oddball; so I kept a low profile. My devout
prayers and practices were kept as secret as possible. But the nuns knew
and probably encouraged what was diagnosed as an incipient religious
vocation.

When I was seven years old, I felt God was calling me to be a nun. My
environment implicitly conveyed the attitude that those who *really* loved
God became nuns if they were girls, or priests if they were boys. Because
of the mutual, intense love between God and myself, I knew God must
be calling me to be a nun. The respect and affection of my peers would
enable me to draw many people to this God I loved. Although I dreaded
the idea of renouncing life's pleasures behind a cloister wall, I trusted
God would make the appropriate arrangements.

"The Good Sisters"

Caryll Houselander, a poet and spiritual writer of the 1950s, comparing "a couple of rather flustered little nuns" to "birds shaking the rain off their feathers," drew the image of "the good sisters." Sweet, kind, cherub-like creatures in ankle-length, black habits and neatly starched coifs, these angels of mercy, like their female counterparts in society, made coffee, not policy. In the mid-1960s, Eugene Kennedy, a leading psychologist wrote, ". . . the sister is prized by a paternalistic and prospering Catholic society as a little girl, innocent and virginal, smiling sweetly, sacrificing silently, just human enough for the mindless caricatures of a dozen motion pictures," Recall the classics: *The Nun's Story* and *The Sound of Music.*

The media capitalized on the stereotype of "the good sister," who with the Second Vatican Council began to crack the cloister wall that had kept her hidden. Almost every hometown newspaper of the early 1960s featured at least one article, complete with photographs, of a nun playing softball with the habit pinned up and wimple pulled back, or of a nun on a roller coaster laughingly enjoying the amusement park with her seventh grade class.

With the relaxation of traditional religious rules, "the good sister" could watch television programs until nine o'clock or even attend an occasional matinee with permission, but not always without a raised eyebrow. In a theater line for a performance of *Alfie,* two nuns were protectively warned by the woman ahead, "Oh, sisters, you don't want to come in here. This is an adult movie." "The good sister" was still very much a child.

Into this religious world of *The Flying Nun* or *Trouble with Angels* I came on September 8, 1960. Amid tears at relinquishing a passionate relationship with a young college man, I surrendered my entire life to God and the service of God's people at the School Sisters of Notre Dame's (SSND) Baltimore motherhouse. The young man's letters, intercepted by the postulant's mistress, were judged dangerous to my germinating vocation. The superior's opening, reading, and possible withholding of mail (a federal offense) was never questioned.

I followed a schedule of 5:15 a.m. rising, private and communal chapel prayer, household chores, meals, school work, set periods of recreation, grand silence after night prayer until the following morning's breakfast, and lights out at 10 p.m. Within the usual daily regimen were such variations as the laughter of family and friends on first Sunday visits, monthly days of prayer and Saturday's hour of singing practice in chapel.

The theological premise of a pre-Vatican II church, that religious life constituted a higher, more noble life-style than the lay state, was concretized by creating differences; for example, a distinct dress, a sacred environment, and the assumption of a new identity separated religious from the body of the Christian faithful. Blue and white striped underskirts and tee-shirts shielded the nuns' modern underwear from pleated yards of a black gabardine work habit or a woollen serge Sunday habit. A cloister or enclosure, a space set aside exclusively for members of the community, was maintained. Religious houses included a chapel, a luxury possessed only by certain upper class Christians. In order to symbolize the departure from one state of life to a higher one, another name "in religion" was given. Because the list of canonized saints on which the religious name was to be based, was overwhelmingly male, the feminine identity of thousands of nuns was wrapped into the package of a "Sister Sebastian Marie" or a "Sister Mary Ambrose." The biological family having been abandoned, family names were naturally obliterated.

I was schooled to attain spiritual perfection, a goal congruent with my personality and natural instincts. My novice mistress, apparently annoyed because she found no rule infraction of which I seemed guilty, in a mixture of teasing and seriousness accused me of pride: Was I striving for an "A" by impeccably observing the daily silence? I took Matthew 5:48 literally: "You must be perfect, just as your Father in heaven is perfect." About a decade later I would nod agreement with hundreds of sisters at a provincial gathering as one community leader, not especially renowned for her liberal stances, assured us that it was "O.K. to make mistakes." But in the early 1960s, seeking perfection, not learning from mistakes, was an authentic Catholic objective.

Perfection was rendered certain by strict adherence to the oft-quoted maxim, "Keep the rule and the rule will keep you." At the hub of the rule, was the public profession of the vows of poverty, chastity, and obedience through which one's entire life was consecrated to God. Unable to reconcile the professions of religious vows with Jesus' words, "But now I tell you: do not use any vow when you make a promise," (Matthew 5:34) I knew simply that God was calling me to religious life. The vows formed part of the packaged deal.

Poverty, interpreted as dependence, was witnessed by the fact that no individual personally possessed money. Never mind that millions of dollars were held corporately in buildings, capital investments, inheritance and retirement funds and other sundry assets. The privatized "God and me" spirituality extended to the material sphere and inhibited a social or global analysis. As long as I dutifully fell to my knees and humbly begged for soap, shampoo, toothpaste or any material need, I was practicing the vow of poverty. My superior determined whether or not my personal comforts contradicted a poor and simple life-style.

Many outside the congregation who struggled financially to feed hungry children or to heat drafty homes correctly perceived the vow of poverty as easy enough to follow. Our material care and security in old age were guaranteed. There was no thought that responsible stewardship included a more equitable distribution of the earth's resources; no thought that it demanded a participation in the project, however staggering, of converting and reforming structures that institutionalize exploitation, domination and selfishness. The realization that religious must witness to a poverty to which all Christians are called had not come. The poverty to which Jesus calls us, an acknowledgment that in the face of another's need we have no right to any excess, means the creation of economic structures to effect a more just and loving world.

Confined to the society of women except for rare occasions, I was hard pressed to appreciate the value of the vow of chastity. Warned, of course, about "particular friendships," we failed, until decades later, to associate these two words with homosexual encounters. For most of us in 1960, the word homosexual was virgin to our ears; if we had heard the word before, its meaning eluded us.

After weeks of explanation in the novitiate concerning the vow and virtue of poverty, we listened to several lectures on human reproduction which culminated in a final statement from the novice mistress to ease our concern: "There is nothing forbidden by the vow of chastity that isn't already forbidden by the sixth and ninth commandments." With that we proceeded to a punctilious explanation of the vow of obedience.

I have always been grateful for my religious instruction in the vow of chastity ever since contemporary moral theologians have begun to reassess and reinterpret the meaning of the sixth and ninth commandments! The chastity of religious, including intimacy and affection, concerns loving relationships with women and men, with gay and straight, with individuals within the congregation and those outside it. As with the vow of poverty, religious must strive to live chastely in order to enable all Christians to do likewise. Chastity must impel us to participate in the building of a loving society in which personal and structural relationships are marked by mutuality and equality.

Obedience to all lawful authority by abdicating one's personal will to a superior, except if a command was sinful, was equated with obedience to God. Although the concept of blind obedience was denounced, an irrational bell could signal the will of God. In my high school teaching days, I promptly stopped chatting with my homeroom students as soon as God's voice ringing in the afternoon bell summoned me to chapel. Since obedience even to a paranoid or insecure local superior was expected, my first year "on mission" provided many tears and lonely hours of silent prayer in chapel. Held hostage by the superior's accusation of disloyalty, I discussed with no one, save God, the tirades and explosions which might charitably be called "human idiosyncrasies" instead of the mental aberrations which they were.

Thank God we have moved from an obedience which controlled people's lives and justified secrecy as a weapon of tyranny and subjugation to an obedience which operates openly and encourages the right of self-determination. Obedience, properly owed to God alone and facilitated by one's religious community, is not a submission of will nor a renunciation of personal responsibility but a cooperation with God and others as manifested through one's gifts and desires, human needs and welfare. Religious obedience, to which all Christians are called, has always entailed a search for God's will and an experience of freedom in following it.

Post-Vatican II Renewal

In 1962 Cardinal Suenens in *The Nun in the World* wrote, "Religious too often seem to be living in a closed world, turned in on themselves and having but tenuous contact with the world outside."In the early 1960s, I was contented and peaceful in my impenetrable religious sphere where flight and separation from secular society were the natural consequences of a hostile and defensive approach to the world. My privatized exclusivity afforded me the luxury of happiness and tranquility; only later would I experience the disturbed harmony which accompanies the responsibility of creating just social structures.

The Second Vatican Council launched religious life, as it did the entire church itself, into the secular world. The world was perceived, not as an enemy to be denounced or avoided, but as the basic building block of God's reign. Solidarity with, involvement in, and acceptance of the world implied a revamping and renewal of religious life. While the religious stance was one of participation in the transformation of humankind, the religious was to stand as a prophetic countercultural sign having a personal and corporate freedom both to condemn and criticize evil and injustice and to praise and vindicate the right and good. Although the mode and context of religious life had changed, it was essentially what it had always been: a dedication of human life to the divine and to the service of God's people.

Endless books and articles of the late 1960s encouraging renewal and adaptation of the religious enterprise, recommended dialogue, collegiality, and decentralization of government. Shedding "the good sister" or "the flying nun" image, nuns were growing into mature persons, ready to make major personal decisions and to assume the responsibility of their consequences. Such a shift in my own self-understanding and personal identity occurred in 1968 when I received a telephone call that my mother was seriously ill with a brain tumor. At age 26, I stood like a child of 12, waiting for the superior's directive.

At the time, we were living in accordance with an interim document called "the blue book." In addition, the strict local superior had been replaced by one who was more lenient. "What are you going to do"? the new local leader asked. With a jolt, I wondered, "Why is she asking *me* what I'm going to do"? Obediently waiting for directions, I received instead an invitation to analyze a situation for myself and to propose a decisive solution. I blinked.

"Well, I guess I should go home," I ventured.

"When are you leaving"? shot back the reply. Without granting permission or determining travel time and arrangements, the response presumed a mature, rational judgment on my part.

This decision-making, clearly a watershed in my personal development in religious life, was at first confined to the professional teaching arena. Afterward, my actions became gradually more self-determined. To this end four years of graduate study on a campus without the presence of a local superior contributed decidedly.

Attaining more visibility and assertiveness, post-Vatican II nuns replaced the old stereotype of gentle teacher or submissive nun with a new image: the nun on the picket line. U.S. women religious threw themselves wholeheartedly into working for the rights of the oppressed, whether by marching publicly in Selma or by demonstrating to support the peace movement and the end of American interference in Vietnam. A self-study of the Sisters of the Blessed Virgin Mary by a Chicago-based research team showed an increased self-awareness and self-sufficiency among the nuns. Between 1969 and 1972 sisters became "more self-confident, cheerful," and also showed "fewer fears."

The Women's Movement

Although much religious literature of the late 1960s and early 1970s was laced with sexist language and concepts which stressed the "proper role" of women and the task of the "feminine nature" in the church, the impact of the secular women's movement was definitely to be felt. The preference of women religious for justice, for the poor, and for the disenfranchised enabled us to identify naturally and easily with the goals of the feminist movement. To address Elizabeth Cady Stanton's denunciation that "the Bible and the church have been the greatest stumbling block in the way of women's emancipation," women religious began a feminist critique of the patriarchal structure of the Roman Catholic Church.

In the mid-1970s a papal document requiring women religious to wear a habit or some identifying garb was addressed to John Cardinal Krol, then president of the National Conference of Catholic Bishops (NCCB) who was commissioned to communicate the papal message to the nuns. Incensed that a letter involving their life-style had been directed to a man and increasingly objecting to man-made rules imposed on women's lives, the nuns virtually ignored the directive. In a repeat performance of content and procedure, the 1983 document from the Congregation for Religious and Secular Institutes (SCRIS) entitled *Essential Elements in the Church's Teaching on Religious Life* informed religious that the lessons learned from their two-decade experience of renewal are abrogated in favor of a return to a preconciliar closed system of religious life.

My own feminist consciousness did not blossom until the mid 1970s. By reading and working closely with members of the National Assembly of Women Religious (NAWR) and the National Coalition of American Nuns (NCAN), I came to understand the extent of the blatant exclusion of women from substantial participation and decision-making at all ecclesiastical levels. Although nuns outnumber brothers and priests by ratios of four or five to one in many dioceses, in decision-making roles priests exceed women religious by as much as ten to one.

In addition to NAWR and NCAN, special interest groups for women religious cropped up: Las Hermanas for Hispanic nuns, the National Black Sisters Conference, the Sister Formation Conference, the National Sisters Vocation Conference, and the Association of Contemplative Sisters. Since a rising recognition of classism as well as feminism prompted vocabulary changes to reflect attitudinal ones, the Conference of Major Superiors of

Women changed its name to the Leadership Conference of Women Religious (LCWR). Each of these organizations enabled members to become painfully aware of the subservient position of Catholic women.

A graph of the impact of the feminist movement upon women religious resembles the normal bell curve. The two percent at one end of the statistical arch, who have experienced little or no effect of feminism, cling to their aphorism that "Father knows best." Like the largest portion of the bell curve, most are questioning why the institutional church forbids its treasured daughters to be altar servers or ordained priests. They are beginning to grasp the importance of sexually balanced language (except where it pertains to God), and expect women to be seminary students or professors. The other two percent tail of the curve constitute the prophetic voices that challenge the mainstream to reconsider, reevaluate and restructure. By boycotting attendance at eucharists at which males preside and planning and participating in their own feminist liturgies, these prime movers are calling for resistance to male domination in the church and are urging women's congregations to forego the canonical status bestowed by male approval for women's community rules. Even though nuns' attitudes toward women are certainly not uniform, we have managed to respect diversity and to maintain a cohesiveness that will be jeopardized if the 1983 SCRIS document is given serious attention and applied literally.

Ministry

It is significant that literature on the traditional vows of poverty, chastity, and obedience dwindled as the renewal progressed. In 1970 Gabriel Moran, a Christian Brother and an accurate predictor of trends, wrote that a discussion of the vows is "no longer viable." Ministry, instead, became a vital concern to nuns' coalitions. Published by NAWR, *Women in Ministry* and *Gospel Dimensions of Ministry* indicated a major shift in apostolic endeavors during the post-Vatican renewal. In 1965 about 60 percent of women religious were teachers; in 1975 the percentage dropped to about 40 percent. Educational ministry, still foremost among today's women religious, is no longer defined as teaching in a Catholic school system. NETWORK, a national sisters' lobbying group, is an example of a current educational ministry. In an obvious trend toward pastoral ministries, nuns are now working with drug addicts, alcoholics, runaways, migrants, the imprisoned, the aged, the deaf, the mentally and physically challenged, and in a host of other service-oriented professions.

Although my formal education was atypical by convent standards because it was uninterrupted, my initial ministry was quite traditional. After assigning me to teach junior high and advanced math classes in senior high, my community administrators asked me to cointinue for an advanced degree. Since dialogue between community representatives and community members regarding future ministry was minimal in the late 1960s, I was surprised to be asked what field I wished to pursue.

I quickly responded, "Psychology." Not surprisingly, I was asked to study mathematics and began a doctoral program at the University of Pennsylvania to research mathematics education.

I believe that God works through people in inscrutable ways. My mother's ill health prompted a choice of school close to home. Concern for her brought me to Philadelphia and concern for a young man named Dominic propelled me to a frontier ministry.

The Cutting Edge

In the spring of 1971 I participated in a home liturgy attended by about 30 people, mostly university students. After the mass as most people milled around in small groups, I found myself speaking with a young man of 25 named Dominic, who excitedly declared that his "sisters and brothers" would enjoy such a liturgy. Dominic's brothers and sisters were the lesbian and gay community, the invisible minority.

Since I knew next to nothing about homosexuality, I was intent as Dominic disclosed his personal story. At first I wondered how someone cold be sexually attracted to another person of the same gender. I gradually came to appreciate that these feelings are natural for Dominic. No one yet understands what causes same-sex orientation so strong as to defy alteration even by a society which advocates and reinforces heterosexuality by capitalizing upon "sex appeal" to sell everything from toothpaste to automobiles.

Dominic's resistance to society's pressures and those of his church was a matter of personal human survival. An intensely pious individual, Dominic had entered a Roman Catholic religious comunity but left shortly thereafter because he could not reconcile his sexual orientation and his religious vocation. He cherished God and the church Christ founded; so did his sisters and brothers who suffered not only from the prejudice and ignorance of a society that called them "queer" but also from the fear and neglect of a church which treated them as lepers. Dominic's two absorbing interests — his religious convictions and his deep concern for lesbian and gay people — were both part of his question, "What is the church doing for my brothers and sisters"? That question would become my challenge to be at the cutting edge of a new and sensitive ministry.

"What is the church doing for my brothers and sisters"? Dominic persisted.

"I don't know," I had to answer.

"Well, why don't *you* do something"? he countered. I know lots of gay people who would love to come to a mass like this." Then he told me why.

For most of Dominic's friends it could mean the first reconnection with the church in many years. Dominic recounted experiences which I heard later reiterated in many lesbian and gay people's lives: Priests screaming in the confessional that a homosexual penitent was going to hell; parents refusing to discuss their children's homosexuality, or even worse, expelling a lesbian or gay child from their homes; parishioners declining to work on a parish project with a known lesbian or gay person.

When I met Dominic, I reminded myself that I had more than enough to keep me busy as a full-time graduate student. I salved my conscience by suggesting a home liturgy in Dominic's apartment for his gay friends. A few weeks later 10 people assembled in his apartment for the breaking of bread. News traveled swiftly by the gay grapevine. Within a few months the group included more than 50 people, some gay, some straight and eventually evolved into a local chapter of Dignity, a national organization for lesbian and gay Catholics and their friends.

Through the insistent prodding of my friend Dominic, I became increasingly involved in a ministry of reconciliation of the church and the lesbian-gay community. I attended clergy conferences designed to explore church attitudes toward homosexuality, met with psychiatrists, psychologists and ministers who counseled gay and lesbian people, and read scores of books, journal articles and other literature on homosexuality.

As I learned, so I helped to teach. I organized a panel at the university to discuss the moral, psychological, sociological and legal aspects of homosexuality; I delivered talks and conducted workshops with numerous groups of students and professionals. Thus began my informal education and field work in lesbian-gay ministry.

"What is the church doing for my brothers and sisters"? Dominic's question continued to haunt me. After I moved to Baltimore to teach mathematics at a local woman's college administered by my community, I volunteered my time in gay ministry as a chaplain for Dignity.

Our province had moved to a new form of ministry placement. Instead of arbitrary assignments or obediences, community members and community representatives dialogued in order to help the individual sister discern God's call for her. After such dialogue and discernment with our provincial leader, I felt that God was calling me to work at the Quixote Center. Others could readily teach mathematics, but others could not easily be found to engage in lesbian-gay ministry, which would be a primary focus of my service at the Quixote Center, in addition to other social justice issues.

At the Quixote Center, I met Robert Nugent, a priest of the Society of the Divine Savior, who also ministered as a Dignity chaplain. Together we developed New Ways workshops, designed to educate non-gay people about the sociological and theological aspects of homosexuality. The name "New Ways" was aptly chosen from Bishop Francis Mugavero's 1976 pastoral letter, *"Sexuality: God's Gift,"* in which the bishop writes to those of a homosexual orientation, "We pledge our willingness . . . to try to find new ways to communicate the truth of Christ because we believe it will make you free."

Convinced of a compelling need for a social justice organization specifically dealing with the concerns of sexual minorities, Bob Nugent and I co-founded New Ways Ministry in 1977. New Ways Ministry seeks to promote justice and reconciliation among lesbian and gay people, their parents, families and friends and the larger Christian community. The ministry is based on the statement by the U.S. Catholic Bishops in their 1976 pastoral letter, *To Live in Christ Jesus,* ". . . the Christian community should provide them (lesbian and gay people) a special degree of pastoral understanding and care."

Because New Ways Ministry has not been approved by the local bishop of Washington, D.C., where its offices are located, tensions and conflicts with ecclesiastical structures have ensued. Despite the fact that cuttingedge ministries usually meet opposition from the church establishment at the outset, New Ways Ministry receives financial and moral support from large segments of the Catholic community, particularly from women's religious congregations. Its staff and volunteer help have included women and men, laypeople and members of religious congregations, heterosexual and lesbian and gay people. All religious on the staff serve with the approval of their religious congregations.

To the pain, apprehension and ambiguity with which any new life-project is fraught, sexual issues provoke fright, panic and even terror. This long overdue ministry to a class considered pariahs or contemporary Samaritans is an essential ingredient in the reparation for the church's social sin against the lesbian-gay community. In his 1980 pastoral letter on homosexuality, Archbishop Rembert Weakland invites us to "Come write in the sand with me. Who is going to throw the first stone?"

I perceive my religious vocation and my service in lesbian-gay ministry to be God's genuine call for me. Both are rooted in an inner conviction of love to serve as a bridge between God and people.

Prophetic Stance

My particular ministry illuminates a common ecclesiastical ailment. Discovering needs unmet at diocesan levels, many women's religious congregations have encountered conflict with the local hierarchy when they seek to minister to these needs. By working in social justice ministries, women religious are often involved in the secular political process or in fringe movements for the nuclear freeze, women's ordination, or military disengagement of the U.S. from Central America. Some of these ministries are structures without the approval of or in direct opposition to certain ecclesiastical figures. We, as church, have reached an authority crisis in which the autonomy of religious congregations concerning their own ministries is being threatened.

Often, though not always, the local bishop is cast in the role of the "royal consciousness" while the religious congregation portrays a prophetic imagination. These two stances have been described by the Old Testament scholar, Walter Brueggeman, in his book *The Prophetic Imagination.* Royal consciousness is identified by adherence to the social and political status quo, to the current and existing government, to the present rule. It is to the king's advantage that the monarchy continue. The royal consciousness legitimates itself by asserting an identification with the divine and subsequently nullifies responsibility to the people. The prophet, however, challenges the kind to accountability in God's name. The prophet Jesus was crucified by the forces of a royal consciousness.

In 1983 this royal consciousness was brought to bear on Sister Agnes Mary Mansour, a Detroit Sister of Mercy. Sister Mansour, who was supported by her religious congregation in her work as Michigan's director of social services but opposed by the local bishop, was forced to resign from her religious order to continue her ministry to the poor. The "royal" authority of any bishop, including the bishop of Rome, conflicts with the autonomy of a religious congregation to determine its ministry. Further, it undercuts the prophetic responsibility of religious to proclaim that representatives of the institutional chruch must be accountable to the people they are called to serve.

Religious Life in the Future

When I entered religious life, U.S. women religious numbered more than 180,000. In 1970, there were approximately 150,000 nuns; in 1984, fewer than 120,000. It is important to know that declining membership is not restricted to U.S. congregations; the religious vocation slump is generally more severe elsewhere. Because the reduction in the number of religious vocations occurred during the period of church renewal, some have linked the two phenomena as cause and effect. This seems to be the view of SCRIS since a studied interpretation of their "essential elements" suggests a return to the world-denying, closed system of religious life.

In a 1983 article on religious orders and future vision, Joan Chittister, OSB, describes five major stages in the life cycle of an institution. Most religious congregations, founded in 19th century Europe or United States, have passed through three phases: First, institutional origin, a time of energy and vision but struggling resources; second, expansion, a period of consolidation and mission in which society admits its own need for the institution's original vision; and third, stabilization, a stage of systemization and social respectability in which the work prospers but the vision fades. Once membership has slipped and morale has declined, the fourth period of breakdown has begun. Most congregations, now in that period of breakdown, will be soon faced with the fifth and final stage, transition, which presents the choice of death, minimal survival, or authentic renewal.

Addressing the life and death questions of religious life in a paper on "A Contemporary Theology of the Vows," Sandra Sneiders, IHM, writes:

> Religious life is at the crossroads. Many are asking if it will survive
> or disappear. Whether it retreats into the ghetto and attracts rigid,

frightened, and structure-seeking dependency types, or moves forward to meet the challenge of prophetic presence and creative involvement in the world and attracts freedom-seeking, radical types, it will probably survive. In fact, one might hypothesize that there are more weak than strong people in any society and that, if survival is the question, the chances for quantitative increase of the ghetto congregations is actually better. But the question is not simply one of survival in the sense of duration. It is a question of meaning. Will religious life continue to be a significant evangelical force in the world? The answer to that question is much less certain.

Still an old-fashioned though post-Vatican II Catholic, I believe that God is calling me to religious life in a congregation which has declined from more than 11,000 to approximately 8,000 sisters. I witnessed our periods of stabilization and breakdown and have never doubted that call. I love and believe in the strong women of my community as we face the three choices of the transitional stage. I pray that we do not merely pantomime the motions of change for minimal survival but that, in faith, we achieve authentic renewal by living the Gospel of Jesus.

Although as a woman religious I am identified with church institutions, in the final analysis, God, not any institution, is paramount. To associate with and to preserve any structure at the expense of serving God and humankind is idolatry. To follow God's call rather than an institutional call, if the two are in conflict, is a moral imperative. I pray always for the grace and the insight to discern God's call.